Pilgrimage to Canterbury

Pilgrims leaving Canterbury, an illumination from John Lydgate's *Segge of Thebes*, painted by a Flemish artist in the sixteenth century. Not an accurate depiction of Canterbury, it shows a typical walled town and great church of the Middle Ages and a mixed group of pilgrims like those who travelled with Chaucer more than a century before. (*British Library.*)

HOWARD LOXTON

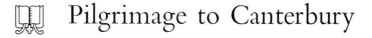 Pilgrimage to Canterbury

DAVID & CHARLES
NEWTON ABBOT   LONDON

ROWMAN & LITTLEFIELD
TOTOWA, NEW JERSEY

© Howard Loxton 1978

British Library Cataloguing in Publication Data
Loxton, Howard
Pilgrimage to Canterbury
1. Christian pilgrims and pilgrimages – England –
Canterbury – History
 I. Title
 248'.29   BX2321.C/

ISBN 0-7153-7508-3

Set in 10d on 13pt Sabon
by HBM Typesetting Limited
Standish Street Chorley Lancashire
and printed in Great Britain
by Redwood Burn Limited Trowbridge
for David & Charles (Publishers) Limited
Brunel House Newton Abbot Devon

Published in Canada
by Douglas David & Charles Limited
1875 Welch Street North Vancouver BC

First published in the United States 1978
by ROWMAN AND LITTLEFIELD Totowa NJ

ISBN 0-8476-6072-9

For Sheila and Frances

I pra you, sers, al in fere,
Worchip Seynt Thomas, this hole marter.
For on a Tewsday Thomas was borne,
And on a Tewsday he was prest schorne,
And on a Tuysday his lyve was lorne,
And sofyrd martyrdam with myld chere.

Carol by John Audeley
in fifteenth-century Douce manuscripts
in the British Library

Thanne longen folk to goon on pilgrimages,
And palmeres for to seken straunge strondes,
To ferne halwes, kowthe in sondry landes;
And especially from every shires ende
Of Engelond to Caunterbury they wende,
The hooly blisful martir for to seke, . . .

Geoffrey Chaucer
Prologue to *The Canterbury Tales*

Contents

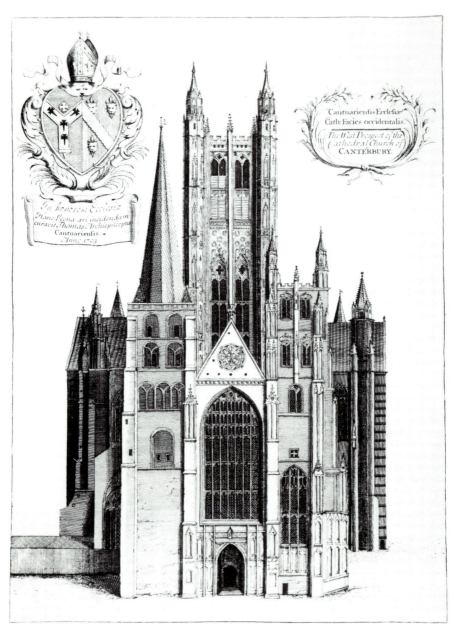

The West Front of Canterbury Cathedral in 1703 and as it would have looked in the later Middle Ages. An engraving from Hasted's *Canterbury*.

Introduction

ON THE EVENING of the twenty-ninth of December in the year 1170 the singing of vespers in the candle-lit cathedral of Canterbury was falteringly halted. As the last echoes faded among the winter-dark vaults, four armoured knights, with drawn swords, entered England's premier church and in the deepening shadows struck down her leading churchman.

Whether this was the culmination of a long-term plan or a sudden and impetuous act on the part of the assassins, it had been anticipated by the victim and was a possibility known to half of Europe. The murder of Archbishop Thomas in Canterbury Cathedral was a decisive move in the politics of Church and State, the results of which were to be felt for many centuries. The four murderers possibly sincerely thought that by their deed they did both King and State a service but, whatever the strength of their reason, they lacked both strategic sense and imagination. In killing the man they named a traitor they made him into a martyr and a saint.

No sooner had the murderers left the Cathedral Church to ransack the archbishop's palace than the terrified monks and townsfolk, who had been watching from the shadows, came out from their hiding places and gathered in the north transept where the body of their abbot and archbishop lay before the altar in the little side chapel of St Benedict. The crown of his head had been sliced off; his blood and brains were scattered about the pavement upon which he had fallen.

Some of the people began to dip their fingers into the pool of blood on the stone slabs and smeared it over their faces, some tore strips from their clothing and soaked up blood, others found bottles and flasks and filled them with the precious liquid. This reaction may seem macabre to us today, but it would not have been thought so at the time, for the churches of Christendom were full of dismembered pieces of the bodies of holy men—to which the faithful attributed miraculous powers. Here was their archbishop, murdered before an altar in the house of God; some of his predecessors had already become saints and the object of pious veneration, their relics preserved here and in the nearby St Augustine's Abbey. In the eyes of these people, who owed fealty to Thomas as both spiritual and temporal lord, the assassin knights who had dared to abuse the rights of sanctuary and desecrate this

An illumination from a collection of letters from and concerning Thomas, copied about ten years after his death. It shows in composite form the four knights outside the archbishop's palace while servants announce their arrival; below are the murder in the cathedral and, to the right, pilgrims before St Thomas' shrine. (*British Library.*)

consecrated place had created a new martyr for their God. As one of those present wrote afterwards, 'at a later time no one was thought happy who had not carried off something from the precious treasure of the martyr's body'.[1]

By the light of candles set upon the altar of St Benedict the monks attended to the body of their abbot and archbishop. Turning it over, they saw that Thomas' face was clean and disfigured only by a thin streak of blood which ran from the right temple across the nose and the left cheek. Lying beneath him they found a hammer and an axe, and nearby were the broken pieces of a sword blade.

Long before this night there had been speculation as to whether Thomas would be entitled to be called a martyr if, and when, he were killed, and even among churchmen opinion had been divided. There were those among his monks at Canterbury who felt that it was his pride that had brought his end —and to the world at large he had often appeared to be a proud and head-strong man. He seemed to have been determined to court death, deliberately refusing all avenues of escape, which would have been easy in the dark church with its many stairways and passages, but was this through dedication to his faith or because he lacked the humility which would permit flight? Many had been shocked that such an apparently worldly man had been made archbishop, and amazed when he had dared to oppose his king. He had showered excommunications on those who crossed him, caused suffering to his supporters and embarrassment for the Pope—and all because he was too proud, or too grasping, or too self-righteous to agree to compromise. He had claimed to be a champion of the Church, yet many of his acts had done it harm. Could violent death counterbalance the apparent lack of virtue? Could his critics, in fact, have been mistaken? Only God could answer; and, that very night, a blind man, with no prior knowledge of the murder, appeared at the cathedral and miraculously regained his sight. A miracle for a martyr! The news of the archbishop's death spread rapidly and as rapidly came back stories of new cures and marvels. Among the common people to whom, perhaps misguidedly, he had long seemed a champion, Thomas was already being treated as among the blessed.

Canonization came two years and two months after Thomas' death, but the procession of pilgrims to his tomb began as soon as the monks allowed the faithful into the presence of his body. Over the next three centuries the pilgrimage to Canterbury became one of the most important in all Christendom.

The murder of Thomas in some ways changed the course of history and is the main reason why most people remember him. But what was it that brought him to such a violent end, and why did that death have such resounding repercussions? The man Thomas earned his place in history without the need of sainthood, and it was his life that gave his death importance as much as the sacrilege it represented. Others died for God without arousing such intense devotion.

Who was this man and why did he become such an important figure? The public facts about his life are well documented and this book will show the path he trod to that last hour before the altar of St Benedict: student, official, cleric, soldier, statesman, prince of the Church and penitent—but was it his deeds or his personality, his duty or his pride, that brought him martyrdom? About the private man we can only guess from those glimpses that are revealed by his contemporaries and his known behaviour: we may each form our own opinion.

There were at least eleven different biographies of St Thomas written within a dozen or so years of his death, several of them by people who were on his staff and some of the others clearly based on information from people who knew him well. But they are the lives of a saint, and sometimes the writers incorporate legendary material or colour their history with what seems appropriate to hagiography. There are many small points on which they disagree but their very contradictions emphasize the consistency with which events and even conversations are frequently reported.

And what of the pilgrims who, right through the Middle Ages, flocked in their thousands to St Thomas's shrine? Why was this particular saint so important to them? Why did they make their pilgrimage to Canterbury? What part did such journeys play in contemporary religion? What did they hope to gain? The reasons, as we shall see, were not always entirely religious, and changed in emphasis with the passing years. We shall follow in the footsteps of the pilgrims too, discovering something of the nature of their pilgrimage, its changing spirit and its practical reality.

Eventually, nearly three and a half centuries after the murder in the cathedral, another great clash between Church and State brought an end to St Thomas' victory—or so at least it seemed—and that must form part of our story too. Yet, after an even greater length of time, Thomas of Canterbury still exerts a fascination, and his Cathedral Church still draws its pilgrims. Time and the hand of Man have destroyed much from those distant centuries, yet much still survives, not only in documents and legends but in actual buildings and artifacts which recall both the life of St Thomas and the journeyings of the pilgrims to his shrine. This book cannot encompass all the records, all the survivals, all the facts, but it will, I hope, answer some of our questions about the pilgrims, the pilgrimage and its Holy Martyr.

PART ONE: THOMAS

1 The Young Lawyer

THOMAS BECKET, as history knows him, was born on Tuesday, December 21st, 1118—Tuesdays were several times to prove key days in his life—in a house to the north of Cheapside where the Hall of the Mercers' Company stands today. There must have been some fears for his survival, for the same day he was taken to the Church of St Mary Colechurch and, at evensong, baptized—the devout believed that an unchristened soul could not enter heaven. His name, unusual for a Norman although it came to be one of the most popular for English boys, was given because that day is celebrated as the feast of St Thomas the Apostle. His father, a merchant from Rouen who had come to London many years before, was known as Gilbert Becket. Surnames were also unusual for Normans and he had presumably gained his—meaning the man from the beck, or little brook—to distinguish him from other Gilberts when he was a boy at Thierceville,[1] in Normandy. In

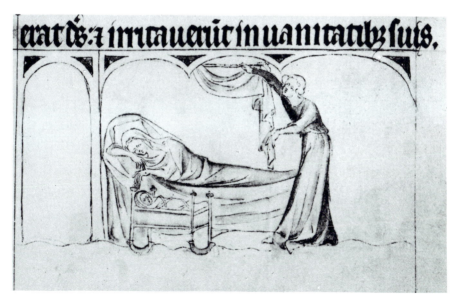

The birth of Thomas, shown wrapped in swaddling bands, lying in a cradle beside his mother's bed. An illustration from a sequence depicting Thomas' life in the Queen Mary Psalter, drawn in the fourteenth century. (*British Library*.)

those days surnames were not automatically handed down from father to son, and it is rare for the name Becket to be used when contemporaries write of Thomas. Indeed, the evidence suggests that he did not like it and never used it himself.

Thomas' mother, the only woman whom he appears ever to have held in real affection, was called Matilda, or possibly Roesa, and came from Caen. Both parents were first generation Normans in England. It was only half a century since the Battle of Hastings and William the Conqueror's youngest son, Henry I, was on the throne of England and held the Dukedom of Normandy.

Gilbert Becket was not a nobleman, but his success as a merchant had enabled him to buy property and so derive his income from rents. This gave him an honourable position in society, for he was no longer in trade, nor did he invest in other people's business ventures (at that time lending money for profit was forbidden to good Christians) and he had no need to work with his hands.

These seem to be the facts, but such a prosaic background did not satisfy some of the storytellers after Thomas' death.

A more romantic legend, told in many versions, including the *Golden Legend* of Jacobus de Voraigne (which William Caxton translated and Richard Pynson printed in 1520), sends Gilbert either on crusade or on pilgrimage to the Holy Land where he is captured by the Saracens. A Saracen princess, his captor's daughter, falls in love with him and promises to 'forsake frends, heritage and countre . . . and become cristen' if he will marry her. Gilbert escapes and 'after thys it fortuned so that this prynces doughter stale away and passed many a wylde place and great adventure and by goddes purveance came at the last to London demandynge and crienge Beket beket, for more englysshe could she nat'. In London's streets she becomes the centre of a jeering crowd and there she is seen by a servant of Gilbert who had shared his captivity, and this servant fetches his master. As soon as she sees Gilbert she falls in a swoon but he takes her up and comforts her. Embarrassed by the situation (no doubt he had never expected to see her again) he sends her to his mother's house and asks the advice of six bishops—conveniently gathered at St Paul's—as to what he should do. They recommend baptism and marriage without delay. Gilbert accepts their advice and the very next night their first-born, Thomas, is conceived.

There is, almost certainly, no truth in the story—but *why* was it invented? Perhaps it was intended to reflect the concept that St Thomas united the Churches of the East and West when he was adopted as the patron saint of the Knights of Acre, and perhaps it gained some credence because exotic blood would help explain some of the unusual features of his character.

There were other legends of omens linked with Thomas' birth, for none of which we have any real evidence, but they were all supposed to have foretold that he would be a luminary of God. One story of his childhood, repeated by his clerk and confidante Herbert of Bosham, who claimed to have had it from Thomas himself, tells how, when the boy lay sick with a fever, a vision of the Virgin Mary appeared to him. She promised that he would recover and gave him two gold keys; the keys, she said, to Paradise, which henceforth were to be in his keeping. Another close acquaintance, John of Salisbury, tells how Thomas' mother brought him up devoutly and to especially venerate the Virgin.[2] Although a devout childhood would be an almost obligatory addition to the writing of a saintly biography, we have no reason to doubt the authenticity of this.

The London of Thomas' boyhood was already England's leading city, although the administration of government was not yet wholly centred there. William the Conqueror had given the burgesses a charter which respected their ancient privileges and Henry I reaffirmed their right to be exempt from certain tolls and taxes and from trial by battle in civil disputes, and assured the citizens a measure of self-government.

In 1099 William Rufus had built a new palace at Westminster—the walls of the Great Hall still stand, though capped by a later roof—and although the court travelled with the king to any part of his lands in England or in Normandy, and government was carried out from wherever he was, London formed a convenient geographical centre for the conduct of affairs.

Westminster Palace was two miles up-river from the city; down-river stood the stern White Tower, begun by the Conqueror to both protect and control the city and the river. The Thames could be crossed by a wooden bridge, which was swept away in a gale a few years later, and most of the houses were built of wood, despite the fact that London had been ravaged by fire in 1077, and again in 1087 when St Paul's Cathedral had been destroyed. It was not until after another fire in 1136, which this time burned down the rebuilt bridge, that the richer citizens began to build their houses of stone and tiles.

The city was surrounded by strong walls, except to the south where the river had undermined them so that only the Thames itself was now relied upon for protection. The fortifications were pierced by seven double gates to give entrance to the city, and towers were placed at regular intervals along the northern walls.

To the people of the time London seemed very crowded, but, despite its growing importance as a centre of international trade, its residents included ploughmen among the merchants and craftsmen, there were gardens and orchards inside the town, and, to the north, there were extensive pastures and fine arable lands. Further beyond was thick forest with deer, boars and wild bulls and the citizens had hunting rights in the surrounding counties and grazing rights nearer at hand.

We have no contemporary description of London but we can get some idea of it from the way it is depicted by a Londoner, William fitzStephen, a scribe to Thomas at Canterbury, who prefaced his life of the saint with a description of his native town—the earliest known description of any medieval city. He tells of weekly horse sales, street vendors and craftsmen, fairs and festivals, wine shops 'kept in ships and cellars', a public eating-house, performances of miracle plays, racing, jousting, football games and celebrated schools attached to the most important of the 136 churches and 13 abbeys. 'The only inconveniences of London,' he claimed, were 'the immoderate drinking of foolish persons, and the frequent fires'.

FitzStephen paints a rosy picture and turns a blind eye on the way in which the poorer people probably lived, for he was proud of London and proud that Thomas was a Londoner. And Thomas was not one of the poorer sort: although he was not a nobleman he had good connections. According to fitzStephen his father came of knightly stock—perhaps he was a younger son—and he had a comfortable house where he could offer hospitality to some of the important people who had to come to London: there were no inns which could offer accommodation fit for a gentleman.

One frequent guest was Sir Richer de l'Aigle, of Pevensey Castle in Sussex. This baron took a particular liking to Thomas and encouraged him to visit Pevensey when on holiday. One source[3] suggests that he actually went to live with him, as sons of noble families went to be a page in another household. On one occasion, when Thomas was out hawking with de l'Aigle, he either fell from his horse when trying to ride it along a single-plank bridge across a millstream or actually dived into the water to rescue a bird. The young man was swept down to the millrace and would have been crushed beneath the wheel but, just as he reached it, the miller stopped its action and pulled him out. Later the story was told to suggest a miracle, with the millwheel stopped by the hand of God. Whether a case of divine intervention or not, the tale shows us that Thomas was learning the pursuits of a gentleman, and in later years he would be well versed in knightly behaviour.

School, for Thomas, was at first most likely one of the London grammar schools which taught the rudiments of Latin.[4] Indeed, at the grammar school he would have been allowed to speak only in Latin, and outside Latin grammar he would learn little else. But this was a necessary first accomplishment for anyone with any pretentions to education, for the books which he would have to read to pursue his studies would all be written in this language. At home he spoke in French (he probably never learned Anglo-Saxon) but although private documents might be written in French most public communications would be in Latin, which could be understood by any educated man throughout Europe. Thomas would not necessarily write it very well—formal letters, books and state documents were written or copied by specialist scribes who had developed a careful and easily deciphered hand. Latin was no dead language to these people. Although Saxon folk would know Latin only if specially taught, quite ordinary people in France, Italy or Spain would be able to follow simple spoken Latin for their own tongues were closely related to it—although not so similar that they would be able to make reply.

All education was in the hands of the Church, and most literate and scholarly people were churchmen—there was no other way for them to earn a living. Clerk and cleric meant exactly the same thing then. A clerk did not necessarily work in the Church but, at a time when wages were not yet the accepted form of payment, his recompense would be the income from the land linked with some Church post, or 'living' (we still use the term today), controlled by his employer.

When he was sufficiently proficient in Latin grammar Thomas was sent to further his education as a boarder at the Augustinian Priory at Merton, south of London, where he would have worn the black habit of the Augustinians although he would not have had to take any religious vows. He seems to have been happy there, for he helped to ensure that it was well endowed in later years. He was taught by Prior Robert and, when Thomas became archbishop, a Prior Robert of Merton became his confessor. They may have been the same man, although it is more likely that the confessor was someone younger, perhaps one of Thomas' fellow students, for he wrote a biography in which he describes Thomas as a bright and intelligent pupil, but one who was lazy and preferred games to study.

From Merton Thomas went to Paris to study at the school attached to the romanesque Cathedral of Notre Dame. Not yet a university—none such existed, although they later grew from the cathedral schools—it nevertheless gave similar academic stature to successful students. The teaching placed an emphasis upon theology but, since Thomas never showed a leaning towards theological disputation in later life, it is possible that his studies concentrated upon another discipline—possibly law, which he was to pursue more deeply a few years later. It is suggested that while in Paris Thomas took a vow of chastity. It certainly appears that he had decided to become a cleric which, although it did not mean that he would become a priest, would entail entering the lower orders of the Church and officially clerics were not supposed to marry. Married clergy were not unknown—in England the Saxon Church had found marriage quite acceptable among its priests, just as the Eastern Church still does—but married clergy would not get far in their careers, for the Pope disapproved most strongly.

When he was twenty or twenty-one Thomas returned home. About this time his mother died and his father was facing financial stringencies. Some of Gilbert's properties, the rents of which provided his income, had been destroyed, possibly in the great fire of 1136 which burned down London Bridge. Perhaps it was his mother's support which had enabled Thomas to go on being a student and now his father felt that he should maintain himself and help provide for his two younger sisters, who were still at home.

His long and superior education would qualify him for a quite important position—he does not seem to have been particularly scholarly and probably saw his future in administration for the crown or for some great lord. However, such jobs were a matter of patronage and not to be had for the asking;

nor did they carry a wage—that was not the way in which such things were organized. Thomas had to bide his time. Meanwhile he found a livelihood working for a wealthy relative who had become a merchant, Osbert (or Osbern) Huit Deniers (Osbert Eight Pence), who was also an official in the administration of the City of London and probably used Thomas to help him in this role.[5]

While Thomas had been gaining his education England had entered a period of confusion and unrest. In December 1135 Henry I had died. Had he left a surviving son the succession might have been clear for, although the Saxon monarchy had been elective (the elective element still survives in the 'acclamation' in a modern British coronation ceremony) and the feudal contract was not in essence hereditary, the idea of succession by blood was strong. The contenders for the crown were now the dead king's daughter Matilda, to whom the king's vassals had sworn fealty ten years earlier as his prospective heir, and Stephen, son of Henry's sister Adela. Taking advantage of popular resistance to the idea of female rule, Stephen gained the support of Londoners and, aided by his brother Henry, Bishop of Winchester, who handed over the royal treasure, was crowned in Westminster Abbey on Christmas Day. Corboil, the Archbishop of Canterbury, performed the ceremony, having been given to believe that on his deathbed the king had named Stephen as his heir.

In 1139 Matilda landed to enforce her claim, although the first major battle between the two forces did not take place until early in 1141. Stephen was captured and Matilda elected queen at Winchester. She entered London for her coronation but was forced to flee before it could take place, and then had to release Stephen in return for her half-brother who had been captured by the other side. For the next eight years Matilda held Bristol and the West while Stephen held the East. Then, in 1148, she retired to Normandy.

Eleventh-century Europe had not yet resolved itself into the nation states of modern politics. In spiritual matters the papacy was striving to establish its supremacy across the whole of Christendom while on the European continent the Holy Roman Emperor, successor to the title of Charlemagne, sought to be a power above his client kings and himself to control the papacy. In France powerful barons, among them the King of England in his role of Duke of Normandy, owed fealty to the King of France but were so strong within their own territories that they were more disunited than they were a nation. In England, however, William the Conqueror had been able to establish a more concentrated power.

Even before the Conquest, Norman influence on English life had been strong, and it is possible that Saxon society would gradually have evolved closer to the Norman pattern, but William I's accession brought in Norman social organisation at one stroke. Weary of war, the Saxon aristocracy either acquiesced, sank back into the common people, or, if they stood out against the Norman conquerors, were dispossessed for their rebellion.

Norman society was based on the feudal system, a system of social inter-dependence based upon land tenure, protection and duty. At the top of the social order came the king who, at his coronation, undertook to protect and provide justice for his subjects in return for the possession of his kingdom. Naturally he could not provide for the defence and governance of the realm on his own so, after setting aside sufficient land to produce the income neces-sary for his personal needs, he divided up his kingdom and gave territory to his noblemen in return for their promise, on oath, to be loyal and to fight in and supply soldiers for his army, or to provide some service in administration. The barons, in their turn, while keeping some aside to meet their private needs, divided up the lands which they had received from the crown and parcelled it out in 'fiefs' to lesser vassals. So it was enfeoffed downwards until the rear vassal was a knight who held a single manor too small to be so divided and which was worked by peasants in return for the right to farm a small part for their own benefit.

At all levels this was a two-way social contract, although the higher up the social scale the greater the material advantage. At the bottom the lord of the manor had control over almost every aspect of a peasant's life and at the top the only way in which the barons could remove an unsatisfactory king was by breaking their oath in outright rebellion—though they might claim justification in that their king had not kept his part of the bargain. A rear vassal always excepted from his duty to his lord such obligation as was implicit to the crown or other overlord but, where the same person held land from two different overlords who had conflicting interests, he might be unable to perform his duty to either of them. This eventually brought about the end of the system, along with the substitution of cash payments for services, which led to personal ownership instead of the feudal situation, where a number of people could all truthfully answer, of the same piece of ground, 'This land is mine, I hold it from my lord.'

In addition to his usual obligation of military service, each feudal lord, if he had enough tenants to justify it, was obliged to maintain his own baronial court and his vassals were obliged to attend it for the judgement of any cases concerning their holdings, their relations with one another or their relations with himself.

There might be many lesser obligations. One Kentishman was required 'to hold the king's head in the boat' when he should cross the Channel, and in another eccentric case a vassal was obliged each Christmas to come before his lord and make 'unum saltum et siffletum et unun bumbulum' (a leap, a whistle and a fart).[6]

In theory, the feudal contract was between individuals and, on the death of a vassal, land would revert to his lord. To renew the contract the vassal heir had to pay a 'relief' or *relevium* and, in the case of lands held directly from the crown, they were actually claimed by the king's officers and only on payment of the relief was the heir recognized and allowed to perform homage,

swear fealty and receive the formal investitutre which gave him legal possession. The land could have been given elsewhere but even the crown did not
feel strong enough to overrule hereditary succession. If, however, the heir
was a minor the lord had wardship and—since the minor could not perform
the services due—retained the income from the lands while being responsible
for the support and education of the late vassal's children as proper to their
station. If the fief passed to an heiress the lord had the right to select her
husband—for he had to be sure that the husband would be capable of
performing the services due (in practice this meant selling the choice to an
interested party or to the heiress' family). If a vassal line became extinct the
fief reverted to its lord, as did the holdings forfeited by a convicted felon.

These were the main features of the feudal system. They are important to
understanding the politics of the time and the principles which guided
Thomas and his contemporaries. There were other rights and obligations
which will play a part in the ensuing narrative, but we have digressed from
it too long and they can be explained as they occur.

We left Thomas in the service of Osbert Huit Deniers, where he remained
for three or four years; but this was not a career for an ambitious young
man and, perhaps because his family's situation had improved, he began to
look for something with a future. One of his father's boyhood acquaintances
had entered the Church as a monk and now had risen to become Archbishop
of Canterbury. He was one of the most powerful men in the kingdom. Thomas
had no plans to become a priest, his interests were too worldly, but members
of the archbishop's staff often stayed at his father's house on their way to the
archbishop's favourite manor of Harrow, just north of London, and they
would have told him of the opportunities in the service of this important
man. Supported by their sponsorship, Gilbert Becket approached Archbishop
Theobald to find a place for his son in the archbishop's household.[7]

Archbishop Theobald needed a large secretariat to deal with the conduct
of Church affairs, manage Church lands, run Church courts, collect Church
monies and sustain the active role he played in national politics. A place was
found for Thomas, who now joined a group of young men whom Theobald
was training for potential high office if they fulfilled their promise.

Thomas, now twenty-five, was an immensely tall young man, well-over
six feet, with an impressive presence and handsome, virile looks. Dark-haired,
with prominent eyes and a powerful Norman nose, he seems to have had
highly attuned senses—he could judge wine and accurately date a vintage with
the finest of palates, even though he preferred to drink a kind of herbal tea—
and he had a charismatic personality which could change quickly from lively
animation to an expression of impressive calm in repose. A chink in his
armour of apparent confidence seems to be revealed in a slight tendency to
stutter. Perhaps, since this picture is drawn from the words of colleagues
describing him much later, we should allow for the possibility that in retro-
spect they would remember his favourable points, and we might also see a

certain arrogance and hot temper hidden behind their words.

Thomas seems to have been liked by most of his colleagues on the archbishop's staff, although neither now, nor later, does he seem to have made any very close friends. While others like him left chatty private correspondence behind them, Thomas never seems to have written a personal letter. Perhaps it was this rather self-contained demeanour which aroused the antagonism of Roger Pont l'Evêque, a colleague in the archbishop's household who was to oppose him many times in later life, and who now contrived to get him twice dismissed from Archbishop Theobald's service. Fortunately, the archbishop's brother, Walter, Archdeacon of Canterbury, saw that he was reinstated and it was not long before Thomas' abilities were being recognized by Theobald himself.

Thomas now took minor orders and was awarded livings at Otford, in Kent, and St Mary-in-the-Strand in London. As was the practice, he would have paid someone else to be his vicar, or substitute, and to carry out the parish duties. In 1143 a new pope, Celestine II, had assumed the triple tiara, and late in the year Thomas may have set off with Theobald for Rome. There the archbishop sought to challenge the right of Henry, Bishop of Winchester, to continue to be the papal legate to England as he had been under Innocent II. As papal legate he was responsible directly to Rome and superseded the archbishop, on some matters, even in his own see. The abbot of St Augustine's Abbey in Canterbury also claimed to be independent of the archbishop and subject only to the Pope.

Celestine had scarcely ascended the papal throne when he died and Lucius II was elected. The case of the papal legacy was heard again and, in June 1144, Theobald returned to England confirmed in his authority over St Augustine's and himself appointed as the papal legate.

Perhaps because he had shown a keen legal mind in Rome, Thomas was now sent to the law schools at Auxerre, in France, and Bologna, in northern Italy, to extend his knowledge of both roman (that is, civil) and canon (ecclesiastical) law.

In 1148 another new pope, Eugenius III, called a convocation of the Church in Rheims, largely concerned with the Second Crusade, but also to discuss Stephen's action of imprisoning bishops who had worked against him in the civil war in England, and the election of Stephen's nephew William to the archbishopric of York—an appointment that Theobald opposed. King Stephen forbade Theobald to leave the country, although he had been summoned to attend. Stephen's command was quite in order, for William the Conqueror had decreed that no tenant-in-chief of the Crown could cross the sea without royal permission. As a baron holding land the archbishop owed the king military service and if, while he was abroad, an army was to be mustered he would not be there to perform his duty. Nevertheless, it was a quibble to use this to prevent him obeying a summons from the Pope.

The archbishop defied the king and secretly took a small boat across the Channel, for which offence he was formally exiled. At the Council, however, Archbishop Theobald spoke up for his king when the future St Bernard asked for his excommunication, declaring that if bishops take to arms and fortify castles they can hardly be surprised if they are treated as enemy prisoners when beaten. The case against Stephen was adjourned, never to be reopened, but Theobald, with Thomas in attendance, stayed in exile for most of the year. The episode is important as a precedent for Thomas' later action.

Although Stephen had managed to keep his crown he still did not have the full support of the country and, when he proposed the coronation of his son Eustace—there were precedents for crowning an heir during the reigning monarch's lifetime to ensure the succession—Theobald was one of the many who opposed it. Thomas was sent to Rome to ensure that the Pope would not give his approval for the coronation. In 1152, after a Council at which many of the nobles swore fealty to Eustace, Theobald still refused to anoint the prince and was shut up under house arrest until he would change his mind. The ageing archbishop and a few followers once again escaped into a small boat on the Thames and sailed for Flanders. The king declared that he would confiscate the property of the archbishopric but, under the threat of excommunication, he relented and recalled the archbishop. The following year Prince Eustace died and Theobald was responsible for arranging a treaty whereby the claims of Stephen's other children were passed over and the king accepted the succession of Matilda's son Henry, provided that he were allowed to live out the rest of his reign in peace.

Thomas' usefulness to the archbishop in all this diplomacy and litigation was recognized by the award of prebendaries at St Paul's and Lincoln cathedrals, which brought in stipends without requiring any duties, and in 1154 he was also made Provost of Beverley and Archdeacon of Canterbury.

The Archdeaconship made him the most important lawyer in the English Church. He presided over the episcopal court, the highest ecclesiastical court in the country; he was responsible for distributing alms and collecting dues and was in effect the 'business manager' of the diocese. It was a job for life, since he was not a priest, and from which, when he came to retire, he could no doubt expect to be awarded a bishopric to provide for his old age. Thomas was now nearly thirty-five, a mature age for those times, but he had achieved a high office which brought respect and a comfortable living—even the continual travelling which the job demanded would have been a pleasure to him, for he loved being astride a horse. His future must have seemed settled and secure but, in a matter of only months, it was to be dramatically changed.

2 The Seal and the Sword

KING STEPHEN died in October 1154. As caretaker of the kingdom, Archbishop Theobald kept the country calm until Matilda's son Henry could be brought across the Channel to take the throne, and it was he who placed the crown upon the new king's head in Westminster Abbey on December 19th. Henry was only twenty-one, but he had already governed Normandy for four years, since his mother had made him Duke, had ruled Anjou and Maine since his father's death[1] the year before and, by his marriage to Eleanor, Duchess of Aquitaine (following the annulment of her marriage to the king of France), was holder of the lands of Poitou and Aquitaine.

Now he had England to rule as well, an England which had been torn by a civil war that had weakened the power of the crown. He was determined that his throne would be secure and his government strong. He needed a reliable and efficient 'civil service' to carry out his plans. To find an able administrator to head his secretariat he asked the advice of Archbishop Theobald, who had already shown his loyal support.

The archbishop recommended his archdeacon, Thomas, and soon after the coronation Thomas became the keeper of the Great Seal, the chancellor to the King of England. Before this time the chancellor had been in charge of all the letter-writing, record-keeping and administration of the court, but Thomas came to be so trusted by the king that, save for the king himself, no one had more power in the administration of the kingdom; and no one was closer to the king. The archbishop was soon writing to his protégé, '. . . it sounds in the ears and mouth of the people that you and the king are one heart and one mind' (cor *unum et animam unam*).

What was this Henry like? He is frequently presented as an uncouth and dirty boor given to hysterical behaviour, but that is far from a true picture. He had been taught by a famous scholar, spoke several languages, read history and politics from Latin texts and may even have been able to write. His appearance was not very prepossessing: short and stocky, rather clumsy and usually shabbily dressed—although he would meet the expense of fine robes and jewels to impress people on state occasions—he did not cut much of a figure next to the tall and finely apparelled chancellor. He ate and drank enormous quantities, but because he was hungry and thirsty not because he relished food and drink, and he took so much exercise that he never got fat. Exotic dishes and grand banquets he found boring: he had no interest in luxury and cultivated living for its own sake. Intensely physical, he was always on the go, riding in a day what most men would cover in four ('like a special courier, and showing no mercy to his companions' is how his contemporary Walter Map put it[2]), hawking and hunting whenever he got the chance, always trying to do three things at once; he rarely sat down to eat but paced about, and if his hands were not doing something else he usually had a book in them. His flaming red hair, which he kept short for fear of baldness (he cared about his looks if not about his clothes), was matched by a fiery temper—he sometimes rolled around on the floor in rage—and his tongue could be as foul as his fingernails were usually dirty (what was left after he had finished biting them). His hands were usually covered with the cuts he got out hunting, but he would play a skilful game of chess when it was too dark to go out hunting but too early to find a partner for his bed. His keen grey eyes missed little and when his temper cooled he had a cunning grasp of politics and statecraft. He had extraordinary charisma calling forth fierce loyalty and, despite his temper and neurotic restlessness, he was 'exceedingly good and loveable' so that no one 'surpassed him in gentleness and friend-liness' (Map again).

In Thomas this colourful and enigmatic personality found not only an able administrator and advisor to help him implement his plans but also a lively and congenial companion. These two strong-willed egoists seem to have found each in each other perhaps the only real friends, whose feelings they could reciprocate, that either ever had. They shared a passion for hunting, a love of action, a determination to get on with life, and if Thomas's modest background made him revel in fine clothes and high living the king was happy to have him take charge at a banquet and to make a show on his behalf. Perhaps he even admired the way in which Thomas could carry off the pomp, and he was certainly amused by the chancellor's lavish tastes. One wintry day, out riding, they met a beggar asking for alms. The king suggested that it would be a worthy act to give the man a cloak and Thomas urged him to do so, but the king demurred and suggested that Thomas should have the credit: 'Laying hands on his hood he tried to pull off the cape the chancellor was wearing, a new and very good one of scarlet and grey, which he fought hard to keep.' In fact, he struggled so hard that the retainers following some way behind rushed up thinking that some mischief was afoot. 'At last the chancellor reluctantly allowed the king to overcome him, suffering him to pull the cape from his shoulders and give it to the poor man.'[3]

For seven years these two were soulmates. Some have suggested that Thomas was sycophantically going along with the king, both in supporting his policies and in sharing his pleasures, but this cannot be so, for Thomas so obviously enjoyed the life and so whole-heartedly devoted his energies to Henry's causes. He was fifteen years older than the king and perhaps for

Henry he was something of a father figure. A homosexual element has sometimes been seen in their relationship—nothing unusual in English royalty; both Henry's uncle, William Rufus, and his son, Richard the Lionheart, are well known to have been homophile—and some of Henry's later behaviour does smack of the rejected lover. However, although to modern eyes Thomas does seem to have taken a rather masochistic pleasure in being whipped this would have been thought devout in his time and there seems never to have been a breath of contemporary scandal about his sexual life—homo or hetero, there just *wasn't* any. Whatever sins of pride he was charged with he seems to have kept his vow of chastity: whenever the king went whoring Thomas seems to have made himself noticeably absent.

The chancellor's official remuneration consisted of a daily allowance of five shillings, one lord's simnel loaf (bread made with fine flour), two seasoned simnel loaves, one sextary (sixth measure) of clear wine and one of household wine, one large wax candle and forty smaller pieces. As a member of the household of the king he would have been housed and fed, but Thomas chose to run his own establishment and, although the ordinary subject would have thought himself laden with riches to receive more than ninety pounds a year, this was in no way enough to pay for the style in which Thomas lived. But he did not have to live on it. He still kept his church posts and their income, and Henry gave him more, including the deanery of Hastings. He received also

The first Great Seal of Henry II, used 1155–8, when Thomas was chancellor.

the wardship of the castles of Eye and Berkhamsted, which brought with them the service of 140 knights. The chancellor's office was responsible for collecting the income from vacant benefices and manors held in wardship by the crown and probably Thomas also used some of these monies to defray the expenses of the job. This was to be held against him later, and even at this time there were churchmen who said that he should have resigned his archdeaconship, for how could he head both the ecclesiastic and royal courts?

Since the tenth century the Church had been building itself into an absolute and highly centralized monarchical power, a vertical hierarchy which replaced the more diverse national churches of previous centuries with the Pope as much a spiritual emperor as the Holy Roman Emperor was a temporal one. As a supranational organization it sought to strengthen its position and protect itself from the control of national governments. The Gregorian programme of reform wanted free election to clerical posts, the inviolability of Church property, freedom of appeal to Rome and clerical immunity from lay tribunals.

Conflict was inevitable, and it first came over who should appoint new bishops. Henry I and Archbishop Anselm worked out a compromise (the same as that made later between the Emperor and the Pope): that the Church would choose the bishop elect but the king would receive his fealty and confer fiefs before the consecration. In effect this gave the king a veto, since the Church was hardly likely to insist on consecrating a man from whom the appropriate endowment had been withheld. Under a strong king, like Henry I, this gave him control, but a weak king, as Stephen had been, was under great pressure to bend with the Church. Since he needed their support Stephen had been forced to make further concessions.

In Saxon England the bishops and sheriffs had sat side by side as the judiciary of the courts of the shires, but William the Conqueror put an end to this and insisted that churchmen should not judge cases where the sentence might be death or mutilation—men of God should not spill blood—, but should set up courts of their own to deal with cases within the province of the Church. These would include any dispute concerning marriage, (including annulments), wills and disputes upon the high seas, which came under no king's jurisdiction. (Divorce, Probate and Admiralty Divisions still form a separate section of the British Courts, set up to replace the Church courts at the time of the Reformation.) They would also claim to judge cases of breach of contract—for contracts were undertaken upon oath—, charges of adultery and non-observance of religious festivals. Under Stephen they had gone further and obtained a concession they had sought, but not achieved, elsewhere. Church courts were granted jurisdiction, to the exclusion of the secular law, in all cases involving ecclesiastics or the property of the clergy. The Church was becoming an independent and rival power.

No doubt, when Archbishop Theobald recommended Thomas to the king, he thought that he was helping someone into high office who would take the Church's side and speak for Church opinion in counselling the king. He was mistaken. Henry wanted to create a strong monarchy and restore the balance to that of his grandfather's time, and Thomas, chief lawyer of the Church, gave his allegiance wholeheartedly to the crown—except for one isolated case when he opposed the king over the marriage of the Count of Flanders to Mary, daughter of King Stephen, who had taken vows and become the Abbess of Barking.

During his first summer as king, Henry besieged the castles of Cleobury, Wigmore and Bridgenorth to suppress a rebellion led by Hugh de Mortimer, and then set about turning out of England all the mercenary forces which Stephen had employed to bolster up the crown. Castles which might prove rallying points for rebels were razed to the ground, while in London Thomas set about the strengthening and restoration of the Tower. Peace came to the land at last and, as one chronicler put it, 'then fled the ravening wolves, or they were changed into sheep; or if not really changed, yet, through fear of the laws they remained harmless among the sheep'.

Now attention turned back to the European continent. Geoffrey, the king's younger brother, claimed to have been promised Anjou as his inheritance, but Henry had no intention of giving up any of his lands. In January, 1156, Thomas accompanied his king across the channel and gained more lessons in siegecraft as their army reduced the fortresses of Chinon, Mirabel and Loudun.

Thomas' next battle in England was a legal one. His leading rival as a lawyer was probably Hilary, Bishop of Chichester, whom he had already encountered in court when, as Dean of Hastings, Thomas had supported his vicar's claim to be exempt from the bishop's supervision. That time Hilary won. Now Hilary claimed the obedience of Battle Abbey. For ten years the abbot had stood out against him, claiming that, although the abbey fell within the bishop's diocese, its founder, William the Conqueror, had placed it directly under the royal protection and that therefore the bishop had no authority. The abbey was built on the site of the Battle of Hastings where, in 1066, the Normans had defeated the Saxon army to claim England for their duke. It was a case that attracted great attention, and which the king eventually agreed to hear in May 1157.

The bishop thought that he had a trump card: he had letters from the Pope in his support; but he had written to the Pope without informing his opponents, a technical irregularity, and, worse, without first obtaining permission from the king—which had been expressly forbidden since the time of William I. King Henry was furious and threw such a tantrum that an adjournment had to be called.

Chichester still stuck to his position, claiming that the king, not being a churchman, had no more authority to release the bishop than he to free a vassal from allegiance to the crown. Thomas made the final speech on behalf of the abbot. It was abundantly clear where the king's feelings lay and the Norman barons who sat with him to advise in judgement were predictably ranged against the bishop—it would have been diplomatic for him to have withdrawn before the case had got this far, for the judgement could scarcely be in doubt. What did surprise the Church was that Thomas declared that abbots and bishops were as much the king's subjects as any secular barons and he could alter and overrule their powers. It can be argued that he was speaking as a lawyer, the representative of his client—but that was not the way the Church now saw it. Whatever the individual opinion regarding the case in point, this statement made by Thomas was a direct challenge to the power of the Church. In giving judgement the king confirmed all the abbot's privileges—'Not,' he told the bishop, 'to set you at naught, but to defend by sound reason those royal rights which you have been pleased, in our hearing, to call frivolous.'[4]

In the spring of 1158 Thomas was sent on his grandest mission yet. The chancellor was to go to Paris, to the court of Louis VII and bring back the infant Princess Margaret as a bride for Henry's eldest son. The prince himself was only three, and the marriage was in the future, but their betrothal was a diplomatic way of settling a dispute over the Vexin, a stretch of land between Normandy and the Ile de France which Henry claimed and which the French king was too weak to defend but would lose face to cede—instead it would form the dowry of the bride.

Thomas was determined to impress the French and organized a lavish train. Louis, for his part, determined not to be outdone in lavishness, had given instructions that the English visitors were not to be charged for anything while they were in Paris, but given everything they asked for, the bill to be sent to him. Thomas heard of this and scotched the plan by sending disguised servants on ahead to buy up surreptitiously all the provisions that they might need. Picture the simple way in which most people lived in those times and then imagine the effect that Thomas created when, as his biographer fitzStephen described, he

'prepares him to display and lavish the wealth of England's magnificence; so that before all and in all things the person of his liege may be honoured in the envoy, that of the envoy in himself. He had above 200 knights on horseback, of his own household, knight's clerks, butlers, serving men, esquires, sons of nobles trained by him in arms, all in fit order. These and their following shone in new holiday attire, each according to his rank. For he had four and twenty changes of rainment whose texture mocks the purple dyes of Tyre, many garments entirely of silk—almost all to be given away and left over sea—and every sort of material, griese [a fur rather like ermine and used for linings; it is not known what animal it actually came from] and furs, of robes also and carpets, such as those with which the chamber and bed of a bishop are wont to be adorned. He had with him hounds, and birds of all kinds, such as kings and nobles keep. He had also in his company eight carriages, each drawn by five horses, in size and strength like destriers [war horses], for each one being set apart a strong young man, girt in a new tunic walking by the carriage; and each carriage had its driver and guard. Two carriages bore nothing but beer, made by a decoction of water from the strength of corn, in iron-hooped barrels—to be given to the French who admire that sort of drink, which is wholesome, clear, of the colour of wine, and of a better taste. One carriage was used for the chancellor's chapel furniture, one for his chamber, one his bursary, one his kitchen. Others carried different kinds of meat and drink; some had hangings, bags with nightgowns, packs and baggage. He had twelve sumpter-horses, and eight chests containing the chancellor's plate, of gold and silver; vessels, cups, platters, goblets, pitchers, basons, saltcellars, tankards, salvers, dishes. Other coffers and packs contained the chancellor's money—coin enough for daily expenses and presents—his clothes, books and suchlike. One sumpter-horse going before the others bore the sacred vessels of the chapel, the ornaments and books of the altar. Each of the sumpter-horses had its own groom provided as was meet. Each wagon had a dog chained above or below, great and strong and terrible, which seemed able to subdue a bear or a lion. And on the back of each sumpter-horse was a tailed monkey, or the ape that mocked the human face. At his entry of the French villages and castles came first footboys, born to eat up the land—about 250—going six or ten or even more abreast, singing something in their own tongue, after the fashion of their land. There followed at some distance hounds in couples, and greyhounds in leash, with huntsmen and keepers. Then there rattled over the stones of the streets the iron-bound waggons covered with great hides sewn together. Then at a little distance the sumpter-horses, their grooms riding on them, with their knees on the flanks of the horses. Some of the French rushing forth from their houses at this great noise asked who this was, and whose train? They answered that it was the chancellor of the king of the English going on an embassy to the king of the French. Then said the French, "Marvellous is the king of the English whose chancellor goeth thus and so grandly." Then the squires carrying the shields of the knights and leading their destriers; then other squires, of fresh youth, and those who carried hawks on their wrist, after them the butlers, and masters, and servants of the chancellor's house; then the knights and clerks, riding all two and two; last the chancellor and some of his nearest friends.'[5]

In Paris, where Thomas and his retinue were lodged at the headquarters of the Knights Templar, he gave a lavish banquet for the French court and a banquet for the creditors of the English students in Paris—it seems that even Thomas had not got enough money with him to pay what the students owed, so he entertained them to discourage them from pressing for payment. If

A feast in a noble household, from an eleventh-century manuscript, probably more like the scene in Thomas' time than are illustrations in later sources. (*Mansell Collection.*)

behaving like a Hollywood spectacular did not really reflect Henry's style it fitted Thomas perfectly and had exactly the effect that was intended—the French were convinced that the English king must be a very grand king indeed!

On the way back from Paris Thomas and his knights managed to capture a bandit who had been terrorising the settlements of the Seine valley, and the following year he took up arms again assisting Henry (who as Count of Anjou was hereditary Seneschal of France) in bringing to heel some squabbling lords in Brittany. This action was at the request of Louis—Henry's liege lord as far as his French lands were concerned, and his future in-law (and also the ex-husband of Eleanor, Henry's queen). The French king joined them on campaign and was delighted by its success—but somewhat surprised, when it was over, to discover that in their submission the barons of southern Brittany had pledged themselves as liegemen to the English king.

In 1159 the chancellor had an even better opportunity to show his military prowess. Henry decided that he would press ancient, and by then disregarded, rights by which the Count of Toulouse should do him homage as subordinate to the Duchy of Aquitaine. Toulouse, who like Henry as Duke of Normandy paid direct homage to King Louis, understandably refused, so Henry made preparations to go to war.

To avoid the cost of shipping men and equipment across the channel and halfway across France, Henry decided to raise troops in Aquitaine and, instead of asking personal war service from his English vassals, to request a cash contribution from them all. This payment of scutage or 'shield money' was not an innovation—it had been used at least as early as the reign of Henry I—but it had not previously been so general and it had not usually been applied to the Church lords, who held their land by knight-service as much as any lay baron. Thomas overcame any resistance they felt about paying up, but was heavily criticized for his action later.

After helping to organize the campaign Thomas joined his king in the field, taking a large following of soldiers onto his own payroll. The Count of Toulouse did not want to risk a battle and sought refuge in his castle at Toulouse. He also sent a message to the King of France for help—feudal aid was owed in both directions. Louis himself came to Toulouse and joined the besieged forces and a diplomatic stalemate was produced. The situation was delicate: it was perfectly in order for the Duke of Normandy to fight the Count of Toulouse, but they were both vassals of the king of France and when Louis arrived it was impossible for Henry to attack for he would then have been attacking the castle which contained his liege-lord. He was not, however, obliged to raise his siege.

For months the siege continued, until Henry ran out of provisions; then a technical way around the situation was conceived. Thomas was a vassal only to Henry, the king of England, not to the same man as the Duke of Normandy. He had not sworn allegiance to the king of France, nor to Henry in any of the continental roles which made him subservient to Louis. Henry would retire and his chancellor would continue the war, with Henry, Earl of Essex, left behind to act as his adviser. 'Donning hauberk and helmet,' Thomas 'put himself at the head of a strong force and stormed three castles which were strongly fortified and regarded as impregnable. He then crossed the Garonne with his troops in pursuit of the enemy and, after confirming the whole province in its allegiance to the king, returned in high favour and honour.'[6]

Now the war moved north to the Vexin, which Louis had begun to regret that he had promised to Henry. It was permissible to defend one's own land even against a liege-lord, so there was no feudal impediment there. Thomas led his company of 700 knights from his own household, 120 mercenary knights and 4,000 soldiers for forty days. He paid each knight three shillings a day for the provision of horses and squires and fed them all at his expense.[7] One contemporary claims that he trained his knights himself, that they were the best in the English army and that 'he used to give the signal for his men to advance or retreat on one of those slender trumpets peculiar to his army, but well known to all those taking part in the battle'.

During this campaign a French knight, Engelram of Trie, issued a challenge to single combat. Thomas, already forty-one in an era when this was considered advanced middle-age, took up the challenge himself. This was not a battle in the field but a formal joust 'with spurred horse and lance', but Engelram had a formidable reputation. Nevertheless it was he who was unhorsed and Thomas took his charger as a trophy.[8]

Since 1158 Henry had been on the European continent, and most of the time Thomas too had been away from England with the king. However disappointed the ageing Archbishop Theobald may have been in Thomas' failure to promote the Church's cause, he wanted to see the man whom he had thought of like a son. Many times he wrote asking him to come to Canterbury, but Thomas was too busy. Perhaps Theobald wanted to remonstrate with him for the worldly life he was leading; or perhaps, as it seems, he wanted Thomas to succeed him (perhaps he understood his archdeacon's complex character better than Henry knew his chancellor's), and if that was so would wish to prepare him for the task; or it may have been no more than an old man wanting to have the ones he loved around him at the end. He even went so far as to threaten Thomas with excommunication if he did not come, and although this cannot have been intended seriously it should have shocked Thomas into realizing how strongly Archbishop Theobald felt.

In 1161 Theobald dictated a letter for his secretary John of Salisbury to send to the king, begging him to come back to England. 'My old age and sickness will not enable me to wait long for your coming,' he writes. 'Will not my Christ give me to see him whom, at my desire, He gave me to anoint.' And he asks the king to send Thomas home: 'He is the only one we have . . . He ought to have come without a summons, and unless your need of him had excused him, he had been guilty of disobedience to God and man. But since we have ever preferred your will to our own, and have determined to further it in all that is lawful, we forgive him his fault. We wish him to remain in your service as long as you stand in need of his services, and we order him to give his whole zeal and attention to your wants. But permit him to return as soon as every you can spare him.'[9]

Thomas did not go. Theobald died in April without seeing his protégé again.

In theory, bishops are elected by the chapter of their cathedral or, in a few places in England at that time—Canterbury being one of them—by the monks. We have already seen how this choice could be vetoed by the crown (and today, in fact, the Prime Minister, in the Queen's name, actually dictates who is to be elected). Henry was in no hurry to suggest a new archbishop—while the post was vacant its revenues all went to him—but someone had to be chosen.

For over a year the Pope, the bishops and the king mulled the matter over. The English bishops seemed to think that Gilbert Foliot, then Bishop of Hereford, would make a good choice; they certainly would not have considered Thomas the Chancellor, even if Theobald had suggested him, for he had been far too harsh upon the Church and would side with the king against them. Then Henry had exactly that idea. The Emperor had a chancellor who was an archbishop; why should not Henry? After all, it was obviously possible to combine both jobs (indeed others had, and later Thomas Wolsey was to combine being chancellor with being a cardinal). The Pope approved the idea—in Rome Thomas was remembered as an expert church lawyer— and Cardinal Henry of Pisa, papal envoy to Henry's court, was told to give his support. The English Church faced the fact that they might have to come round to agreeing.

But there was one implacable opponent of the idea: Thomas himself. As Thomas said to churchmen who came to sound him out, there were poor priests in England whom he would rather see appointed. He certainly was not living in the style of an archbishop elect and showed no sign of wanting to change fine clothes and a grand life for ecclesiastical discipline and sobriety.

In Spring 1162 Henry summoned Thomas to his castle at Falaise, birth-place of William the Conqueror, and asked him to accept the archbishopric. Thomas's reply shows just how clearly he understood the situation. Looking down and pointing at the colourful attire he was wearing he said, 'What a religious and how saintly a man you would appoint to the holy see, and over so renowned and pious a body of monks! I assure you that, if God should so dispose it, you would soon turn your face away from me and the love which is now so great between us would be turned into most bitter hatred. I know that you would make many demands, for already you presume over-

The Norman castle at Falaise, where William the Conqueror was born and Henry pressed Thomas to accept the archiepiscopacy. (*French Government Tourist Office.*)

much in ecclesiastical affairs, and this I cannot bear with equanimity, so the envious would find occasion to stir up endless strife between us.'[10]

Henry certainly did not conceive any change in their relationship: Thomas would go on being his great support and being head of the Church would make it easier to bring in the reforms he hoped for. Perhaps Thomas did not relish giving up a worldly life; but, although people believed that churchmen should live—and dress—more soberly, there would be nothing to stop him from continuing to live like a great baron. Perhaps the biographer, wise after the event, puts words into Thomas' mouth he would not have uttered. Yet, if Thomas had not felt that accepting the archbishopric must change both his attitudes and his loyalties it is difficult to see why he should have refused. His recorded acts show little personal affection for other people, yet it does now appear that it had not just been a sense of professional dedication but a real affection for the king which had kept him firmly supporting policies which a change of role would make him repudiate.

Eventually, after further pressure brought by the Cardinal of Pisa, Thomas finally accepted and left for England. At Canterbury the monks went through the formal ceremony of election, at Westminster the bishops gave their assent—although not altogether enthusiastically—and Prince Henry, now aged seven, gave the royal approval on behalf of his father, who stayed in Normandy.

Now, in accordance with the compromise worked out with Henry I, Thomas swore fealty to Prince Henry, as proxy for his father, and then Henry, Bishop of Winchester, precentor of the province, speaking for the assembled electors, asked that the prince give Thomas a discharge from all obligations contracted during his chancellorship and thus free Thomas from worldly ties. This was not part of the usual formula and it is, perhaps, a little strange since Thomas was still chancellor, and the king was expecting him to remain so; but Young Henry, as his contemporaries called the prince, agreed.[11]

The actual rite of consecration needed some diplomacy. The Archbishop of York, as the highest ecclesiastic in the country, Winchester, as precentor, Walter of Rochester, as archbishop's chaplain, and the most senior bishops of Wales all claimed the right to perform the ceremony.

A compromise was reached. Thomas, as yet a deacon only and not a priest, had still to be ordained so the Bishop of Rochester performed the ordination: Thomas, previously only a church administrator, now became responsible for the souls of men. The following day—a Tuesday, that recurrent day in Thomas' life—in the presence of the bishops of Ely, Bath, Salisbury, Norwich, Chichester, Chester, Exeter, Lincoln, Rochester, Llandaff, St David's, St Asaph and Hereford, the Bishop of Winchester performed the consecration and enthroned Thomas in the chair of St Augustine in Canterbury Cathedral.

The consecration of Thomas as Archbishop of Canterbury, a painting by Jan van Eyck (1421). (*Mansell Collection.*)

3 The Mitre and the Ring

TO THE LAST moment Thomas seemed to resist the idea of becoming archbishop. Henry of Winchester, who himself would have become archbishop
in 1136 if St Bernard had not overruled his election, reassured and exhorted
him at the consecration. 'My son, you must accept,' he said. 'If you have done
wrong in worldly tasks, then serve the Lord of Heaven the better and more
eagerly. You have been a wolf to the sheep, now become their pastor and
priest. You must and you shall change from Saul, the persecutor, into Paul.'[1]

Can the wolf turn into the shepherd quite so easily? Can a man lightly
shed the mantle of courtly pomp and take up an ecclesiastical abstinence? If
we are to believe some of the first biographers of Thomas a dramatic change
was not really necessary, for he already led a secret life of penance and
privation. But we should remember that they were writing not just the life
of a man whom they had known but the life of a saint. They could offer us a
sudden and dramatic conversion, like that of St Paul, but they do not, and it

The cathedral and priory of Christ Church during the archiepiscopacy of Thomas, drawn
from a plan prepared about 1165 to show the newly installed water supply brought from
a conduit house which collected spring water in a field about a mile northeast of the
priory. It flowed through a series of settling tanks and by pipe across a vineyard (*vinea*)
and an orchard (*pomerium*) belonging to the Black Canons (who were allowed a tap in
return for a basket of apples each year), crossing the town ditch by an aqueduct and
thence into the precincts.

The largest building on the plan is the cathedral itself, with the golden figure of the
Archangel Michael rising from the central tower. Most of the monastic buildings are
labelled in Latin on the original although not all the text is included here. Below the
cathedral to the left are the infirmary buildings with their own chapel, kitchen and
lavatories. Here the aged and sick were cared for. Centre is a cloister divided by a fence
enclosing the *herbarium*. To the right is the monks' cloister, surrounded by their
dormitory, dining hall and the *cellarium*. Next to the hall (lower on the picture) is their
kitchen beside which is a turret labelled 'the room where fish is washed' (*camera ubi
piscis lavator*), and between hall and kitchen are two windows labelled on the original
'window where the portions are served out' (*fenestra ubi fercula administrantur*) and
'window through which platters are tossed out for washing' (*fenestra per quam ejiciuntur
scutelle ad lavandum*).

To the right of the kitchen are the guest quarters (*domus hospitum*). Also identified
are the monks' lavatories (*necessarium*), with a bathhouse to the left, and the New Hall
(*aulis nova*), where more guests were accommodated. The precincts are encircled by the
monastery wall (*murus curis*) and the city wall (*murus civitatis*) with a road between
them. The archbishop's personal accommodation was to the west of the guest house,
off the plan.

36

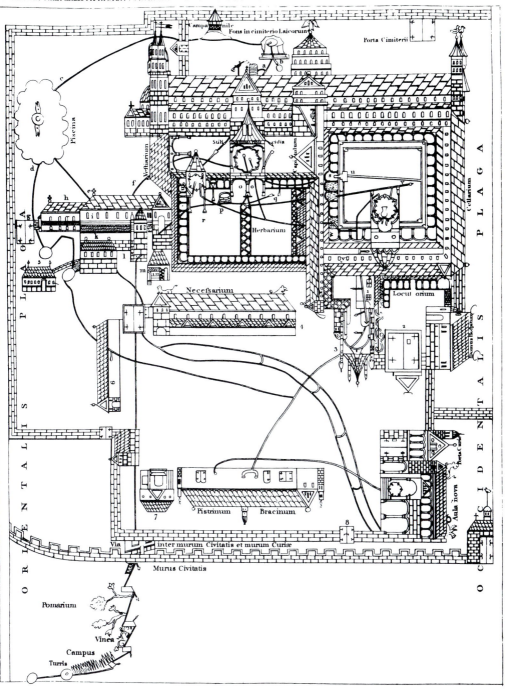

Campanile
Fons in cimiterio Laicorum
Porta Cimiterii
Piscina
Herbarium
Aula
Capella
Herbarium
Necessarium
Locutorium
Cellarium
PLAGA
Domus Hospitum
Pistrinum   Bracinum
Aula nova
Porta Curiæ
PLAGA
Via inter murum Civitatis et murum Curiæ
Murus Civitatis
ORIENTALIS
OCCIDENTALIS
Pomarium
Vinea
Campus
Turris

seems unlikely that, to the world at large, there was a very noticeable change in Thomas' way of life. It is not the picture of virtue that his biographers paint that gives credence to their monkish histories, but the glimpses we have of pride, anger and impatience that give humanity to their portraits.

As archbishop, Thomas continued to keep a grand establishment. Important though he was as chancellor he was not born, nor had he been made, a nobleman: but now he was created the greatest baron of the English Church. He still kept a lavish open house and his table still boasted rare and delicately flavoured dishes, but laymen—the archbishop's knights and his guests—sat apart at a separate table where they would not be bored by Latin homilies and ecclesiastic conversation.[2] Among the pages who waited upon them—as in the hall of any great lord, the sons of noblemen sent to other households to learn behaviour—was Prince Henry, whom the king had sent to live in Thomas's household when he was very young.

The Archbishop of Canterbury was also Abbot of the Priory of Christ Church, and Thomas' dress upset some of the monks. One of them had a dream in which God appeared to him and said 'Hurry to the chancellor, tell him that I command him to put on monastic garb without delay.'[3] The clerks argued against monastic dress, the monks for, but Thomas decided to wear the robes of a canon when not in his episcopal vestments. Some historians suggest that he wore them over his usual clothes. He seems to have suffered from the cold and the number of garments he wore gave some people the impression that he overate. The group of talented clerics which Thomas gathered about him as his staff and secretariat probably, like Thomas previously, wore secular dress. Herbert of Bosham, for instance, was known as a stylish dresser and is described at a later meeting with King Henry as wearing a tunic of green Auxerre cloth and a full length, decorated cloak in the same cloth 'in the German fashion'.[4]

William fitzStephen and Herbert himself describe the magnificence of Thomas's hospitality and detail the daily routine of the archbishop's life.[5] He would rise in time for the first service of the day, in the early hours of the morning, and afterwards, in secret, wash the feet of thirteen poor men. Then, after a short sleep, he would study Holy Scripture with Herbert and later pray alone. If he were celebrating Mass, which he did not do daily, he prepared himself by saying the prayers of St Anselm and then performed the service with speed and devotion. He followed this by hearing any cases brought to his court and then, about midday, went to hall for dinner.

Instead of being entertained at mealtimes by troubadours and jesters Thomas now heard readings from sacred books as in any monastic refectory. Even on feast days, when his kitchens excelled themselves, Thomas ate frugally and drank little wine, preferring some kind of *tisane*, a taste perhaps picked up during his studies in France.[6] This was probably always his way: even his ostentation as chancellor had been directed towards impressing others rather than indulging himself.

Soon after becoming archbishop, Thomas decided to stop being chancellor 'God's eyes!' swore Henry to the messenger who brought Thomas's resignation, 'I have got letters and full permission [from the Pope] for him to be both chancellor and archbishop. Will he not keep it?'

'He feels the cares of two offices will prove too burdensome,' replied the emissary.

'I feel, he does not care about serving me!' retorted the king.[7]

Henry had good reason to feel let down—Thomas did not appear to want to resign his archdeaconry or other offices. Indeed, he needed their income to maintain his magnificent household and to keep up his conspicuous charity: he doubled the amount which Theobald had distributed in charity, and that was already several times more than the alms given by their predecessors.

The king's plans had gone very awry, but at first all seemed well. Thomas continued to take an active part in the governing of the country—his name appears as signatory of charters—and indeed he would be following in Archbishop Theobald's steps in acting as caretaker for the crown. Meanwhile on his own part, Thomas set about obtaining all the rights and revenues that he felt due to him as archbishop. This was not unnatural avarice. At any time when a see was vacant it was likely that minor infringements had taken place and a new incumbent would also try to reclaim any farms or manors which had been alienated during his predecessor's time. In particular, Thomas found Rochester and Tonbridge castles both in the possession of others. He wasted no time in litigation and did not hesitate to repossess by force any lands to which he believed the archbishopric had an inalienable right. He met little resistance from people without influence or power but, when he lay claim to the property of grander lords, complaints began to be made to the king.

Thomas could also gain income from the 'first fruits', the tax, rather like an agency commission, which was due from a cleric to the person who awarded him his benefice; and Thomas found William de Ros, the lord of Eynsford, had appointed a priest to a living Thomas considered in his own gift. He tried to throw the priest out and install his own, claiming his 'first fruits' tax of course. William was a tenant-in-chief of the king and, although the court denied him the advowson, he still resisted the archbishop. There were to be repercussions.

The hagiographers tend to present a picture of either an archbishop suddenly reformed, like Paul, or perhaps a man already of saintly practice in his earlier life; but today we cannot give credence to all the later tales of these obviously partisan reporters. Many historians have seen the apparent change in Thomas' attitudes as being simply the attitude of a man who is determined to do whatever job he has to the best of his ability, and indeed his switch of loyalty makes good sense when compared with a business executive changing companies, a football player changing clubs, or a politician moving on from one alliance to the next. The diplomacy of the twelfth century was very much a matter of changing loyalties—but it was also governed overall by the duties inherent in the feudal system and, especially to a man who had risen from lowly rank, feudal allegiances would have seemed very important. Thomas was as aware of rights and privileges as he was of duties, whether those of precedence or of income, and especially if those rights and privileges were his. As chancellor he had pressed the claims of the crown and the exchequer against the Church: they were the chancellor's rights as proxy for the king. As archbishop he pressed the rights of clergy against the lay power, but just as strongly he defended his own rights and those of the archbishopric against those of any other churchman.

At first, the king pushed aside any complaints against his new archbishop and when, in January 1163, Henry returned to England, Thomas went with Prince Henry to meet the king at Southampton. In the next months Thomas was largely with the king. Together they attended the dedication of Reading Abbey and officiated at the translation of St Edward the Confessor to his new shrine in Westminster Abbey; on Palm Sunday they were at Canterbury for the monks' Holy Week procession and Thomas joined in the negotiations at Dover for a treaty with the Count of Flanders. In April, Henry set off on a campaign against a rebellion in Wales, while Thomas set off for Tours to attend a council called by the Pope. One of the objects of this council was to excommunicate the Empire's anti-pope.

Pope Alexander III did not have the allegiance of all Christendom. France, Spain, Sicily, southern Italy and England acknowledged him as head of the Church, but the German Emperor supported a rival pope, recognized by Scandinavia, Hungary, Bohemia and Northern Italy. Alexander had been unable to establish himself in Rome and presently had his court at Tours.

Thomas set off for Tours as magnificently as he had travelled to Paris as chancellor. The whole city turned out to meet him, and Alexander himself rose to greet Thomas on his arrival. At the conference Thomas was seated at the Pope's right hand, while at his left was Roger, Archbishop of York— Thomas's old rival from their days in the household of Archbishop Theobald.

King Henry's show of power quieted the rumblings of rebellion in Wales and, in July, soon after Thomas' return from France, a council was called at Woodstock. Henry wanted to raise money and proposed that a previously voluntary payment of two shillings per hide of land made to the king's sheriffs should be converted into a regular tax for crown use—the exact nature of this 'sheriff's aid' is uncertain but it seems to have been a form of *ex gratia* sum for doing the job fairly well, which the sheriffs themselves kept. As chancellor, Thomas had been able to give the king his advice in private, now he gave it in public. He opposed the proposal on the grounds that it would encourage the sheriffs to seek bribes and make illegal exactions to restore their income. Henry did not like being crossed and lost his temper, but Thomas won the day.

They were soon in opposition again. A number of cases had been brought to Henry's notice in which clerics had escaped the punishment which would have been theirs had they been judged in lay courts. Here was a loophole through which wrongdoers could escape the royal law. Worse, clerks who held no office, and therefore had no superiors to discipline them, were able to roam the country and they, or others pretending to be clerics, were committing robberies and murders, and even when caught and convicted were receiving sentences which were insufficiently deterrent. There were also occasions when ecclesiastical judges were blackmailing people with the threat of charges, sometimes trumped-up ones, in the ecclesiastical courts.

Once a clerk had been sentenced by the church court and degraded from his order he was turned over to the secular law—but this led to a major disagreement for, whereas some of Henry's supporters believed that this implied that he could then be tried and punished by the king's courts, Thomas read this as meaning only that the criminal lost his protected status and would be under the jurisdiction of the lay courts for any subsequent crimes.

In one case a canon of Bedford had been tried in the Bishop of Lincoln's court for the murder of a knight, and was acquitted. The sheriff of the county tried to reopen the case and the canon retaliated with abuse which the sheriff claimed, by insulting him, was insulting to the crown. The king wanted him punished. Thomas refused to allow the case to go before the king's court. He insisted upon hearing the case in his own court, although he allowed laymen to attend as observers. The ex-canon admitted that he had insulted the king's officer and because of this the court, while it declared that he could not be retried for the murder, demanded a very serious sentence. But Henry was not satisfied.

Thomas' claim to Tonbridge Castle also was due to be heard in July but the archbishop, sensing the king's mood, did not press his case against the Earl of Clare who held it. He did, however, excommunicate William de Ros for resisting him at Eynsford. William held only seven knights fees—but he did hold them from the king, and Henry took an interest in the case. In theory, an excommunicate was not only denied the comfort and intercession of the Church, but all Christians were forbidden to give him aid or associate with him for fear that they could become contaminated. Most vassals holding fiefs directly from the crown were important barons and advisers to the king —it would be extremely difficult for him to avoid them without disrupting the government of the realm. It had been established by William the Conqueror that such tenants-in-chief could only be excommunicated with the knowledge and consent of the king. Thomas had not obtained the king's agreement. Henry demanded that the excommunication be withdrawn. The archbishop did eventually comply, but not soon enough to cool the royal anger.

Another case concerned a clerk in the Worcester diocese who was accused of the rape of a girl and the murder of her father. When Henry heard about it he instructed that the man be tried in the lay court, but Thomas ordered the bishop—newly appointed and in fact the king's young cousin—not to hand him over. Henry probably thought that Bishop Roger would do his bidding but, as he was to show again later, he proved to be a consistent supporter of his archbishop.

Thomas made some attempt to assuage the king by inflicting harsh sentences in his court—a London clerk who stole a silver cup was, for instance, 'deprived of his orders and branded into the bargain to please the king'.[8] But by now he knew that conflict was inevitable and that a great number of the barons was ranged against him. Perhaps as early as September[9] 1163 he was writing to the Pope, now living at Sens: 'The malice of the times increases daily, our injustices, and Christ's, . . . become greater and greater. Wave follows wave in this sea of calamity, so that we see nothing but shipwreck ahead . . .' With this letter he sent a messenger to give detailed information, warning him to 'keep this entirely confidential: almost everything we say in public or in private is reported to the king'.[10]

Henry called a Council at Westminster for October 1st. Ostensibly it was supposed to deal with the claim of Canterbury to primacy over the see of York, but this does not actually seem to have been discussed. The king launched straight into an attack on clerical immunity and corruption in church courts, ending by demanding 'your consent, my lord of Canterbury, and that of all the other bishops, that when clerks are caught in criminal acts, and convicted by judgement or confession, they be stripped of their orders, and the protection of the Church, and handed over to the officers of my court to receive corporal punishment'.[11]

Thomas gained permission to consult with his bishops before replying. Most of them were prepared, at first, to yield to the king's demands for, they argued, if a man held holy orders and was not deterred from crime by his greater privileges, then he deserved double punishment. But, Thomas insisted, 'God does not judge twice in the same case: now the sentence of the Church is either just or unjust. You will not allow that it is unjust . . . Besides, the liberties of the Church are in our keeping, our duty is to guard them, or they will be subverted.'[12] Eventually he won his bishops round to his support and they returned to the king's presence.

'It would be wrong,' Thomas answered the king, 'for you to demand, or us to grant, anything that goes beyond the customs set form in the Canons of the Church, nor ought we to consent to any new laws.' The bishops rehearsed their interpretation: that the criminal clerk would be indictable as a layman for offences committed after his degradation, and they referred to their rights to send men out of the kingdom or on penitential pilgrimage.[13]

'I am only asking that you observe the customs observed in the times of my predecessors,' the king replied, cutting short discussion. Thomas acknowledged that they would observe them 'saving their order (*salvo ordino nostro*)'—that is, as far as would be lawful for a churchman.[14] The qualification infuriated Henry. He asked each bishop in turn and each replied as

Thomas had except for Hilary, Bishop of Chichester, who used the reservation 'in good faith (*bona fide*)' instead. In a fury Henry turned upon them, refusing to listen to any further attempts to placate him, and stormed out of the hall.

Before dawn the king left for London, but first he sent a demand to Thomas for the return of the castles and fiefs he had received as chancellor and had not given up despite his resignation. He also removed Prince Henry from the archbishop's household. Yet Henry then decided to make an attempt to reason with Thomas and summoned him to Northampton. Thomas, misjudging what was appropriate, arrived with a great retinue and the king refused him admittance to the town, telling him to wait outside. Henry rode out to meet him and Thomas spurred his charger forward so that he should be the first to give salutation. But, strangely paralleling the personalities of these once close but proud and strong-willed friends, their horses mistook the charge across the field and began to rear and manoeuvre into positions as though their riders were about to fight. The king and the archbishop were forced to turn them back towards their own followers and change to less fiery steeds before they could approach each other.[15]

But the chance had gone. Although the king reminded Thomas of the honours and privileges he had bestowed upon him, and Thomas protested his loyalty to the crown, neither would give way over Thomas' qualification of *salvo ordino*.

Henry sent messengers to the Pope, and Innocent III advised Thomas to give way. Eager though the Pope was to build the power of the Church, at a time of schism within the Church itself he did not want to risk a break between Church and State in England—and his need for the support of the king of England and Duke of Normandy, Anjou and Aquitaine coloured papal reaction throughout the ensuing dispute.

Pressure and entreaty from the pope and the English bishops eventually convinced Thomas that he should give the king his agreement and, in December, he sought out Henry at Woodstock. There he gave his acceptance of the ancestral customs 'in good faith'[16]—using the same formula as Hilary of Chichester, who had been party to discussions with the king and no doubt had convinced both parties that this really was a harmless phraseology.

Henry was glad to have Thomas' compliance, but his defiance had been before the court and now he asked that the archbishop should give his word before the assembled barons and bishops of the realm. He called a meeting of the council in January. By the time Thomas attended the council, at Henry's hunting lodge at Clarendon, near Salisbury, he had changed his mind. When Henry asked for his submission to be made in public he replied that he must consult his bishops. The king was furious and flew into one of his rages. The situation did not improve when Thomas and the bishops dragged out their discussions for several days. Friendly barons meanwhile tried to coax them into acceptance, or sometimes warned them of dire consequences if they did not agree. Eventually the clergy agreed to give way. Henry had won.

To their surprise Henry immediately queried exactly what these customs were and ordered them to be set down in writing. While both parties were agreeing to a vague body of accepted custom, which each interpreted in their own way, there could be peace between them, but Henry's list enumerated those in force in the time of Henry I—not the ones which Thomas had known in the reign of Stephen—and the document infringed the rights which the Church had come to think were customary.

Although they did not demand that the state court should try the guilt of a cleric, they declared that he should be arrested by state officers and brought before a state court for indictment, eventually to be returned to the state for sentence and punishment. They also reverted almost to the position under William I with regard to suits concerning the right of presentation to churches and those concerning church land not held by *frank-almoign* tenure; these were to be held in secular courts. These Constitutions also clearly defined the feudal position of bishops as vassals of the king.

Such features were offensive to Thomas and he avoided affixing his seal, asking for time to study the document. In view of the popular idea of Thomas as protector of the poor it is interesting that he did not object to one clause in particular which made it more difficult for a peasant to take holy orders, his only way of rising in station or leaving his village; for entering the Church freed him from his villein status.

Thomas, believing that he had failed Mother Church, made a public display of contrition—thereby directly affronting the king—by suspending himself from officiating at the altar and by performing harsh penances. He wrote to the Pope confessing his error and received a reply absolving him and instructing him to celebrate Mass, and gently suggesting that he was reacting rather theatrically.[17] After receiving the Pope's letter he tried to see the king again at Woodstock, but was refused admittance and returned to Canterbury.

Meanwhile the king had sent a copy of the Constitutions to the Pope, along with a request that the Archbishop of York be made the papal legate to England. The Pope would not give the Constitutions his approval, objecting to ten of them, but he did grant Roger of York the legateship, although writing to Thomas telling him that he and the Church of Canterbury would be exempt from Roger's jurisdiction.

Now Thomas began to get frightened. Rumours that reached him suggested that he was in real physical danger. Twice he tried to leave the country—in doing so expressly breaking item IV of the Constitutions. On the first occasion foul weather forced the vessel to turn back and on the second the sailors, fearful of what the king might do if he found out that they had aided the archbishop's flight turned the ship back shortly after leaving port.

While Thomas continued to opposed the Constitutions and defend criminous clerks from lay power, Henry instructed his officers that they should be 'seized without mercy and condemned by their own parishioners, even shamed and maimed like any lay person'.[18] Thomas was stubborn but Henry was determined. If Thomas could not be brought to heel he must be discredited—and if possible removed from office.

One of the officers of the Exchequer, a baron called John who held the hereditary office of marshal, was in dispute with the archbishop over land he claimed. He lost his case in the archbishop's court and appealed to the king's court in accordance with the Constitutions. Thomas was summoned to appear to answer the case and failed to do so. His biographers disagree as to whether he sent a message to say that he was too ill to attend or, as is more likely, that he sent evidence to prove his claim[19] and refused to attend, for he would want to avoid so apparent an acceptance of the Constitutions. Henry was not satisfied, and called the archbishop to appear before his court for the case to be judged at Northampton in October. In fact Henry seems to have seized upon this case as an excuse, for the suit of John the Marshal was never judged: on the day appointed for the trial he was, in fact, still in London on the king's business. At Northampton Thomas was charged with contempt of court for his non-appearance at the earlier hearing and found guilty of failing to carry out his feudal duty to the king. He was sentenced to be 'at the king's mercy'—in practice this usually meant a fine, on this occasion of £500, for which the bishops stood surety, Gilbert Foliot, Bishop of London, excepted.

Now, instead of proceeding to the retrial of John the Marshal's case (which Thomas would probably have won), Henry began to make a series of unexpected demands for monies which he claimed were due to him from Thomas. First was the income from the castles of Eye and Berkhamsted: Thomas claimed that it had been spent on the repair of these castles and of the Tower of London, but the king insisted that this had been done without his authority and the archbishop agreed to pay £300 (the equivalent of at least fifty times as much today). Three barons—including William of Eynsford, who would hardly have supported the archbishop who had excommunicated him if he thought Thomas in the wrong—stood surety. The following day Henry demanded the return of a loan made during the campaign in Toulouse and a further sum borrowed on the king's security. Thomas claimed that the first was a gift and that both had been spent on the king's service but, since he could produce no confirmatory evidence, the debt was supported by the court. Five laymen this time stood surety for Thomas. Now the king demanded the revenues received when Thomas was chancellor from the vacant bishoprics and abbeys then in his charge. Probably Thomas had used such monies to maintain his household as chancellor, and would have thought it reasonable to expend them in the costs of office, but he could not be expected to suddenly produce accounts for his expenditure. He had been given no notice of the demand and he had been formally discharged of all outstanding responsibilities by Prince Henry after his election. But the king insisted and Thomas again asked for time to consult with his bishops.

The bishops met next day at St Andrew's Priory, where Thomas was lodged. Gilbert Foliot bade the archbishop remember 'the condition from which his majesty raised you, and what benefits he conferred upon you, also the ruin which hangs over the Church and all of us, if you persist in your opposition to the king, for then you would not only resign your see, but ten times as much, if it were in your power, and perhaps the king would reward your humility by giving it you back again.'[20] Henry of Winchester suggested that the king's motives were pure avarice, that cash would solve the problem, and he offered his own wealth to Thomas—but Henry refused an offered settlement of 2,000 marks (perhaps not surprisingly since the king was claiming fifteen times as much: more than £300,000 at present values). Roger of Worcester was the only other bishop to stand out against Thomas' resignation. Discussion and argument continued all that day and the next. When Thomas fell sick with a persistent renal condition and the following day could not even stand, a message was sent to the king who, suspicious, sent two noblemen to check up on him.

By now rumour was rife. The king, it was said, planned to throw Thomas into prison for life, to blind him, to cut his tongue out—he would be condemned for treason. The bishops begged him to yield to the king and resign. Thomas sent off appeals to the Pope and instructed the bishops that they must refuse to sit in judgement on him and that they should excommunicate any lay persons who offered him violence. When they had gone he went into the church of the priory and celebrated the Mass of St Stephen, the first martyr, which begins with the introit 'Princes also did sit and speak against me' and includes a reference to 'Zachary murdered between the temple and the altar' in the reading from the Gospel—he was daring the king to kill him.

In fact, Thomas was wildly overdramatizing the situation, for Henry wanted his compliance, not his end: but Thomas clearly relished theatrical effect. Now he announced that he would walk barefoot to the council, in all his vestments and carrying his cross. His household calmed him down a little. He did not wear his full robes and he rode upon a horse but, after dismounting inside the royal castle, he took the episcopal cross from his cross-bearer and flourished it before him. The Bishop of Hereford, and even Gilbert Foliot, tried to take it from him—there was no point in deliberately stirring the king's anger by such a show—but Thomas was too strong for them.

Henry retired to an upper room when he heard that Thomas was coming and he stayed there with his barons while Thomas stayed below. King and primate were not to meet that day. Henry returned to his demand that Thomas account for the sums received when chancellor and asked about the appeal which the archbishop had made to the Pope—a further contravention of the Constitutions. Thomas answered with a reminder of his release from debts and liabilities at his election, he pointed out that he had been called to answer a suit of John the Marshal's and explained that, since he considered his bishops had condemned him more seriously than was meet for a single absence from court, he had appealed against them, forbidding them to judge him on any secular suit arising from the time before he became archbishop.

Henry flew into a rage and demanded that the bishops sit in judgement. Some of them tried once more to perusade Thomas to give way before the king. Even Henry of Winchester begged him to resign, but he could not be moved. They could not support him for fear of the king, they could not judge him for fear of excommunication. Eventually, they reached an understanding with the king that they would appeal to the Pope to be released from the archbishop's prohibition and he accepted that they would not sit in judgement. Instead a lay court alone decided the archbishop's case. There is no record of either the court's decision or its sentence, although cries of 'Traitor!' were heard in the hall below and presumably Thomas was found guilty of treason. The barons who came down to announce the court's decision to Thomas hesitated to tell it and before they could come to the point the archbishop, interrupting, declared, 'I will hear no judgement. . . . As the soul is more worthy than the body, so are you bound to obey God rather than an earthly king. Shall the son judge or condemn his father? The Pope alone is my judge. I have appealed to him.'[21]

Then, cross in hand, Thomas swept out of the hall to shouts of abuse and further calls of 'Traitor!' By the door his dramatic exit was ruined when he tripped over a bundle of firewood, but he safely reached his horse and mounted. The castle gates were locked but, miraculously it was later considered, one of his attendants found a bunch of keys and the first he tried opened the lock. There was no attempt to follow him and Henry sent out a proclamation that no one was to molest the archbishop. In fact, the townspeople milled around him cheering and asking for his blessing—rumour had already reported him killed. Whether because of his fame as chancellor, a belief that as archbishop he would protect the poor, or because of his reputation for distributing largesse, Thomas was popular among the lower orders.

But, although the poor folk flocked to him, some of his knights, servants and clerks were eager to leave his service lest the king's retribution strike them too. Their empty places at his supper tables he filled with beggars. By chance the supper reading included the phrase 'If they persecute you in one city, flee to another', and at the words Herbert of Bosham says that he and the archbishop exchanged glances. Thomas sent messengers to the king asking his permission to depart—although whether to leave for Canterbury or to take his appeal to the Pope is not clear—but Henry refused to give an answer until the morrow. Thomas then ordered that his bed should be set up behind the high altar—perhaps to give himself the protection of sanctuary or perhaps to keep vigil—although during the singing of the last service of the day at about nine o'clock he seemed to be asleep. A few hours later, when the monks returned for matins, he had gone.

With three companions, and in disguise, Thomas rode through a night of gale and pelting rain, his only baggage the pallium—the vestment worn across the shoulders bestowed upon archbishops by the Pope—and the archiepiscopal seal. The rain was so heavy that twice he stopped to cut pieces from his sodden woollen cloak to reduce its weight. Next morning the riders reached Lincoln. Dressed as a lay brother, and using the name Brother Christian, Thomas made his way by boat and foot slowly southward until he reached the manor of Eastry, a possession of Christ Church near Sandwich, where he could wait for a boat to get him across the channel. On All Souls Day the refugees made a rough crossing in a small boat, landing near Gravelines in Flanders. Thomas was not to see England again for six years.

4 The Obstinate Exile

THOMAS' OPPOSITION to the marriage of the Count of Flanders, in whose lands the fleeing archbishop now found himself, had made the count no friend. Thomas' height and striking appearance made him easily recognizable and his disguise did not sit well upon him so that he had to be doubly cautious. He was exhausted by the difficult crossing and unaccustomed to making his way on foot, but the only mount that could be procured was an unsaddled mule. At Gravelines an innkeeper recognized him, but promised to keep his identity a secret.

By boat the refugees reached the abbey of Clairmais, near St Omer. They were headed for the nearby monastery of St Bertin but a delegation which King Henry had sent to the Pope was already there so they delayed. At St Bertin they met Sir Richard de Lucy, Henry's justiciar, returning from a pilgrimage to St James de Compostella. He offered to reconcile Thomas, if he would return, with the king, but the archbishop spurned his help, and said he would go straight to the Pope.[1] For a time Thomas recuperated at St Bertin, where Herbert of Bosham and others of his clerks joined him. He sent Herbert after the royal ambassadors to see what case they were putting against him.[2]

The English envoys, led by the Archbishop of York, the Bishop of London and other bishops and the Earl of Arundel, presented a letter to King Louis at Compiegne asking him not to help 'Thomas, who was Archbishop of Canterbury'.

'Who *was* archbishop?' answered Louis. 'Who has deposed him? I am king as much as the English king, but I have no power to depose the least of the clerks in my kingdom.'[3]

Louis went on to say that Thomas would be most welcome in his realm and he would have gone to meet him if he knew where he was. The Earl of Arundel reminded him of the way in which Thomas, as chancellor, had waged war against him, but Louis replied: 'A man who served his lord so loyally would have served me well, if he had been my man. And if he conquered lands and castles for him, that is the greater reason why he should hold him dear.'[4] Louis was going to give his vassal (Henry, as Duke of Normandy) scant support against the Church.

Soon after, Thomas met the French king at Soissons where he was promised support in his cause and financial help in his exile. Meanwhile, Herbert of Bosham reached the Pope at Sens and outlined Thomas's case, then the English bishops and their party arrived, asking the Pope to give a judgement —which he refused since Thomas was not present to be heard. He declined to order Thomas to return to England but did agree to appoint legates to investigate the case, although reserving judgement to himself.

After three days' discussion, during which they took every opportunity to bribe the cardinals and to make secret offers to the Pope, the envoys left. Then Thomas arrived at Sens. This was no longer a stumbling, exhausted refugee. He came with a train of 300 mounted men, not as extravagantly appointed as on his previous missions in France, but able to hold his head high.

Pope Alexander greeted him with the kiss of peace and seated him at his right hand. At dinner, when water was brought, the Pope asked Thomas to bless it. He did and poured out . . . wine, or so the biographer records! The Pope asked the servant what he had brought and asked for more, and it happened again.[5] Instead of the gifts customary from suppliants, Thomas presented the Pope with a copy of the Clarendon Constitutions to show the cause of his exile. Some sources say that he offered to resign his archbishopric, an offer which, if made, was certainly refused for the Pope confirmed him in his see.

After about a month at Sens, Thomas and his companions, at the Pope's suggestion, retired to a monastic life at the Cistercian abbey of Pontigny. There, at Thomas' request, the Pope sent him a monk's rough woollen habit which he had personally blessed. With this monk's wear Thomas adopted the strict life of the Cistercian order and its sparse diet—one meal a day from autumn to spring, and that without meat, which was kept for the sick. He instructed his chaplain to scourge him regularly and beneath his monastic garb he wore a hair shirt and hair breeches to increase his discomfort (he may have worn these in England, but they were a secret from even his close associates until after his death). In fact, the Cistercian monks were not allowed breeches and if discovered they would have been denounced as an infringement of the order's rules. When they needed mending the Virgin Mary is said to have helped him keep his secret by appearing to him and doing a running repair. Of course, his biographers may be exaggerating the privations which Thomas persisted in inflicting upon himself, but there is no doubt that they made him ill. Although no glutton, he was used to fine and well-balanced food and a life in comfortable surroundings. He developed a bone disorder in his cheek which only a primitive operation ended, and after that he was prevailed upon to modify his diet.

Meanwhile, to these self-imposed penances revengeful Henry added the distressing sight of wretched refugees. He expelled all Thomas' relations and all his household from his realm and made them swear to present themselves

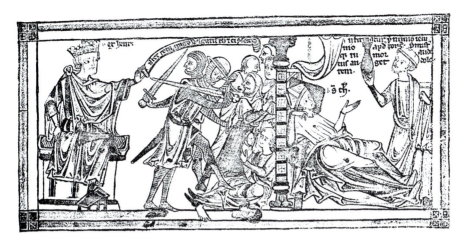

Two incidents from the life of Thomas illustrated in a thirteenth-century French biography. Henry II orders the exile of Thomas' kin and, right, Thomas falls sick from the rigours of life at Pontigny.

to Thomas in his place of exile. Many are said to have found their way eventually to Sicily, and the Italian families called Bechetti claim descent from them.[6] Some of Thomas' leading clerks came and stayed at Pontigny, and with them he spent his time in studying scripture and law, and in planning how to win his battle with the king.

All the parties to the dispute were caught up in the complex political uncertainties of the age. The Pope, Alexander III, was for much of the time himself an enforced exile from Rome and was continually threatened by the power of the German Empire in support of the anti-pope. Henry II was struggling to establish a more ordered and secure government over his lands on both sides of the channel, living in fear of discipline or rejection by the Church but seeking an alliance with the Emperor and playing with support for the anti-pope if he would support the royal claims. Louis VII, supporter of Alexander as Pope, befriender of Thomas partly because of his opposition to Henry, was nevertheless trying to avoid a clash with English and Norman power. The English clergy were caught between their feudal allegiance to the crown and their canonical duty to their archbishop. And Thomas himself, lacking any military power but with the weapons of excommunication and interdict to wield, was uncertain of how far to trust either Pope or king to support him, and was himself subject to papal discipline. All wanted a speedy end to the dispute, except perhaps for the Archbishop of York and the Bishop of London, whose positions were the stronger for Thomas' absence, and many of the English barony who, with Thomas removed from Henry's side and the king's power weakened by the dispute, could more easily resist the control which Henry wished to exercise.

For six years there were hints of compromise, threats and counterthreats.

Three fat volumes of 700 letters, copied by later scribes and often lacking authentic dates, record the discussion and argument that passed across Europe. In spring 1165 Alexander was invited to return to Rome and in June his strengthened position encouraged him to declare the judgements at Northampton 'utterly void'.[7] But at the same time he instructed Thomas to do nothing hasty and to take no measures against the king or his land until the following Easter.

During those nine long months Thomas sought the aid of Henry's mother the Empress Matilda, the king of Scotland and many others, but took no action against his king. However, when Easter came he wrote to Henry in an almost evangelical vein saying that it was his devotion to his duty that forced him to admonish the king, yet he feared the king's anger if he spoke out. He goes on to speak of the Church as the 'daughter of Zion held captive, the spouse of the great King oppressed by many', begs him to free her and refers his 'dear Lord and most serene prince' to the fate of Solomon before ending with the request 'above all things to be present and converse with you'.[8]

Meanwhile the Pope, on Easter Day, appointed Thomas papal legate for all England except for the province of York. When Thomas received the news in May he asked a friend to seek the intervention of the Empress Matilda, giving the warning that he was about to 'unleash the sword of the Spirit' against Henry and England: a threat of excommunication and interdict. The message was passed on to Henry, as he hoped, and the king, who was holding a council at Chinon, flew into a rage. A further letter from Thomas begins more temperately with a protestation of his wish to see his king again and a reminder of past services, but goes on to warn Henry of the danger of consorting with schismatics and bids him 'Remember the profession, which you made and placed in writing on the altar at Westminster, to preserve the Church's liberties, when you were consecrated and anointed king. Restore the Church of Canterbury, from which you received your promotion, to the state in which it was in the days of our predecessors, with all its possessions . . . and allow us to resume our duties in the aforesaid Church, without trouble or molestation. If your majesty will consent to this, I am prepared to serve you with all obedience as my beloved lord and sovereign, as far as lies in my power—saving the honour of God and of the Roman Church, and my own Order. But if you do not these things know for a certainty that you shall feel the severity of God's vengeance.'[9]

The threat was clear, and by now Henry knew that he would find no support in England for an abandonment of Alexander III; so he took the only course open to him—he sent messengers to notify Thomas that he appealed to Rome against the possibility of excommunication. By the time they arrived, Thomas, probably knowing that their coming was imminent, had left on pilgrimage to Soissons, and from there he went to the great church at Vezelay where he celebrated Mass on Whitsunday before the crowds of pilgrims visiting the shrine of St Mary Magdalene. (The vast

After the meeting at Montmirail both King Henry and King Louis reject Thomas but the ordinary people seek his blessing. From a thirteenth-century life.

crowds at the famous shrine ensured publicity for what he planned to do and, because the church was a direct dependency on the Pope over which the French king had no control, it avoided putting Louis in an embarassing position.) To this audience Thomas expounded the history of his quarrel with the King of England and then, with due solemnity, lit a candle, inverted it and dashed out its flame upon the ground—so pronouncing John of Oxford excommunicate for taking an oath to the anti-pope while representing Henry in an embassy to the German emperor.[10] In the same way he proceeded to anathematize Richard of Ilchester (an envoy with John) and the schismatic Archbishop of Cologne, Richard de Lucy and Jocelin de Balliol, who had helped to frame the Constitutions of Clarendon, and Ranulf de Broc and two others for seizing the possessions of the see of Canterbury. Despite advice against it he had intended to excommunicate the king, but news came that Henry had been taken ill and he withheld the sentence. Instead he issued a warning that if the king did not repent his turn would come.

The response to this dramatic development was a flurry of appeals from England. Thomas wrote to his English bishops demanding that they support his censures and in turn the bishops, in the person of Gilbert Foliot, wrote to the Pope and back to Thomas urging moderation and seeking to justify the king's position. Thomas called some of his bishops out to Sens but both king and Pope forbade their going. Henry threatened the general chapter of the Cistercian Order that they might find all their English possessions confiscated if they continued to harbour Thomas in the abbey at Pontigny and in November Thomas moved to Sens.

Alexander instructed Thomas not to issue any more excommunications and agreed to appoint legates to go to England. He promised that they would have full powers to judge in the disputes between king and archbishop, and between the archbishop and the other churchmen, and powers to absolve those of the king's household who had been excommunicated—who, further, if in danger of death could be absolved by any of the bishops. Henry was bidden to keep these matters secret and Thomas was told a somewhat different version. Why had Alexander gone so far towards meeting Henry's demands? Because the threat from the German emperor was once again becoming serious.

Thomas was suspicious and anxious. He did not like the choice of cardinals for legates. He was restrained from sending some rather hysterical letters to the Pope, but his pleas did cause Alexander to instruct the cardinals not to enter England until peace had been made between the king and Thomas. In fact it took the legates nearly six months to make their way from Rome, partly because Louis VII, fearing that their purpose was to depose Thomas, was hesitant to grant them a safe conduct through his kingdom, and partly because they did not wish to become involved in a war which had broken out between Henry and another of Louis's French vassals. Meanwhile Alexander's position grew worse. The Germans invaded Italy and at the end of July the Pope was forced to flee from Rome disguised as a pilgrim, while the Vatican became a bloody battleground. The Emperor's victory was not to last. Fever struck the imperial forces and, after losing 25,000 men, they abandoned the Holy City.

At last, at the beginning of November, Thomas was summoned to a conference with the legates near Gisors. The legates found Thomas intractable and he despaired of getting a just settlement from them. A few days later they met with Henry at Argenton where the king showed his fury that they had not been able to make Thomas yield; when they parted he burst into tears and pleaded with them to intercede with the Pope to rid him of Thomas altogether. The cardinals, in fact, forbade Thomas to place an interdict upon the English, but a few months later the Pope sent messengers threatening Henry with dire consequences if he did not come to terms with the archbishop. Nevertheless, it was not until the beginning of 1169 that any major development took place.

In January, Henry II and Louis VII met at Montmirail, not far from Chartres, to make a peace treaty which was to be accompanied by the betrothal of Prince Richard (later Richard the Lionheart) to Louis' daughter. Louis and the Pope's representatives arranged for Henry to meet Thomas and convinced the archbishop that he should desist from using the qualification 'saving my order' which had proved such a stumbling block in the past. Thomas offered to substitute the formula 'saving the honour of God' but it was still felt that this might provoke the king and they hoped to convince him that he should accept the king's demands without it.

When Thomas was shown into the royal presence he rushed forward and threw himself upon his knees. The king took his hand and raised him to his

54

feet. Then Thomas began a long speech heaping blame upon himself, but not forgetting to throw in some criticisms of the king, and concluded: 'On the whole matter which lies between us, here in the presence of our lord the king of France, and of the archbishops, princes and others who stand around us, I throw myself on your mercy and your pleasure—*saving the honour of God.*'[11]

The effort of all the mediators had been in vain. Henry furiously denounced Thomas as proud and ambitious, even accusing him of reaching out for the crown, suggesting that he had, in fact, deserted the English Church. Turning to the king of France he concluded: 'Whatever his lordship of Canterbury disapproves he will say is contrary to God's honour, and so on all occasions he will get the advantage of me; but lest I be thought to despise God's honour I make this proposition to him: There have been many kings of England before me, some greater and some of less power; there have been many good and holy archbishops of Canterbury before him. Now let him behave towards me as the most holy of his predecessors behaved towards the least of mine, and I am satisfied.'

All present exclaimed: 'The king humbles himself enough!' and King Louis, turning to the archbishop, demanded, 'My lord, do you wish to be more than a saint?'[12]

It seemed that Thomas had lost the support of the king of France and it was a despondent party that returned to Sens. But it was only a matter of days before Louis discovered that the King of England had already broken one of the promises made at Montmirail, and he swung back in favour of Thomas' cause, begging the archbishop's forgiveness for deserting him.

There were more attempts at arranging a meeting between the parties but Thomas refused to change his stand for, as he wrote to Pope Alexander, 'If the Constitutions be conceded the authority of the holy see in England will be reduced to little or nothing.'[13] The Pope strengthened his stand, appointing two new legates to deal with the case while Thomas, freed from the ban on taking action, pronounced excommunications on Gilbert Foliot, Jocelyn of Salisbury, Ranulf de Broc and most of the others he had excommunicated three years earlier; moreover he succeeded in getting the excommunications delivered to St Paul's in London, despite the king's ban on communications with Thomas and tight controls at all the English ports.[14]

A meeting between Henry and the papal envoys got nowhere and the king issued further decrees forbidding communication with or appeals to the Pope or the archbishop, dispossessing all those who supported them and recalling clerics abroad. All his subjects over fifteen years old had to swear to observe these decrees—and Peter's Pence (the papal tithe) was to be paid into the royal exchequer.[15]

In October another meeting was arranged between Thomas and Henry at Montmartre, overlooking the city of Paris. Henry, fearful that his kingdom might be placed under interdict—which would mean no church services, no weddings and no funerals, although not excommunicating individual citizens —was prepared to concede almost everything and Thomas it seemed was prepared to make no qualification of 'saving the honour of God' or 'his Order'. But Thomas felt some guarantee of the king's good faith was necessary and the Pope advised him to ask for the kiss of peace.

All went well until Thomas made this request. Henry replied that, although he would have been very ready to do as the archbishop asked, he had formerly sworn that he would never kiss him. He must refuse for he could not break his oath. Oath-breaking was not something that had previously seemed to worry Henry overmuch. However, the Pope did not want to let such an advance be lost and wrote to Henry absolving him from his oath. He proposed that if Henry still would not give the kiss then Thomas should be persuaded to accept it from Prince Henry in his stead.

Fifteen-year-old Prince Henry was, however, the reason for a new rift between the parties. Henry wanted to have him crowned as his successor, just as King Stephen had wished with his son Eustace. Thomas had been instrumental in preventing that during the previous reign but he might have felt less strongly about his ex-ward and a king who had been a dear friend if their present relationship had been different. However, he certainly would not have permitted any infringement of his own rights and they included the right of coronation. Permission had been given eight years earlier, when there was no Archbishop of Canterbury, for the Archbishop of York to crown the prince, and now it was proposed to claim this authority again. Thomas asked the Pope to forbid it and he did. Nevertheless, the coronation took place— Roger of York denied receiving the papal letter.

Thomas wrote imposing an interdict on England, but the letter was probably never despatched for Henry, feeling that he had won a battle, was disposed to encourage moves to peace.

Five weeks after the coronation Henry and Thomas met at Fréteval, between Tours and Chartres. When the king saw Thomas approaching with the Archbishop of Sens he rushed forward to greet them and, when the Archbishop of Sens left them together, they talked, as Thomas later wrote to the Pope, 'with such intimacy that it was as though there had never been any discord between us'. Henry even spoke of going on a pilgrimage or crusade to Jerusalem and leaving the 'Young King' (Prince Henry) and the kingdom in the archbishop's charge. The Constitutions and claims for property were not discussed but Thomas asked permission to inflict ecclesiastical punishment on the Archbishop of York and the suffragan bishops involved in the coronation. 'To this the king assented,' records Herbert of Bosham,[16] 'and the archbishop . . . jumped from his horse and threw himself humbly at the king's feet [Thomas' own version says he knelt]. But when the archbishop was going to mount his horse again, the king held the stirrup for him.'

Thomas began to make plans for his return to England, including the purchase of a stock of wine for the cellars at Canterbury and his numerous manors, but delayed leaving until, as he wrote to the Pope, 'our envoys bring word that retribution is being made. . . . It is not that I fear the king will break his promises but that evil advisers may again mislead him.'[17]

In October the Pope instructed the archbishops of Sens and Rouen to visit Henry and call on him both to implement his promises and to revoke the Constitutions of Clarendon: and a threat of interdict was once more unsheathed. Then he authorised Thomas to reimpose the previously planned censure if the reconciliation did not prove to be genuine. Thomas replied that he would 'grasp this shadow of reconciliation' and 'hold fast to the favour of this man as much as possible, consistent with the liberties and honour of the Church, and will make trial by experiment whether he can be brought back to tranquillity'. He goes on to 'intreat your holiness to omit all mention of the king's excesses' in letters of correction to the Archbishop of York and the suffragan bishops, and 'although the Bishop of London has been the standard bearer of this sedition . . . entreat you to give us power to pardon him and the Bishop of Salisbury, if we find that they cannot be punished without renewal of the schism'.[18] For once Thomas seems to show a greater sense of diplomacy than concentration on claiming his own rights or dramatising the threat to his person. He still hoped to receive the kiss of peace which would show the world, and Henry's barons back in England in particular, that he and the king were reconciled and that it would not gain royal favour to act against him.

Thomas heard that Henry was to have a conference with the Count of Blois at Tours and decided that this would be an opportunity to talk with him again. When the king heard that he was coming he sent out an escort to greet him and then rode out himself, but their meeting was cool. Next day the king was to meet the count at Amboise, where he first heard Mass in the chapel of the castle. On his arrival he was told that Thomas was already there. In those times it was the practice that at the point in the Mass when the celebrant said 'The Peace of the Lord be with you always,' he gave a ritual kiss to the person of highest rank in the congregation who would then kiss the next in rank, and so downwards, uniting the whole congregation in the blessing.[19] If they were both present the king would not be able to avoid giving Thomas the kiss, and it is probable that it was the archbishop's intention so to obtain it. But the king's chaplain found a way to avoid this happening by saying a requiem Mass, from which the *Pax* is omitted, despite the fact that the day was the feast of St Wilfrid of York, a famous English saint. After the service Thomas directly asked the king to give him the kiss but Henry still refused, though saying, 'On another occasion you shall have it as much as you wish.'

A short time later they met again at Chaumont, near Blois, where Henry was very amicable and spoke of Thomas serving him as before. 'Why will you not do as I want?' he exlaimed, 'If you would I would hand over everything to you.' But Thomas later told Herbert of Bosham that to him these words sounded like those of Christ's tempter in the wilderness: 'All these things will I give to you if you fall down and worship me.'[20]

The king urged Thomas to speed his return to Canterbury and promised to meet him in Rouen to settle his debts and that he would accompany him to England, or follow as quickly as possible. As they parted Thomas declared: 'My lord, my heart tells me that when I leave you now I shall never see you again in this life.'

'Do you think me faithless then?' replied the king.

'*Absit a te, domine*,' (Let that be far from you, lord), answered Thomas.[21]

Henry now wrote to England announcing their reconciliation but did not concede to all Thomas' claims: he instructed his son to restore to the archbishop and his men all the possessions which they held three months before their departure, but he left the Young King to judge the rights of Thomas or the de Broc family to Saltwood Castle.

In fact Henry did not meet Thomas in Rouen, but wrote explaining that he had to go to Auvergne to support his vassals against an attack by the King of France but that he sent John, the Dean of Salisbury (whom Thomas had previously excommunicated!), to be his companion. The king had given no kiss of peace and had not paid Thomas' debts, to settle which the Archbishop of Rouen lent him £300, but Thomas set off for the coast with a retinue of a hundred horsemen and the wine and other goods which he was taking back from France.

When he reached the coast, at Wissant, near Boulogne, he heard that the Archbishop of York and the Bishops of London and Salisbury had already got wind of the letters of excommunication which he carried and were preparing to cross to Normandy to appeal against them. In addition they had organised de Broc and other knights to set up armed watch at all ports, ready to search the archbishop's baggage as he landed and confiscate the documents before they could be presented. Thomas had them taken across ahead of him. The messenger evaded de Broc and his men and the excommunications were delivered to their subjects at Canterbury itself. Others newly arrived from England warned Thomas against returning and spoke of enemies who would either make him prisoner or murder him. 'It is of no consequence,' Thomas declared, 'if I am torn limb from limb. For seven years my Church has been deprived of a pastor; it is my request, perhaps my last to my friends, that if I cannot return to Canterbury alive, they will carry me there dead.'[22]

A sailor gave reassuring news of the popular enthusiasm for the archbishop's return but his captain warned of the fury and confusion aroused by the new excommunications. Thomas refused to reconsider or delay, but orders were given not to sail on the expected crossing and instead to set course for Sandwich, a port belonging to Christ Church, Canterbury, where it was hoped the inhabitants would prove loyal liegemen. Sandwich had been given to the priory by King Cnut and each year the townsfolk, as rent, supplied clothing for the monks and sent 40,000 herrings to the cellarer.

The plan did not work. The king's supporters were waiting at Sandwich harbour and the armed men who rushed towards the ship put down their weapons only when the Dean of Salisbury, known by them to be a supporter of the king, called out that anyone who harmed the archbishop would be guilty of treason.

There is little doubt that these men genuinely feared Thomas' intentions. Gervase, the Sheriff of Kent, angrily declared that the archbishop had 'come back bringing fire and sword. You want to take the crown from the king. [The Young King, a misunderstanding of Thomas's attitude to the coronation.] You have excommunicated the Archbishop of York and bishops for serving the king. If you do not change your attitude soon something will happen that would be better not happening.'

'I have no intention of undoing the king's coronation,' Thomas replied. 'I would happily give him four more kingdoms if I could. I have punished men who, by usurping the right of consecration, have defied God and the prerogatives of the Church of Canterbury. Is it bringing fire and the sword if I inflict due justice on the sins of bishops? Threatening me with death will get you nowhere for I have come to risk life and limb for justice and for truth.'[23]

5 Dark December

THE HOSTILE RECEPTION which Thomas encountered on his landing was a further ominous warning of the danger which he faced from the barony, but the enthusiastic welcome of the ordinary people of Sandwich warmed his heart and all along the road to Canterbury people expressed their joy at his return. If Herbert of Bosham is to be believed the scene was like that of Christ's entry into Jerusalem. People strewed their clothes upon the roadway; whole villages came out, led by their priests, to greet him; music, singing and pealing church bells sounded all along the way and, at Canterbury, the cathedral had been decorated by the townsfolk and a public banquet had been arranged. In the evening Thomas preached in the Cathedral church and exchanged the kiss of peace with his monks and followers.

Next day Ranulf de Broc and the Sheriff of Kent, together with representa-

Thomas returns from exile to the threats of Henry's knights and the joy of the townspeople of Sandwich. From a thirteenth-century life.

tives of the three bishops, called upon Thomas to request that he lift the excommunications and suspension. If he did so the bishops promised to make their submissions to him—'saving the honour of the king'.

The formula was too close to the one which Thomas had been forced to abandon and agreement would have been too like defeat—if he allowed his suffragans to use such a limitation it would be admitting the subservience of the Church to the king. However, he did not refuse, but offered absolution to the Bishop of London and the Bishop of Salisbury if they would swear before him to obey all future demands of the Pope, for the power to absolve them was really the Pope's not his. He made no mention of the Archbishop of York. Since the royal party considered all the sentences unlawful, because they had been imposed without the king's consent, no compromise was possible.

The Archbishop of York, Roger de Pont l'Evêque, Thomas' enemy since youth, persuaded the bishops that they could not accept the terms and they all set off for France to seek King Henry's aid. Meanwhile Roger sent a messenger to the court of the Young King (Prince Henry) to tell him that Thomas intended to depose him.

Thomas, too, sent a messenger to his one-time page to ask for an audience, and himself set off more slowly *via* Rochester and London for the court, which was gathered at Winchester. Ahead, with the messenger, went a present of three fine warhorses which he had brought over from Flanders. Elegant, swift, high-stepping and lively, they were caparisoned in gaily decorated harness. They were a splendid gift, but they could not turn the Young King from the advisers who surrounded him. Although the messenger was himself well received, he was told to tell the Archbishop that he would hear from Prince Henry later. At the same time two knights were sent to instruct Thomas to return to Canterbury.

As Thomas neared London a great crowd of clergy, theological students and citizens came out from the city to greet him. They were proud of the fellow Londoner who had become so famous. The archbishop planned to stay in Southwark, south of the river, in the palace of the Bishop of Winchester, and he had just dismounted at St Mary's Church (now Southwark Cathedral) to a choral welcome from the canons of the church when there was a commotion and cry from the crowd. It was a mad woman, named Matilda, who screamed out repeatedly 'Archbishop! Beware the knife!'

The next day, before the archbishop could cross the river into London the queen's brother arrived as messenger from Prince Henry and ordered Thomas to return to his diocese and to stay there. The popular enthusiasm shown for Thomas, and the rumour which had spread that he proposed to nullify the Young King's coronation, together with Henry II's accusations that he had ambitions to the throne, may have made the barons, and even Young Henry, fear that the people might rise behind him in rebellion. Although such an idea must have been far from Thomas' mind it would not be unreasonable among those who had seen a nobody rise to high office, wealth and influence, and then dare to outface the king and threaten a whole nation with God's wrath.

Saddened by the rebuff and fearful of what it might imply, Thomas nevertheless set out first for his manor at Harrow (where he had first entered Archbishop Theobald's service), which probably gave the impression that he was on his way to force a meeting with Young Henry. He was there, and preparing to return, when news came that Ranulf de Broc had seized a ship which was bringing back some of the wine Thomas had bought in France, and, it was said, killed some of the crew and imprisoned others. Thomas sent more messengers to Young Henry to ask for restitution and, on the Young King's orders, the vessel was restored and the sailors freed. Yet another outrage of the de Broc family was reported. Robert de Broc, coming upon some sumpter horses belonging to the archbishop on their way to Canterbury, had encouraged his nephew to dock the tail of one of them—in other circumstances perhaps a mere childish delinquency, but at the instigation of de Broc a calculated insult.

Taking five soldiers to protect him from attack—from thieves or possible assassins—Thomas made his way back to Canterbury through Wrotham. On his way he confirmed many children, descending from his horse to do so (a consideration not practised by all bishops; many would give a general blessing from the saddle).

Even back in Canterbury the insults of the de Brocs persisted. Not only did they still continue to occupy Saltwood Castle, they hunted in the archbishop's woods, chasing his deer with hounds that came from his own kennels. Ranulf de Broc had been in charge of the palace, and Thomas would not easily forget that it was Robert de Broc who had carried out the expulsion of all his relatives with such severity.

On 19th December Thomas held a service of ordination in the cathedral and on the 21st, his fifty-second birthday, he celebrated a festive High Mass: it was the feast of St Thomas the Apostle. On Christmas Eve he officiated at a Midnight Mass and on the day of the Nativity preceded the celebration of the Eucharist with a sermon on the text 'Peace unto all men of goodwill'.[1]

The church of Thomas' archiepiscopate was not the Christ Church of today but Anselm's church. The nave and transepts, the western and the central towers, were those that Lanfranc built, the splendid choir was that raised by Priors Ernulf and Conrad when St Anselm decided that his predecessor's church needed enlargement. Completed in 1130, its outer walls still form the lower parts of some of the present building. A plan drawn about three years before Thomas' return to show the layout of a new water supply gives a clear idea of what the outside looked like, and one must imagine the rounded arcades of Norman arches right through the church, inside and out.

Gervase, a contemporary monk at Canterbury, describes how during High

Mass the archbishop sat upon the patriarchal chair, carved from a single stone, which was placed in an apse behind and above the altar, descending down the eight steps to it when the time came for the consecration of the holy elements. At the eastern corners of the altar two wooden columns, gracefully decorated with gold and silver, carried a great beam whose ends rested on the capitals of two pillars. On it, above the altar, were an image of Christ and figures of St Dunstan and St Alphege, and seven chests, faced with gold and silver, in which were the relics of many saints. Between the columns was a gilded cross, surrounded by a row of sixty transparent crystals. From the middle of the choir a golden crown was suspended carrying twenty-four candles, and beneath the lantern tower, hanging in the centre of the transept crossing, was another gilded cross. The nave was separated from the tower by a screen with a second loft, in the middle of which the altar of the Holy Cross faced out to the nave, while on the rood above were another great cross and figures of St Mary, St John and two angels.[2] The ceiling of the choir was finely painted, and frescoes decorated many of the walls—remains of some of them can still be seen in the apse of St Gabriel's Chapel, preserved by being bricked up from the twelfth century to the nineteenth. Although the architecture was heavier and the church darker than today's, it too had steps descending from the transepts to the crypt (which is little changed) and rising to the higher levels with many passages and corridors behind the upper levels of the arcading. Thomas would be wearing his magnificent archiepiscopal robes, the altars would be shining with their finest plate and all would be as impressive and solemn as he could make it.

In his sermon Thomas urged his flock to lead virtuous lives and to honour the Church and her ministers. He referred to the way in which he had been abused and how he still had to suffer insult, and warned that worse might be to come. Canterbury already had one martyred archbishop, St Alphege: there might soon be another. Returning to his text he spoke of those men without goodwill and ended his sermon with the ritual upturning of candles and, dashing them to the ground, pronounced Robert de Broc excommunicate, renewed the ban on Ranulf his brother, and anathematized the holder of the churches at Harrow and Throwley who denied him repossession.

Thomas' biographers report many earlier occasions when he had referred to the possibility of martyrdom, but now he had made a public prophecy of its likelihood. It seems that Thomas was preparing himself for such an eventuality and his close associates were as aware of it as he. Yet it would be wrong to think that he must have set himself firmly on such a course. He perhaps still hoped for a peaceful settlement with the king. Indeed, by speaking of martyrdom he may have hoped to intimidate his enemies, who would surely fear the idea of murdering a saint.

Thomas now sent Herbert of Bosham and the crossbearer Alexander Llewellyn away from Canterbury. He told them to go to France and tell

King Louis and the Archbishop of Sens how Henry's peace had proved 'no peace, but turbulence'. They were two of his closest clerks and known to have advised him to stand firmly against the king. He must also have been saving them from sharing his danger, although against their will. He also sent a messenger to the Pope but, strangely, made no attempt to communicate with Henry: perhaps he really did believe that the opposition of the barons and the Young King reflected King Henry's orders.

Meanwhile, the Archbishop of York and the Bishops of London and Salisbury had reached Bures, near Bayeux, where Henry was celebrating Christmas. Their letters had preceded them and other news was coming through from England, but hardly any that would speak of Archbishop Thomas with favour. Henry had thought himself at peace with the archbishop, or so he had written to his son, but instead a very distorted picture was presented by Roger of York (the other two bishops were too fearful of contaminating the king with their excommunicant status to speak). He gave details of their excommunication and described Thomas marching through the country with an army of soldiers and rousing up the people. He even went so far as to say: 'You will never have a tranquil day so long as Thomas lives.'[3]

The excommunications—Henry had not expected Thomas to carry the disciplining of those involved in the coronation so far, for he too was a participant—and the news of warlike agitation threw Henry into one of his towering rages.

Garnier describes the whole court swearing to kill Thomas, 'pledging each other that they would pull his tongue down past his chin and pluck both eyes out of his head', but this is not substantiated, although some very intemperate suggestions were made. Certainly it was now decided that the Earl of Essex and others should go to England to prevent Thomas from leaving the country again and to either put him in prison or set him under house arrest at Canterbury until he removed all the penalties inflicted upon his opponents.

Most of the court were used to Henry's undisciplined displays, shouting, tearing his clothes, rolling around in the rushes and gnashing his teeth on hanks of straw, but there were four knights who, when he cried out 'Will no one free me of this wretched priest?'[5] took him at his literal word.

It is not clear when these four—Hugh de Moreville, William de Tracy, Richard le Breton (or de Brito) and Reginald fitzUrse—left the court. All except Brito were, in fact, vassals of Archbishop Thomas from the time when he was chancellor. They sailed separately from different ports but, having crossed the channel, made for Saltwood Castle. They were no impoverished adventurers but barons of some substance, known well to both the king and Thomas. They left secretly without asking the king's permission, almost certainly before the decision to arrest Thomas was made, and when they were missed a party was sent to try to stop them. Why? Who was afraid of what?

On Holy Innocents' Day, December 28th, the four knights were gathered at Saltwood Castle, where they were welcomed by the brothers de Broc, and news of their arrival soon reached Thomas at Canterbury.

The knights gave out that they had come on the king's orders to arrest the Archbishop of Canterbury, and the following morning they rode to Canterbury with a body of soldiers raised in the neighbourhood by the de Brocs. They did not go straight to Christ Church but to St Augustine's Abbey, where the abbot was no friend of Thomas and had refused even the Pope's orders to vow obedience to the archbishop. After dining and drinking well at St Augustine's, they sent out some of their men to rouse the townspeople to arm themselves and report to the archbishop's palace to serve the king or, if they would not, to keep away and not interfere. Then, with a small band of soldiers, the four set off for Christ Church.

We do not know exactly what they planned. Perhaps only to arrest Thomas and hold him at the king's pleasure, perhaps to force him to lift the excommunications he had imposed. There is no certainty that they intended any violence against him, but they could reasonably expect that the man who had led an army when he was chancellor would not be likely to submit without a fight.

When they arrived they found that the archbishop, having finished his dinner, had withdrawn with some of his household to an inner chamber to deal with business matters, leaving the rest waiting in the main hall of the palace.

At Christ Church there was a secular clerk called Edward Grim, recently arrived from Cambridge to see the archbishop. By chance, he now became closely involved with the events of the next few hours and later recorded his memory of them in one of the biographies of Thomas. Let his words now tell what happened, with occasional comments from other sources.[5]

The four knights, with one attendant, forced their way in. They were received with respect as servants of the king and well known to the archbishop's household; and those who had waited on the archbishop, being now themselves at dinner, invited them to share their table. They scorned the offer, thirsting rather for blood than for food. By their order the archbishop was informed that four men had arrived who wished to speak with him on behalf of the king. On his giving consent, they were permitted to enter. For a long time they sat in silence and neither saluted the archbishop nor spoke to him. Nor did the man of wise counsel salute them immediately they came in, in order that . . . he might discover their intentions from their questions. After a while, however, he turned to them and, carefully scanning the face of each, he greeted them in a friendly manner; but the unhappy wretches, who had made a pact with death, straightway answered his greeting with curses and ironically prayed that God might help him. At these words of bitterness and malice the man of God flushed deeply, for he now realized that they had come to work him injury. Whereupon fitzUrse, who seemed to be their leader and more prepared for the crime than the others, breathing fury, broke out in these words: 'We have somewhat to say to thee by the king's command; say if thou wilt that we tell it here before all.' But the archbishop knew what they were about to say and answered, 'These things should not be spoken in private or in the chamber, but in public.' Now these wretches so burned for the slaughter of the archbishop that if the door-keeper had not called back the clerks—for the archbishop had ordered them all to withdraw—they would have killed him with the shaft of his cross which stood by, as they afterwards confessed. When those who had gone out returned, he, who had before reviled the archbishop, again addressed him saying, 'When the king made peace with you and all disputes were settled, he sent you back to your own see, as you requested; but you, in contrary fashion, adding insult to injury, have broken the peace, and in your pride have wrought evil in yourself against your lord. For those, by whose ministry the king's son was crowned and invested with the honours of sovereignty, you with obstinate pride have condemned with sentence of suspension. You have also bound with the chain of anathema [i.e., have excommunicated] those servants of the king by whose counsel and prudence the business of the kingdom is transacted. From this it is manifest that you would take away the crown from the king's son if you had the power. But now the plots and schemes you have hatched in order to carry out your designs against your lord the king are known to all men. Say therefore whether you are prepared to come into the king's presence and make answer to these charges.' The archbishop replied, 'Never was it my wish, as God is my witness, to take away the crown from my lord the king's son or to diminish his power; rather would I wish him three crowns and help him to obtain the greatest realms of the earth, so it be with right and equity. But it is unjust that my lord the king should be offended because my people accompany me through the towns and cities and come out to meet me, when for seven years now they have been deprived through my exile of the consolation of my presence. Even now I am ready to satisfy my lord wherever he pleases, if in anything I have done amiss; but he has forbidden me with threats to enter any of his cities and towns, or even villages. Moreover, it was not by me, but by the lord pope that the prelates were suspended from office.' 'It was through you', said the infuriated knights, 'that they were suspended; do you absolve them?' 'I do not deny', he answered, 'that it was done through me, but it is beyond my power and utterly incompatible with my dignity to absolve those whom the lord pope has bound. Let them go to him, on whom redounds the injury and contempt they have shown towards me and their mother, the Church of Christ at Canterbury.'

'Well then,' said these butchers, 'this is the king's command, that you depart with all your men from the kingdom and the lands which own his dominion; for from this day forth there can be no peace betwixt him and you or any of yours, for you have broken the peace.' To this the archbishop answered, 'Cease your threats and still your brawling. I put my trust in the King of Heaven who for his own suffered on the Cross; for from this day forth no one shall see the sea between me and my church. I have not come back to flee again; here shall he who wants me find me. It is not fitting for the king to issue such commands; sufficient are the insults received by me and mine from the king's servants, without further threats.' 'Such were the king's commands,' they replied, 'and we will make them good for whereas you ought to have shown respect to the king's majesty and submitted your vengeance to his judgment, you have followed the impulse of your passion and basely thrust out from the Church his ministers and servants.' At these words Christ's champion, rising in fervour of spirit against his accusers, exclaimed, 'Whoever shall presume to violate the decrees of the holy Roman see or the laws of Christ's Church, and shall refuse to come of his own accord and make satisfaction, whosoever he be, I will not spare him, nor will I delay to inflict ecclesiastical censures upon the delinquent.'

Confounded by these words, the knights sprang to their feet, for they could no longer bear the firmness of his answers. Coming close up to him they said, 'We declare to you that you have spoken in peril of your head.' 'Are you then come to slay me?' said he. 'I have committed my cause to the great Judge of all mankind; wherefore I am not moved by threats, nor are your swords more ready to strike than is my soul for martyrdom. Go, seek him who would fly from you; me you will find foot to foot in the battle of the Lord.' As they retired amidst tumult and insults, he who was fitly surnamed 'the bear' [Urse] brutishly cried out, 'In the king's name we command you, both clerks and monks, to seize and hold that man, lest he escape by flight ere the king take full justice on his body.' As they departed with these words, the man of God followed them to the door and cried out after them, 'Here, here will you find me'; putting his hand on his neck, as though marking beforehand the place where they were to strike . . .

As they left the monastery the knights removed the porter and stationed one of their own men at the gate. Then, at a given signal (William fitzStephen records), the men they had gathered in a house opposite the gate 'rushed forth as one man, passed through the open gate of the courtyard, bolted it behind them and with a loud and terrifying clamour shouted "Knights of the king, the king, the king!"'. FitzStephen also describes Reginald fitzUrse putting on his armour in the courtyard where he also seized a hatchet from a carpenter who was repairing some steps.

Ere long, [continues Grim] came the murderers in full armour, with swords, axes and hatchets, and other implements suitable for the crime on which their minds were set. Finding the doors barred and unopened at their knocking, they turned aside by a private path through an orchard till they came to a wooden partition, which they cut and hacked and finally broke down.

FitzStephen says that thus Robert de Broc forced his way into the hall and threw open the door to the rest, inflicting severe wounds on those who tried to stop him. (Monk Benedict's account says they got in through a window.)

Terrified by the noise and uproar, almost all the clerks and the servants were scattered hither and thither like sheep before wolves. Those who remained cried out to the archbishop to flee to the church; but he, mindful of his former promise that he would not through fear of death flee from those who kill the body, rejected flight . . .

FitzStephen says that there was already a clamour from the church, presumably from townspeople as well as monks who had gathered there, who were by now aware that the knights and soldiers were hounding the archbishop. However it was time for vespers and the monks tried to persuade Thomas to go with them to the service and the safety of the church.

. . . But when he would not be persuaded by argument or entreaties to take refuge in the church, the monks seized hold of him in spite of his resistance, and pulled, dragged and pushed him; without heeding his opposition and his clamour to let him go, they brought him as far as the church. But the door, which led to the monks' cloister, had been carefully barred several days before, and as the murderers were already pressing on their heels, all hope of escape seemed removed. But one of them, running forward, seized hold of the bolt, and to the great surprise of them all, drew it out with as much ease as if it had been merely glued to the door.

Grim was a new arrival and did not know the monastery, so this may be a misunderstanding—several other accounts speak of a 'breaking of the lock' without implying a near miracle as Grim does. Why had the door been barred some days before? Dr William Urry, for many years archivist at Canterbury, suggests that there was a speaking tube through from the outside to the cloister (there is an opening in the wall today through which it is suggested cellarmen could pass things to monks in the cloister): those inside would then be able to open the door on the identification of who was coming. One report describes the fleeing monks going into the chapter house—in their confusion and panic to reach sanctuary they probably rushed into the first door they reached. A French verse biography, based on information collected at Canterbury suggests that Thomas was actually carried, but fitzStephen suggests a more orderly departure. 'He [Thomas] ordered the cross of the Lord to be borne before him. It was borne by a certain clerk of his named

Henry of Auxerre. When he had reached the monk's cloister, the monks wished to shut the door fast behind him. But he was displeased and would not allow it. He walked on behind them last of all, at a slow pace, driving all before him, as a good shepherded doth his sheep. . . . Once indeed he cast his eye back over his right shoulder, perchance in case he should see the king's men dogging his footsteps, perchance lest someone should bolt the door behind him.'

What was Thomas thinking? Was he making sure that all his flock got to the safety of the church taking all the risk himself since it was him the knights were after? Or was he afraid that the monks might try to deprive him of the glory of martyrdom which he felt coming?

After the monks had retreated within the precincts of the church, the four knights came following hard on their heels with rapid strides. They were accompanied by a certain sub-deacon called Hugh, armed with malice like their own, appropriately named Mauclerc, being one who showed no reverence either to God or his saints, as he proved by his subsequent action. As soon as the archbishop entered the monastic buildings, the monks ceased the vespers, which they had already begun to offer to God, and ran to meet him, glorifying God for that they saw their father alive and unharmed, when they had heard he was dead. They also hastened to ward off the foe from the slaughter of their shepherd by fastening the bolts of the folding doors giving access to the church. But Christ's doughty champion turned to them and ordered the doors to be thrown open, saying, 'It is not meet to make a fortress of the house of prayer, the Church of Christ, which, even if it be not closed, affords sufficient protection to its children; by suffering rather than by fighting shall we triumph over the enemy; for we are come to suffer, not to resist.' Straightway these sacrilegious men, with drawn swords, entered the house of peace and reconciliation, causing no little horror to those present by the mere sight of them and the clash of their armour. All the onlookers were in tumult and consternation, for by this time those who had been singing vespers had rushed up to the scene of death.

Thomas was now on the steps leading up to the choir, either dragged there by the monks, hustling him towards the greater sanctuary of the altar, or himself thinking to offer his life in the most sacred part of the church. He urged the monks to return to their service and perhaps intended to participate and be seen to be struck down in the service of God. As the knights came forward the crowd dissolved, taking refuge by more distant altars of the church or hiding in dark corners. Only Robert of Merton, William fitz-Stephen and Edward Grim stayed by him.

FitzStephen points out how easy it would have been for the archbishop himself to have evaded his pursuers, for it was by now getting dark; inside the cathedral things would be only very dimly seen except where there were candles burning to throw a stronger light: 'both time and place offered the opportunity to escape without being found. It was evening. The long night of the winter solstice was at hand. The crypt was near, full of winding passages, mostly very dark. There was another door close by, through which he might have taken a spiral staircase to the arched chambers in the roof of the church. Perchance he would not have been found: or in the meantime some change of circumstance might have occurred.'

In a spirit of mad fury [continues Grim] the knights called out, 'Where is Thomas Becket, traitor to the king and the realm?' When he returned no answer, they cried out the more loudly and insistently, 'Where is the archbishop?' At this quite undaunted, as it is written 'The righteous shall be bold as a lion and without fear', he descended from the steps, whither he had been dragged by the monks through their fear of the knights, and in a perfectly clear voice answered, 'Lo! here am I, no traitor to the king, but a priest. What do you seek from me?' And whereas he had already told them that he had no fear of them, he now added. 'Behold, I am ready to suffer in His Name who redeemed me by His Blood. Far be it from me to flee from your swords, or to depart from righteousness.' Having thus said, he turned aside to the right, under a pillar, having on one side the altar of the blessed Mother of God, Mary ever-Virgin, on the other, that of the holy confessor, Benedict . . . The murderers pursued him. 'Absolve', they cried, 'and restore to communion those whom you have excommunicated, and the functions of their office to the others who have been suspended.' He answered, 'There has been no satisfaction made, and I will not absolve them.' 'Then you shall die this instant,' they cried, 'and receive your desert.' 'I, too,' said he, 'am ready to die for my Lord, that in my blood the Church may obtain peace and liberty; but in the name of Almighty God I forbid you to harm any of my men, whether clerk or lay.'

Then they made a rush at him and laid sacrilegious hands upon him, pulling and dragging him roughly and violently endeavouring to get him outside the walls of the church and there slay him, or bind him and carry him off prisoner, as they afterwards confessed was their intention. But as he could not easily be moved from the pillar, one of them seized hold of him and clung to him more closely. The archbishop shook him off vigorously, calling him a pandar and saying 'Touch me not, Reginald; you owe me fealty and obedience; you are acting like a madman, you and your accomplices.' All aflame with a terrible fury at this rebuff, the knight brandished his sword against that consecrated head. 'Neither faith,' he cried, 'nor obedience do I owe you against my fealty to my lord the king.' Then the unconquered martyr understood that the hour was approaching that should release him from the miseries of this mortal life, and that the crown of immortality prepared for him and promised by the Lord was

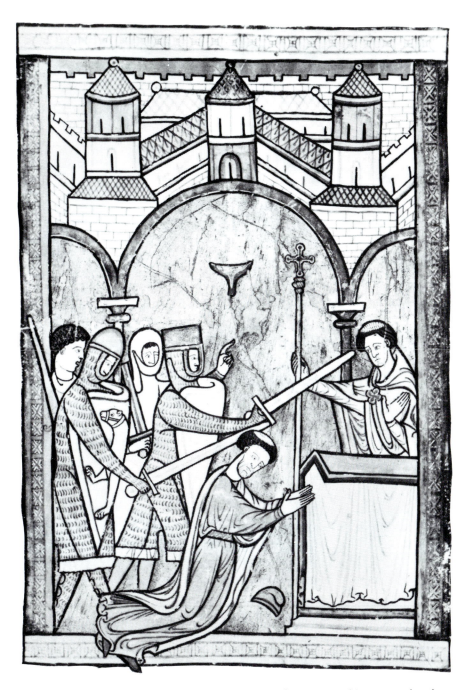

The murder of Thomas, from a psalter manuscript made twenty to thirty years after the event. Reginald fitzUrse, identified by the bear upon his shield, is striking a blow while Edward Grim still stands steadfast with the archbishop's cross. (*British Library*.)

already nigh at hand. Whereupon, inclining his head as one in prayer and joining his hands together and uplifting them, he commended his cause and that of the Church of God to St Mary and the blessed martyr, St Denys. Scarce had he uttered the words than the wicked knight, fearing lest he should be rescued by the people and escape alive, leapt suddenly upon him and wounded the sacrificial lamb of God in the head, cutting off the top of the crown which the unction of the sacred chrism had dedicated to God, and by the same stroke he almost cut off the arm of him who tells the story. For he, when all the others, both monks and clerks had fled, steadfastly stood by the saintly archbishop and held his arms around him, till the one he opposed to the blow was almost severed.

Next he received a second blow on the head, but still he stood firm and immovable. At the third blow he fell on his knees and elbows, offering himself a living sacrifice and saying in a low voice, 'For the Name of Jesus and the protection of the Church I am ready to embrace death.' But the third knight inflicted a terrible wound as he lay prostrate . . . The fourth knight warded off any who sought to intervene, so that the others might with greater freedom and licence perpetrate the crime. But the fifth—no knight he, but that same clerk who had entered with the knights [Hugh Mauclerk]—that a fifth blow might not be wanting to the martyr who in other things had imitated Christ, placed his foot on the neck of the holy priest and precious martyr and, horrible to relate, scattered the brains and blood about the pavement, crying out to the others, 'Let us away, knights; this fellow will rise no more.'

In all his suffering the illustrious martyr displayed an incredible stead-fastness. Neither with hand nor robe, as is the manner of human frailty, did he oppose the fatal stroke. Nor when smitten did he utter a single word, neither cry nor groan, nor any sound indicative of pain. But he held motionless the head which he had bent to meet the uplifted sword until, bespattered with blood and brains, as though in an attitude of prayer, his body lay prone on the pavement, while his soul rested in Abraham's bosom.

6 The Hooly Blisful Martir

THE DEED DONE, the four knights who had murdered Thomas rushed out of the church shouting, 'The king's men, the king's men!', and, according to the eyewitness biographers, ransacked the archbishop's palace, breaking open chests and cupboards, searching for incriminating documents, while de Broc and his soldiers looted both palace and clerks' quarters, taking books, gold plate, jewels and coin, and loaded them up onto the archbishop's own horses to carry them away.

According to fitzStephen's account a great storm cloud now filled the sky, thunder pealed and the very air turned red; but such manifestations seem more desired than real, and fashioned on the biblical description of—as the writer himself puts it—'when Christ was suffering in his own body'. But, whether there was a miraculous colouring of the heavens or not, the religious brethren and the townsfolk of Canterbury were filled with horror and with dread. At first the body lay deserted, not even a candle by it, but then it was realized that the soldiers had gone, although they could be heard outside and in the palace. In the dark cathedral the monks and clerics came out from the shadows and gathered by the body of their abbot and archbishop. There were some who felt that, terrible though it was, their archbishop had brought his fate upon himself—even, perhaps, deserved it—and although the desecration of the church and the sacrilege of murdering a priest filled them with horror not many felt for Thomas personally; he had been away for six years, during which his stand against the king had made life difficult at Canterbury.

Osbert, the household chamberlain, cut off a strip of his shirt and bound the severed portion of the archbishop's head back into place; then the body of Thomas was carefully carried from the transept to the sanctuary, where it was laid upon a bier before the high altar. In the transept of the martyrdom the blood and brains were carefully collected or soaked up with cloths, and Arnold, the abbey goldsmith, washed the remaining blood from the chapel pavement, although a dark stain remained to be pointed out for many years. Below the bier, bowls were set to catch any remaining drops of blood and every fragment of stained cloth, each drop of spilled blood, became a wonder-working relic.

When it was realized that the murderers had left the precincts, the priory servants and the townsfolk of Canterbury—'and only the poor,' says Herbert of Bosham in his account [1]—rushed to the cathedral to see their new martyr, but few dared to mourn openly that night for fear of the de Brocs. When the lay people had gone the doors of the cathedral were locked because the desecrated building could no longer be used for worship.

Benedict, a monk of Christ Church who later became prior, and then abbot of Peterborough, had a dream that night in which he claimed [2] that he saw Thomas rise up, dressed in his full vestments, and approach the altar as if to celebrate the Mass. In his dream he asked Thomas: 'Are you not dead?' To this the archbishop answered: 'Dead I was, but I have risen again.'

Not all the monks could believe that this was a vision but they were convinced of Thomas' piety when Robert of Merton, Thomas' confessor, showed them that below his outer vestments and under his monk's habit their dead archbishop wore a hair shirt and hair drawers to mortify the flesh. To intensify the penance this uncomfortable underwear was crawling with lice. Such evidence of penitential devotion convinced many doubters that, despite the public image of his life, this indeed had been a holy man. Perceiving this 'double martyrdom', the monks 'fell to the floor, kissing his hands and feet, calling him Saint Thomas, declaring him a martyr of God. Everyone hurried forward to see him in haircloth whom they had seen as chancellor in purple and byssus.' [3] The hair shirt was so contrived that it could easily be removed to bare his back for the discipline of the scourge which, according to Robert of Merton, Thomas had received three times on the morning of his martyrdom.

Already rumours were flying about that the church had a new saint. Next morning Robert de Broc sent a message to the monastery that they must quickly and secretly bury the body or he would drag it from the church and have it publicly degraded and torn apart. The monks hastily prepared it for burial and placed it in a new empty tomb 'which was hewn out of the rock' [4] in the crypt, between the altars dedicated to St Augustine and St John the Baptist. Later it was told how, before its internment, the body of Thomas rose and made the sign of the cross over itself and the surrounding monks. It was also testified that a blind man, coming from London and hearing of the murder of the archbishop when he reached Canterbury, made his way to the cathedral where he touched his eyes with the martyr's blood and received his sight. [5] These particular miracles do not seem to have been recorded by the eyewitnesses of the murder, but William fitzStephen records the curing of a Canterbury woman striken by paralysis. Her husband, who told the tale in floods of tears and barely audibly, was among the townsfolk in the cathedral who saw the martyrdom, and he had dipped some of his clothing in the martyr's blood. She 'begged that the blood might be washed off and caught in water so that she might drink its healing draught. It was done and she was at once cured. This was the first of the signs God wrought for his Martyr the same night. Hence, I suppose, came the custom (through divine

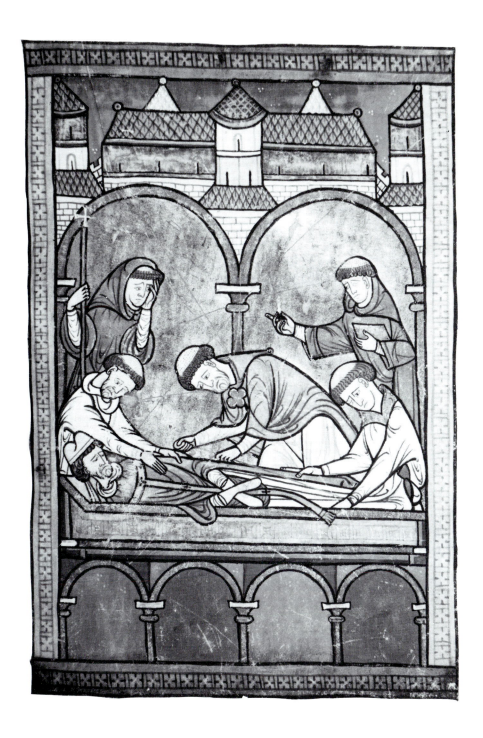

The burial of Thomas in his archbishop's vestments, including the pallium, from the same manuscript as the illustration on page 71. (*British Library.*)

inspiration) of infusing a portion of the blood of St Thomas in water . . .'[6]

News of miracles, both at Canterbury and far away, where people had called upon the name of Thomas or he had appeared to them, were soon spreading across the country—as quickly, almost, as the news of the archbishop's death.

The sacrilege of Thomas's murder caused a wave of revulsion across Europe. King Henry was told of it on January 1st and dissolved into tears at the messenger's words. His grief was wild and inconsolable. He refused to leave his room for three days, he refused to eat, he sat staring in front of himself as if in a trance, or he howled his heart out. When at last he had regained his self-control he called upon his court to witness that he had not wanted Thomas's death, but he knew that he would be blamed and sent embassies to the Pope to plead his innocence.

No doubt the bond between Henry and Thomas had been very close and the king's grief was very personal, but he had more than lost a one-time close friend and loyal adviser, he had lost all hope of winning his struggle against the power of the Church. Now he stood in much greater risk of excommunication than he had at Thomas's hands. Now it was he who would have to make concessions. The Archbishop of Sens imposed an interdict on all Henry's continental territories, a sentence which the Pope confirmed, but England was spared and Henry was not excommunicated, for he promised to carry out whatever penance the Pope decreed was necessary. Meanwhile he had made himself inaccessible to anyone wishing to deliver an excommunication by taking an army across the sea to Ireland, declaring that he was launching a crusade to bring the Irish back into the fold of the Roman Church.

The Pope also showed a very personal grief for Thomas, and retired to his private apartments for a week. He, too, must have felt a partial responsibility for Thomas's death for he had urged him to return to England. But Pope Alexander was on the winning side. Not only did the world support the cause of the dead archbishop—the cause of Church power—the martyrdom also added to Alexander's power and prestige against the rival pope supported by the German emperor.

Meanwhile, in Kent, the de Brocs set men to watch the bridges and crossroads around Canterbury to take the names of any who came on pilgrimage to the tomb, and others hung about the alehouses to arrest any that they heard speak well of the archbishop.[7] But this did not stop the devout from coming: already people were treating Thomas as a saint and stories of miracles began to multiply. Men like Richard de Lucy and Jocelyn, Bishop of Salisbury, who had been Thomas' opponents, publicly expressed their disbelief—although both later were to change their minds after they had personal experience of Thomas' miracles. Lucy saw a priest from one of his manors whose paralysed arm was restored[8] to health. Jocelyn was convinced by the cure of a boy leper who had been brought up at the monastery of Abingdon,[9] and himself called upon Thomas as he sat watching by the sickbed of Thomas' old enemy Gilbert Foliot, Bishop of London. After he made a vow to Thomas on Foliot's behalf, the bishop was cured.[10] At length even one of the de Broc's brothers, William, was cured of a fever and an intestinal complaint after four years of suffering. He drank three times of St Thomas' Water, twice vomiting it up, and was completely restored to health.[11]

In Paris the learned clerics at the university argued about Thomas' claim to martyrdom. One 'swore that he had deserved to die (though not die in such a way), and judged the constancy of the blessed saint to be mere obstinacy.'[12] But it was agreed that the many miracles confirmed his sanctity. Two of the canons of St Frideswide's, in Oxford, would not believe in Thomas' sanctity until an appeal to the saint miraculously cured one of their brethren of constipation.[13]

Until Easter 1171 the cathedral was closed and pilgrims were admitted only privately to the tomb in the crypt, but there was a rising undercurrent of reproach that the monks were keeping the blessings of their martyr too closely and, no doubt, people were feeling much less afraid of the archbishop's enemies—by now everyone must have heard that the king had not been pleased at the murder. On the Friday after Easter the crypt was opened

The crypt of Canterbury Cathedral, little changed since Thomas was buried there. (*British Tourist Authority.*)

to the public, and soon it was the setting for a regular flow of pilgrims, while many sick lay about the church, hoping for a cure. And cures there were, each adding to the martyr's fame and attracting further pilgrims in its wake.

It was not until the feast of St Thomas the Apostle, December 21st, 1171 (which would have been Thomas's fifty-third birthday), that the cathedral church was reconsecrated. For nearly a year the altars had been left stripped of cloths and vessels and the holy images covered as though every day had been the day of the Crucifixion. A solemn Mass was celebrated by Bartholomew, Bishop of Exeter, in rededication and the regular celebration of the Holy Office once more resumed.

Henry II stayed in Ireland while his emissaries made peace with the Pope. He did not return to France until the spring of 1172, when terms were finally agreed with the papal legates, although even then Henry refused some of their demands almost to the end. On May 21st, in the cathedral at Avranches, in Normandy, he met with them to accept his sentence. The church was destroyed in the French Revolution but an inscribed stone still survives to show the spot by the door where, in the presence of his son, the Young King, and with his hands upon the Gospels, he swore that he had neither commanded nor desired the killing of the Archbishop of Canterbury, although admitting that it was due to his angry words that it had been carried out. In penance he was instructed to provide and equip, at his private expense, two hundred knights to fight in the Holy Land for a whole year under the command of the Knights Templar (a sentence later commuted to the foundation of three religious houses); he was to return all lands and possessions to the Church of Canterbury, and all possessions confiscated from Thomas' supporters; further, he was to be prepared, if the Pope so wished, to go to Spain to fight the Moors; and in addition he was instructed to fast, give alms, and perform other secret penances. Tactfully, no direct mention appears to have been made of the king's claims made at Clarendon, perhaps because the Pope had already declared them unacceptable and the king had promised to follow the Pope's directions.

On September 2nd Alexander III issued a papal bull confirming the agreement made at Avranches and declaring that the oath made by the bishops at Clarendon was void.

A hero who had won such a victory for the Church, who was already being treated by the common people as a martyr and a saint, was an obvious candidate for canonization, but before anyone can officially be declared a saint there has to be evidence that God intends the promotion of one of the faithful. From the eleventh century it became necessary to investigate the life and acts of the proposed saint and, especially, to record those miracles and wonders which identify the ones whom God has singled out for sainthood. It had been the custom for the local bishop to be the judge of suitability; now the decision had to be made by the Pope. Those who claimed to have witnessed or been the subject of miracles were very closely questioned.

Details of sickness, its duration and manifestation were required of those who claimed to have been healed, and every attempt was made to expose fraud. Of course, in an age of faith, many things which had quite natural causes were attributed to miraculous intervention. The devout were eager to gain the closeness with heaven which even a miracle against them would bestow, and were not so interested in looking for rational explanations. There were liars and frauds who hoped to gain material benefit by deliberately recounting false miracles, and there must have been many cases where fortuitous circumstance was interpreted as saintly intervention—as for instance in the case of a knight who, having dismounted in the forest of Ponthieu, lost his horse. He invoked the aid of St Thomas and, after making his way on foot for the rest of the day, found his horse standing in a clearing and hurried to announce this as a miracle to the local clergy.[14] They were convinced enough to pass the information on to Canterbury where it was inscribed in the book recording the miracles of St Thomas. Naturally, when records were being kept with the idea of substantiating a claim to sainthood we can assume that the clerks entering each incident were eager to recognize as many miracles as possible out of partisanship for the prestige of their own church.

Two papal legates were instructed by the Pope to go to Canterbury to investigate what was happening there and the claims being made. Written evidence of the many miracles and cures was sent back to Rome and the legates also took back with them a piece of the martyr's bloodstained tunic, a portion of his brains and some fragments from the pavement in the transept where he had died; these were given to the Church of St Maria Maggiore in Rome.

Alexander III—despite his own experience of Thomas' obstinacy—did not take much convincing and, on February 21st, 1173, he declared Thomas, late Archbishop of Canterbury, to be a saint and martyr. It was little more than three years after his death, a much shorter lapse of time than usual even in the twelfth century. The Pope called for a suitable shrine to be erected to house the archbishop's remains and himself sent two marble columns taken from the ruins of Carthage as a contribution towards its construction. Henceforth December 29th, the day of his death, was to be celebrated as the feast of the new saint.

While Thomas was being wreathed in glory, Henry was facing rebellion—and rebellion led by his own family: Young Henry and his brothers Richard and Geoffrey, egged on by their mother and by the King of France, and supported by many of Henry's discontented barons. In life many of these nobles had been Thomas' enemies but now they were happy to encourage those who said that the rebellion was a divine punishment on the king. There was a dangerous possibility of England being lost completely to the rebels, and Henry decided that he must take an army against his enemies—but he too heard the talk of retribution, and knew that he had to show his subjects publicly that he was reconciled with England's new saint. It was a private need also, perhaps, for who had been closer to Thomas than he?

On July 8th, 1174, the king made landfall at Southampton. Next morning he set off to ride to Canterbury. On the journey he took only bread and water for his sustenance and, riding hard (sleeping we know not where), he reached Canterbury by early light on July 12th. At the village of Harbledown 'as soon as he catcheth first sight of the city,' as the Icelandic *Thomas Saga* puts it, 'he dismounteth from his horse'[15] and walked towards Canterbury until he reached the Church of St Dunstan, outside the walls, where he 'putteth away his kingly rainment' and, clad instead in a simple woollen kirtle (some writers say sackcloth), he

> walked barefoot . . . the whole way to the martyr's tomb. There he lay prostrate for a great while in devout humility, and of his own will was scourged by all the bishops and abbots there present, and each individual monk of the abbey of Christ Church. There he stayed, in prayer before the holy martyr, through all that day and night. He took no sustenance, nor went out to relieve nature, nor would he permit a rug or wrap of any kind to be provided for him but remained as he had come. After the celebration of Lauds he made a tour of the altars in the choir of the cathedral and the bodies of the saints interred there and then returned below to the tomb of St Thomas in the crypt. Early on Sunday morning he heard Mass. Finally he drank of the water of the holy martyr and was honoured with the gift of a phial.'[16]

Henry was known to drive himself hard physically and, though patience was not a virtue he had much store of, he must have spent a night in vigil as the culmination of his preparation to become a knight—but on this occasion his naked back had been flogged with five strokes of the lash from each of the prelates present and three strokes from each of eighty monks. Over 250 lashes are not easily borne. Perhaps his chastisers laid on lightly for fear of the king's person, or from charity—and indeed there is no report of him suffering any immediate effects from his scourging, although he fell ill when he returned to London—but the humiliation and the physical strain must have been great. Perhaps he was succoured by some mystical communion with the saint, perhaps it all seemed worthwhile as a propaganda exercise.

In modern times a theory has been put forward[17] which would have put Henry very deeply in Thomas' debt and make this vigil and abasement the acknowledgement not of Henry's guilt but of a conscious sacrifice on Thomas' part. Hugh Ross Williamson, taking the pagan concept of the king who becomes the sacrificial victim for the good of the community as expounded by Dr Margaret Murray,[18] sees this ancient ceremony re-enacted in the death of Thomas. William Rufus, shot under peculiar circumstances in the New Forest in 1100, is also singled out as a king sacrifice. There is evidence to suggest both that William was a follower of the 'old religion' and that he was expecting death.

At its simplest, the concept is that of a fertility cult with the king as its head. As Fraser puts it in *The Golden Bough*, 'The life-giving spirit of God was caused to enter into the chosen man at a special ceremony, which later developed into the enthroning of a king, and still later into the coronation. After the ceremony the Divine Man was credited with the power of giving or withholding fertility . . .'. Since the Divine spirit was subjected to the physical condition of the body it entered, weakness or illness would threaten disaster, so the remedy was to kill the king, release the spirit and place it in a new, strong body. When the death was by bloodshed it was vital that the blood should fall upon the ground.

William Rufus was killed in a 'hunting accident' by an arrow fired by Walter Tyrrel, his close friend—and possibly his lover, for the king was a practising homosexual. William is said to have called out just before his death: 'Shoot, in the Devil's name, shoot quickly,' and his body was taken to Winchester in a charcoal-burner's cart, dripping blood all the way.

Can a similar scenario be seen behind Thomas' death? Hugh Ross Williamson suggests that Thomas was given high office and boundless privileges in return for accepting the role of substitute sacrificial victim in the king's place, and was made archbishop in order that he should perform the ceremony of coronation of the Young King, but that when the time came for him to die he backed out on the bargain and fled for his life. Seven years later he returned to England having become reconciled to Henry just in time for the death which he, like William Rufus, anticipated. Henry's avoidance of giving the Kiss of Peace is seen as the king's avoidance of reaccepting the sacrificial role himself, and Thomas's remark at their parting: 'My lord, we shall never meet again on this earth,' as his sign of acceptance of his role. The way in which Henry held his stirrup is then seen as his homage to his substitute king. In contradictions in the reports of the murder as to the number of steps in the short flight on which Thomas stood at the time of his martyrdom Mr Ross-Williamson sees both a record of certain mystic numbers concerned with the rite and the deliberate falsification of them to disguise a pagan ritual as a Christian martyrdom. The cap worn by Thomas, in later manuscript illustrations of the murder and the burial of the archbishop, he compares with the Phrygian cap seen worn by devotees in carvings of Mithraic ritual.

Could there be any truth in such an interpretation? Thomas was a close friend of the Templars who, when the Order was disbanded, were accused of practising black magic, worshipping the devil and homosexual acts. It would not be impossible for older religions to survive masquerading inside the Christian Church—but if this was the case the Church certainly found a way to turn the whole affair to its Christian advantage! In fact, the supporting evidence is so meagre as to be discountable—but even then one might argue that it was in the interest of the pagans to keep everything secret and of the Christians to suppress it totally, so that we could hardly expect to find any proof extant.

Almost equally tied up in myth is the fate of the four knights who murdered Thomas. The '*Lives*' of the saint have them sent off to soldier in the Holy Land, and all being buried there except Tracy; he, having been prevented from reaching Palestine, was seized by a madness in which he tore his own flesh from his body, and died in Calabria. In fact—because they had killed a priest and in a church—Thomas' claims for church jurisdiction made them subject, like Thomas' clerics, to Church law and, although a later agreement with the Pope would have allowed Henry to bring them to trial, it seems that they went free. They appear later to have been accepted back in court and their descendants became landowners in the West Country and northern England.[19] Tracy, for his part in the crime, actually gave the manor of Daccomb, in Devonshire, to the monastery of Christ Church.

The king's penance seemed to show immediate results. Even while Henry was carrying out his vigil the King of Scotland was captured and the balance turned against the rebels in the north. 'God be thanked for it,' cried Henry, 'and Saint Thomas the Martyr and all the saints of God.'[20]

The king had already appointed one of Thomas' sisters, Mary, Abbess of Barking, and now he begged the forgiveness of another sister, Roesia, and in recompense for the sufferings he had caused her gave her the profits of the King's Mill at Canterbury. He gave money to Christ Church, and promised more, and endowed the leper hospital of St Nicholas at Harbledown, where he had dismounted to perform his penance, with an annual income of twenty marks, which was to be paid from the royal dues on rents from stalls in the Buttermarket and elsewhere in Canterbury. In 1234 Henry III arranged that the city should be held in 'fee farm' by its citizens, who then collected all the monies due to the crown and kept them, in return for a regular payment of sixty pounds to the royal Exchequer. They also became responsible for the penitential payment which was deducted from the sixty pounds. A mark was worth thirteen shillings and fourpence so the annual payment of ten marks is now £13.33p in decimal currency. The hospital, like other ancient institutions endowed with money rather than with property, now comes off very badly, for twenty marks was originally a considerable sum. The city loses too, for, although the payment is still made, no rents have been paid for stall pitches in the Buttermarket since the nineteenth century—so the citizen pays the penance through his local taxes!

During the winter of 1175–6, after Henry had suppressed rebellion in England, the Pope sent Cardinal Pierleone to clear up those points not already settled between Church and State and to wrest further concessions from the king. Henry gave up all claims to judge criminous clerks, except for transgressions against the forest laws and questions of lay service for lay fiefs. Free communication with Rome was guaranteed, and bishoprics and other

The flagellation of King Henry II by the bishops and the brethren of Christ Church; a stained-glass window from Duke Humphrey's library, Oxford. (*Bodleian Library.*)

vacancies were to be filled without undue delays. Murderers of clerics were, however, to be tried in the royal courts.[21] Strangely, Saltwood Castle, which had seemed such an important possession to Thomas, was not fully returned to the See of Canterbury until the reign of King John.

Peace in Henry's dominions was not to last. His wife, Eleanor of Aquitaine, and his sons, Young Henry, Richard, John and Geoffrey—could there ever have been a more quarrelsome family?—were continually plotting against him. After Henry's two eldest sons had died Richard joined the French king in a war against him. When Henry died of fever in 1189 he was only fifty-six, but prematurely aged. It is said that his last faithful knight had to borrow money to get a coffin for his corpse and that his servants stripped the body before it was cold.

Only a few months after Henry II's penance at Canterbury a fire broke out in the cathedral and destroyed the choir, spreading to the infirmary and various buildings in the Green Court. Gervase, a Christ Church monk, describes how the brethren 'to relieve their miseries . . . fixed the altar, such as it was, in the nave of the church, where they howled, rather than sung, matins and vespers.'[22] The priory chose William of Sens, who had just completed the fine cathedral in that French town, to rebuild their church for them in the new style, but it was many years before it was ready for the body of St Thomas to be placed in a new shrine as the Pope had commanded. Meanwhile the tomb in the crypt remained the centre of pilgrimage and the monks continued to record the miracles that happened there or were reported to them. Two monks were responsible for the records: Benedict, he who had dreamed of a resurrected Thomas, and William, who had been ordained by Thomas just before his martyrdom and who wrote a life of the saint. Sometimes both record the same miracle, sometimes different ones, and many hundreds are listed and authenticated (at least sufficiently to satisfy them).

One of the earlier miracles concerns a knight called Stephen who came from Hoyland and who for thirty years had been troubled by a nightmare in which a demon leaped upon him and tormented him.[23] By calling upon the help of St Thomas he freed himself from this apparition and came, dressed in 'despicable garb' to show his humility, to give thanks at the tomb. (You can

Effigy of Henry II on his sarcophagus at Fontevrault. (*French Government Tourist Office.*)

see him, lying in bed, in a window in the Trinity Chapel at Canterbury.)

Henry of Fordwich,[24] whose case is also recorded, was a madman dragged by his friends to visit the tomb with his hands tied behind him. He stayed there all day, struggling and shouting, but became quieter with evening and, after spending all night in the church, was taken home again with his sanity recovered.

More practical was the cure of William Patrick,[25] a serving man who had a violent toothache. He had a vision in which a figure, claiming to be a clerk of the archbishop's, bade him open his mouth and, after wafting air into it with his mantle, touched his cheek with its border, banishing the pain. Later, at the tomb, William described the mantle—it was the pallium of the archbishop and the investigator accepted this as proof of the miracle's authenticity.

Usually a much more rigorous proof was demanded, especially when a miracle happened somewhere far away. This is one which occurred when William, King of Scotland, was passing through Roxburgh, a town on the river Tweed. He sent the Bishop of Glasgow and his archdeacon to interrogate John, the Provost's grandson, to whom it happened, and they took down his story 'on peril of anathema and edict' if he should distort the truth. John was turning a horse away from the river after taking it to drink when it took fright and leaped into deep water. He was thrown out of the saddle into the river while the horse made for the bank and home. It was getting dark, there was little hope of rescue, and as the torrent pulled him into the deepest parts of the river John began to sink. He prayed to St Thomas: 'Let not thy servant perish: for I have but lately visited the sacred threshold of thy martyrdom. Come to my aid, thou Champion of God, let not thy pilgrim die.'

He was then sucked down into a kind of hollow. 'While thus out of sight, deep down, fixed in the mud, behold, eight figures of reverend presence were borne upon the waters, walking side by side.' Benedict's record (probably copied from the bishop's report) is very careful not to take pious imagination for fact: 'He imagines that he arose and followed them . . . but in truth was borne up to the surface of the waters and was following by swimming.' At last, nearing the bank, he caught hold of a willow bough, but it broke off and pulled a stone from the bank down on top of him, pushing him back into the stream. After a time the eight figures appeared again and he felt them to be lifting him up ('Imagining himself to be walking he was swimming in the waters,' writes Benedict). Then he found himself lying on a bridge, six or eight feet above the water, much further than he could have climbed. The water he had swallowed 'leaped back by the same passage by which it had flowed in' and while he was painfully vomiting he heard one of the figures, clothed in pontifical robes, say: 'To thine own good wast thou mindful of me yesterday when thou didst fall in. Behold thou hast been snatched from death. Be thou a good man: and do good while thou art able.'

When he raised his eyes to see who spoke the figure vanished. Too numb and cold to rise, he crawled to the toll house of the bridge—where at first they would not let him in because they thought that he was a ghost, for he had already been reported drowned. Once inside he dried out before their fire.[26]

Another entry describes Matilda, a violent madwoman, who had made her pilgrimage all the way from Cologne and went home cured. Cripples came and threw away their crutches, blind men saw, and there are descriptions of the restoration of mutilated, and even amputated, limbs. The water of St Thomas was taken home to work more miracles—and in one case even fraudulent water of St Thomas is recorded as causing a miracle to be performed, because of the deep faith of the recipient.

A prisoner in goal in Stafford, on a charge of manslaughter, was given some water of St Thomas to drink by a returning pilgrim: the saint caused the man's fetters to fall off, no matter how many times they were refastened, until the goalers took the man before the king who, after being convinced that it was not a devil's work, decreed: 'If Thomas has freed him, let none trouble him. Let him go in peace.'[27]

In Holland, a peasant caught in the great flood of May 1173 was forced to leave two children and a cow behind in his cottage and entrusted them to St Thomas' care. Returning when the waters fell he found them safe. '"A man in white clothes," said the little ones, "brought us bread for ourselves and hay for the cow." And they not only described the Martyr (to the best of their power): they also shewed as a proof of their story, the remains of the bread and the hay.'[28]

It was not only the sick and those in danger who called upon St Thomas' aid, and miracles took many forms. He put money into the pockets of pilgrims who needed it for alms. Two children who mislaid a cheese given to them as a present for their mother invoked his aid, and both had a dream which showed them the disused milk churn in which one of them had hidden it for safety.[29] He restored to life a cow which had already been skinned and buried[30]—although he also killed another belonging to a farmer who failed to offer it to his shrine when it was suggested by a neighbour. Indeed St Thomas could be quite vindictive on occasion. One lame boy who fell asleep upon his tomb saw him in a dream saying, 'Why do you lie on me? You shall certainly not recover. Go hence. I will do nothing for you.' Benedict tells how the monks bade the boy devote himself to prayer—but it had no effect in changing the saint's decision.[31]

There are a number of miracles concerning the recovery of falcons and one concerning an especially fine falcon called Wiscard, which belonged to the king. Its eye had been pierced by the bill of a crane. The falconer made a vow to St Thomas, who told him, in a dream, to look for twelve pimples on the hawk and open them. Next morning he found three or four and, calling his friends, said that if he could find all twelve it would be no fancy but a real vision. He did find them and, when he carried out the saint's instructions, 'the bird opened its eyes and called for its food'.[32]

The miracles recorded after Thomas' canonization tend to be more fantastic, and hearsay evidence seems more easily accepted, but when pilgrims reported happenings at home the monks of Christ Church usually wrote to the local bishop or civic authority asking for an investigation to be made. Correspondents reporting distant miracles sent as evidence depositions made by witnesses and testimonials to their good character.

During the years 1171–77, when these detailed records were kept, Canterbury was growing into a major centre of pilgrimage, next in importance after the Holy Land, Rome and Santiago de Compostella. New shrines were always an attraction and, although at first it was largely the poor who flocked to St Thomas, soon the greatest could be counted in their number. Of the 665 pilgrims recorded in the miracle collections the social standing of more than two-thirds is described: of them more than a quarter were of the knightly class and about eight per cent were members of the nobility. In 1179 came Louis VII of France, Thomas' old protector—the first French king to set foot on English soil—to give an offering of a magnificent jewel, the Regale of France, at the tomb, while to the monastery he made a gift of 100 hogsheads of wine each year in perpetuity. In 1197 came Richard I (Coeur de Lion) with William III of Scotland, also known as 'the Lion', who founded the famous abbey at Arbroath in St Thomas' honour. King John also made the pilgrimage and in 1220 his son, thirteen-year-old Henry III, came for the 'translation' of the body to the new shrine.

However, according to the *Chronicle* of Ralph of Coggeshall, the popularity of Canterbury had fallen within ten years of the martyrdom and the Holy Cross, more recently acquired by Bromholm Priory, in Norfolk, was attracting pilgrims who used to go to Canterbury. Such whims of fashion seem to have been the case with all except the three great pilgrimages to Jerusalem, Rome and Santiago, but Thomas' continuing influence was assured because his cult was taken up all over England and across the seas. Henry's daughter Joan, who married the king of Sicily, founded the Cathedral of Monreale where there is a fine mosaic portrait made about 1190. A church was founded in his honour in the Holy Land at Acre—so that he is sometimes known as St Thomas of Acre. He became particularly popular in Iceland, where a biography was written in saga form. His relics began to find their way to churches far away. When Benedict, who had guarded the shrine, became abbot of Peterborough in 1179, he took with him two vases of Thomas' blood, part of the clothing of the archbishop and flagstones from the place of martyrdom from which to build an altar. Another custodian, Roger, was offered the abbacy of the rival St Augustine's monastery in Canterbury if he would bring part of the martyr's skull with him—he did. Sens had the vestments which Thomas had worn—and has them still. The present Westminster Cathedral has one of his mitres. Carlisle Cathedral claimed to possess the sword of Hugh de Morville and another murder weapon was in a London church. Parts of Thomas' clothing were scattered among churches all over England: Chester had a girdle, Bury his boots and a penknife. Other vestments were at Bourbourg, St Omer and Douay. In Verona there was a tooth, while in Florence a convent claimed to have an arm—and in Lisbon two arms were supposed to be those of Thomas! Windsor, Peterborough, St Albans, Derby, Warwick and Glastonbury all had relics, and St Thomas Abbey in Erdington, Birmingham, claimed earlier this century to have 'great and precious relics of the saint's body and that amice which he wore around his neck at Holy Mass'. With three arms missing one might wonder what remained at Canterbury. However, such questions would not have troubled a medieval mind as much as they do the sceptic of today. If Christ could multiply the loaves and fishes why should he not replicate a limb or add a thousand-fold to the timber of the cross?

In 1218, when the rebuilding of the choir and eastern chapels of Christ Church Cathedral were nearing completion, Archbishop Langton proclaimed to the world that the body of St Thomas would be translated to a new shrine on July 7th, 1220. The Pope declared that pilgrims to Canterbury for this occasion could gain a plenary indulgence—a total remission of all penance due.

For over forty years the masons and the carvers had been intermittently at work whenever funds and weather permitted. William of Sens had fallen from the scaffolding as he directed operations and had been succeeded, when he proved too ill to carry on, by another William, an Englishman, who built the chapel of St Thomas on the site of the old Trinity Chapel and added an eastern circular chapel. The crypt in which Thomas rested had been untouched as new walls rose above it, but when the eastern chapel was built its new crypt came very close, and (says Gervase) 'a wooden chapel, proper enough for time and place, was prepared over and around his tomb; without whose walls, the foundation being laid of stone and mortar, eight pillars of the new undercroft, with their capitals, were furnished. The architect prudently opened an entrance from the old undercroft into the new one. With these works the 6th year [of the rebuilding] ended and the 7th began.'[33]

The new choir, which came into use at Easter, 1180, and eastern chapel were made much higher than before and decorated with carving and shafts of black Purbeck marble. 'In the old capitals, the workmanship was plain, in the new the sculpture is excellent,' considered Gervase. 'In the circuit without the choir the vaults were plain, here they are arched and studded . . .' The wooden ceiling was replaced by light, high vaulting. The towers on either side of the choir were retained and, in order to continue the ambulatory aisle right to the east, this necessitated the narrowing of the new structure, giving a visual impression of even greater length than the 258 feet which it now reached from west to east, the grandeur being further increased by the way in which the choir rose from the nave and the sanctuary from the choir, with the setting for the shrine being on a higher level still. Beneath the soaring pointed arches of the new style the shrine, which was the focus of it all, was splendidly adorned with the jewels and precious stones that were the offerings of the wealthy.

Preparations for the thousands of pilgrims expected were elaborate and extravagant. The abbeys and monasteries of Canterbury and along the routes to the city were provisioned to feed and shelter an unprecedented number of travellers. Free hay and fodder were provided for the asking at points all along the way from London. At every gate of Canterbury and in four quarters of the city, tuns of wine were ready to be distributed free on the great day itself.

At midnight on July 6th, after hymns and prayers, Archbishop Langton, the monks and the prior of Christ Church, opened up the tomb. Each in turn reverently kissed the martyr's head and the remains were prepared for their removal. They were then carefully guarded through the night. Next morning a great assembly, led by the King and attended by the highest dignitaries of Church and State, gathered to celebrate High Mass and witness the enshrinement of the martyr. Pandulph, Cardinal of Milan (the Pope's legate), the Archbishop of Rheims, Archbishop Langton, Hubert de Burgh, (Lord High Justiciar of England), and four other great nobles carried the relics from the crypt to their new resting place. (The cost of providing so lavishly for this great occasion so bankrupted the monastery that it was many years before the debt was cleared.)

The anniversary of the Translation now became the most important feast for pilgrims—travel in July was much easier than in the bleak days of December—but they came throughout the year. By the middle of the thirteenth century the great days of the pilgrimage had passed and in the fourteenth century a miracle at the shrine was such a rare occurrence that it warranted a letter of congratulation from the king.[34] But Canterbury was on the London–Dover route and many travellers would take the opportunity to visit the shrine. London to Canterbury was not such a gruelling journey: it could be a lively holiday for travellers like those in Chaucer's *Canterbury Tales*. The great and famous still came to kneel at St Thomas' shrine: among them were many of England's kings, including Edward I, to whom the crown of Scotland was presented before the shrine; Henry IV, who was buried close beside it; and Henry V, returning from the Battle of Agincourt. Edward the Black Prince, who also is buried near the shrine, came here in 1356 after the Battle of Poitiers with the French king, John the Good; Manuel II, Palaeologus, Emperor of the Eastern Empire, came in 1400, while in the west to raise support for the defence of Byzantium; and Sigismund, Holy Roman Emperor, came in 1416. And St Thomas was still worth calling to one's aid—in 1402 the Venetian Senate issued a decree permitting Lorenzo Contarini, captain of a fleet of Venetian galleys setting sail for Flanders, to leave his command at Sandwich and visit Canterbury to accomplish a vow,

The choir and eastern chapels of Canterbury Cathedral. In medieval times the high altar would have been on the level below the final flight of steps and the shrine of St Thomas in the centre of the further chapel, behind the position of the modern high altar. (*British Tourist Authority.*)

provided that he did not sleep away from his vessel.[35]

In 1320 a plenary indulgence was granted by the Pope and this hundredth anniversary of the Translation declared a Jubilee. Every fifty years thereafter the monks applied to the Pope for a Jubilee plenary indulgence, which naturally attracted an extra surge of pilgrims. This was not an automatic grant. The Pope had to be petitioned, and 'persuaded'. Plenary indulgences became a useful source of papal revenue. By the end of the fifteenth century the right to give a plenary indulgence through a particular year would cost the church a payment of four or five hundred gold florins, plus a fat royalty from the proceeds—usually about a third.[36] In 1420, an indulgence was refused by Pope Martin V and the monks declared their own—four learned doctors of theology summoned by the prior declared this to be quite legitimate.[37] In 1520, Pope Leo X asked more than Christ Church could afford and, despite their pleas that many Englishmen were unable, because too sick or too poor, to go to Rome or Santiago (where Italians and Spaniards and other closer peoples could gain a plenary indulgence) and that 'the English are the most attached to old habits and traditional devotions, and they will not easily be deprived of them without great uproar',[32] they were denied one. The agent putting their request in Rome was told by Cardinal Campeggio that 'it is not possible that the Pope will grant you this for no money or favour'.[38] It was Pope Leo's ready sale of indulgences—at the right price—to finance the rebuilding of St Peter's which brought down the wrath of Martin Luther.

Jubilee or not, King Henry VIII, who gained his title of Defender of the Faith for his attack on Luther, went to Canterbury in 1520 and stood before the shrine with his guest and nephew, the Emperor Charles V. Henry seems to have been a devotee of St Thomas—each year he sent a sum of twenty shillings to the shrine[39]—yet it was he who in 1538 caused the shrine to be destroyed and brought an end to four and a half centuries of pilgrimage.

7 To be a Pilgrim

THE WORD PILGRIM comes from the medieval French *pelegrin*, which in turn comes from the Latin *peregrinus*, which meant a stranger and might originally have referred to any traveller. But the idea of pilgrimage is much older than the word itself. More than 3,000 years ago the devout Hindu would travel to the ancient city of Benares (now known as Varanasi) to wash away his sins in the waters of the Ganges, most holy of Hindu rivers. Pilgrimage is a concept that appears in many faiths—the journey to Mecca is a vital part of every Moslem's religious life; and it is a practice that even the least religious of us continue in paying homage to the memory of the talented and the famous. Does the modern 'pilgrim' to the birthplace of William Shakespeare, the tomb of Napoleon or the portals of the Parthenon hope to gain virtue by his outing in an air-conditioned coach? Does he hope that some of the genius of the great will be transferred to him? Does she feel that the glory of the past will illuminate her life? Or is the trip—'It's Tuesday, this must be Rome'—merely a means of gaining prestige among the folks back home? During the Middle Ages one benefit probably *was* enhancement of prestige, at least for the poorer sort of folk, but the role of pilgrimage was a very real one in their religious life.

In AD 70 the Roman army of Titus had almost levelled Jerusalem, but in the early centuries after the establishment of Christianity in the Empire the places in which Christ had lived and taught exerted a particular fascination for the devout. People believed that they could still identify the cave in which he had been born in Bethlehem, the tomb in which he had been laid and the place where he ascended into heaven. To bathe oneself in the River Jordan was to be rebaptised indeed, and the idea of baptism and rededication is an important part of the pilgrim's attitude. As Benedict of Canterbury puts it, the pilgrims to a shrine are 'rebaptised in the font of their own tears'.

Those who came to the Holy Land might well settle there, as did St Jerome, who lived at Bethlehem for thirty-five years and wrote that a pilgrim should 'not merely live in Jerusalem but live a holy life there'. For St Jerome the holy life was more important than the place, and a renunciation of worldly life was the true pilgrimage. This is the concept of the pilgrim which is reflected in the teaching of the Buddha, and which made John Bunyan call his allegory *A Pilgrim's Progress*. It was a process of self-exile, whether in an enclosed community or as a perpetual wanderer. Irish monks, in particular, took up the concept of the wandering pilgrimage, the idea spreading to Saxon England and during the sixth and seventh centuries to the continent. Although ecclesiastical authorities found them a threat to church discipline, and sought to control them, aimless pilgrimages of this kind were common for several hundred years.

In his *Sermons*, written at the beginning of the fourteenth century, Franco Sacchetti presented the pilgrim's journey as an allegory of Christ's life with its dangers and betrayals. And on reaching the Holy Land many pilgrims would literally try to follow in the steps of Christ from Bethlehem to Galilee, fasting in the desert, bathing in the Jordan and treading the route of His Passion along the Via Dolorosa to Calvary—a route marked out in the medieval streets of Jerusalem.

Devotion and meditation at the scenes of Christ's life were linked with a veneration for physical relics connected with Him and with His saints that, like the Cross on which Christ was crucified (which the Empress Helena claimed to have discovered in 326), could be divided and taken to the far corners of the world. The cult of relics was already established by the middle of the second century, when the bones of a martyred bishop were carefully preserved as of inestimable value. During the persecutions of Diocletian, relics were eagerly collected, and later the catacombs of Rome were considered particularly holy places. (Although most of the thousands who pass through them today are probably gaping tourists, a visit to them was one way for a good Catholic to gain an indulgence during the last Holy Year.) There were those who criticised the veneration of relics and remains, seeing it as a continuation of pagan idolatry, but St Jerome defended the practice, claiming that the relics were not worshipped, but were venerated only in honour of the faith they witnessed. St Augustine considered that they should be venerated even as one would venerate a holy man when living. With this veneration came the belief that through such relics cures and miracles could be worked, and the holiness inherent in them was such that, as Gregory of Tours recounts,[1] if they had sufficient faith, pilgrims who hung a piece of cloth inside the tomb of St Peter would find, when they withdrew it, that it was heavier because it had absorbed so much of the divine grace exuded by the saint.

It became the custom to place a relic in a new church, or even in an altar at its consecration—and relics of the apostles and martyrs were among the things 'necessary for the worship of the Church' which Pope Gregory the Great sent to St Augustine's mission in England. In 787 the Second Council of Nicaea decreed that relics were henceforth necessary for the consecration of new churches and that any consecrated without them should acquire some as soon as possible. This position was opposed by iconoclasts such as Claudius, Bishop of Turin, who in 823 ordered images to be burned, ridiculed the idea of virtue in relics, and criticised the idea of pilgrimage to tombs and to the Holy Land. Yet the greater number of Christians, in the West at least, thought that contact with relics, whether in church, worn on the person, or in a private relic collection—and some people began to amass relics as recent generations have collected stamps—would bestow virtue upon the faithful.

A visit to a shrine might be in hope of help—of a miracle—or in thanks, or to keep a promise made when asking heavenly help against sickness or danger. It also came to be considered a worthy act in itself, a good deed to set in the balance when it came to judgement. Even before St Augustine's time it was held that complete remission of sins might be obtained by going to the tomb of a martyr and meditating there. Whereas the free, wandering pilgrimage, or the self-exile to the Holy Land had carried unmeasured merit and might be perpetual, pilgrims now returned to take up their former life and an attitude began to develop which accorded different values to visits to different shrines.

Beginning once more in Ireland, pilgrimages came to be given as a penance to sinners, especially to those who had committed public rather than private sins—murder, sacrilege and sexual transgressions (especially those of the clergy)—for which it was felt public atonement should be made. For those whose sins were private ones, a penitential pilgrimage might be the result of a vow, voluntarily undertaken because of a weight upon their conscience, or in return for favours received. People began to think of making vows as a practical form of bargaining—help me and I will say so many prayers or visit your shrine—a pilgrimage could become a form of 'contract' with a saint.

In the early Church, penance had to be carried out before a believer could be absolved from sin, but from the end of the tenth century it became usual for absolution to be given at the time of confession; and by performing good works, or going on a pilgrimage, in this life, it was thought possible to reduce the punishment awaiting in the next. Forgiveness of sins is an essential part of the Christian belief, but forgiveness of the contrite sinner did not mean that he would escape punishment in the next life any more than he would escape human punishments if found guilty of crimes against earthly laws. However, acts of penance, like good works, could increase a Christian's credit balance. In fact, theologians concluded, the virtue of Christ, the saints and the martyrs gave a surplus which was available to others, who might earn a share in proportion to the contribution which they gave themselves. This theory of the Treasury of the Church was based upon apostolic teaching (especially the Epistle to the Hebrews) and clarified by St Thomas Aquinas at the beginning of the thirteenth century. More recently the doctrine was restated by Pope Paul VI in 1967: the Treasury consists of: (1) Christ's merits before God; (2) prayers and good works of the Blessed Virgin Mary; (3) prayers and good works of saints; and (4) prayers and good works of all those who have made their lives holy.[2] Since Christ gave the keys to paradise to St Peter, and hence to his Church, the Church becomes responsible for deciding upon the form of penance required to earn a portion of the corporate Treasure.

At the beginning of the eleventh century many Christians were very aware that they were approaching a time one thousand years from the crucifixion of Christ and believed that the Millennium would be the Day of Judgement. In consequence, there was a particular surge of pilgrimages by people who saw little time left in which to build up as much remission as possible. The destruction of the Holy Sepulchre by the Caliph Hakim led to a mass pilgrimage in 1009.

In fact, the end of the world did not come, and instead Europe entered a (relatively) more peaceful period after the preceding centuries of invasion by northmen and barbarians. Travel became much easier and safer, and pilgrimage to distant places, if not easy, at least less arduous.

In addition to the journey to the Holy Land and the tombs of the early saints in Rome another major shrine gained great popularity—Santiago de Compostella, in the northeastern corner of Spain, where the decline of Moorish power had opened up the route from France. Here was the body of St James, 'discovered' early in the ninth century. St James' pilgrims took as their symbol the cockleshell, picked up at first from the nearby beaches and later manufactured as a badge which was often used to indicate all kinds of pilgrimage. Keeping the way open to Santiago encouraged the pressure against the Moors in Spain and soon a new kind of pilgrimage was emerging: a military pilgrimage—the crusade—against the Infidel wherever he might be, in Spain or in the Holy Land. The first big crusade was called by Pope Urban II in 1095. It was a new way to salvation for both 'the knightly order and the vulgar masses'[3] and, in fact, attracted many unarmed followers who believed that God would enable them to capture Jerusalem as a reward for their piety. Taking part in a crusade earned the participant a measured quantity of indulgence, but failure to carry out a vow to join a crusade was punishable by excommunication—and in some cases punishable in the civil courts. An heir might even be bound by the vow of the deceased. Few were excused, although those prevented by illness or infirmity were allowed to send a substitute. Recruitment by vow providing insufficient numbers, mercenaries came to be used in the crusades and, gradually, an increasing number of dispensations permitted substitutes, until in 1240 Pope Gregory allowed all crusading vows to be commuted for a money payment, whether or not the potential crusader was capable of fighting in person.

Apart from those for such 'long-distance' crusaders, indulgences were available only in certain places and at certain times, and the degree of remission varied according to the value which had been accorded to the place of issue. Quite fairly, those who made the greatest effort often gained most from an indulgence: a pilgrim from far off who went to Rome gained greater benefit than one from close at hand.

Papal indulgences were not widely granted, but bishops were much more free and some churches issued indulgences without any real right to do so. In 1215 the Lateran Council placed a limit on the indulgences which bishops could issue—of forty days for the feast of a patron saint or one year for the anniversary of a dedication. Before the end of the century, however, the Pope was permitting almost every church in Rome, and every altar of the great basilicas of the apostles, to issue generous indulgences and, in 1294, Celestine V for the first time officially issued a plenary indulgence (a *total* remission of sin) for a pilgrimage; previously they had been limited to partial indulgences giving a restricted period of remission, although the chapel of St Mary of the Portiuncula at Assisi was already claiming to have been given the right to issue a plenary indulgence in the middle of the century.

If a person confessed their sins as death approached, but did not live to complete their penance, it could be performed by someone else on their behalf, and was usually effected by giving alms from the belongings they left behind. In 1205 this was carried further when the Synod of Arras decided that penance could be as effective for the dead as for the living. It became quite usual for the wealthy to leave money in their wills for Masses to be said on their behalf, or for a pilgrimage to be made by someone else.

If a pilgrim could be proxy for the dead then why not for the living? In fact the sick, and those otherwise prevented by legitimate reasons from carrying out a vow, could reasonably rely upon the kindness of another to carry it out for them. The records of the early Canterbury pilgrimages include a man who came to fulfil a vow made by his mother, who had become a nun in a closed order and so could not perform it herself, and a case where a sick man who sent a messenger with a candle for the shrine miraculously recovered at the same moment that the candle was lit at Canterbury.

In the fifteenth century it became accepted for a proxy pilgrimage to be a purely commercial transaction. Just as the crusader had paid a mercenary soldier to fight on his behalf, a pilgrim would be found who would pass on all the indulgence gained in return for cash. Even earlier there had developed a kind of professional pilgrim who had no other occupation but relied upon charity from others—many of them must have chosen this as an easier way of life than the possible alternatives, and would use tales of their devout travels, and the wonders and miracles they had seen, to arouse the sympathy of listeners sufficiently to make them dip into their purses. Many of them were frauds and their tales inventions, although, with continual repetition, the pilgrims may have almost convinced themselves of the veracity of their tales. When, instead of relying on charity, they could also offer a straightforward business deal, their security increased; but their existence helped to bring pilgrimage into disrepute.

A dispensation to permit another to carry out a pilgrimage, to attribute the benefit from pilgrimage to the dead or to another person living, was always easier to obtain than the equivalent release from a crusading vow, but from that cash commutation the idea of an outright money payment for an indulgence grew. In an ideal sense, and in the view of the Catholic Church today, this was a contribution of alms and therefore a suitable good work to earn remission, but that was not the way the less theologically minded sinner saw it—they were buying 'trading stamps' to cash in for entry into paradise, and this was to be a major argument in the attack of Martin Luther against the established Church. Many Protestants think of indulgences as being one of the differences between their beliefs and those of the Catholic Church, but the Anglican (Episcopalian) Church has never actually abrogated them.

In 1350 Pope Clement VI insisted that the faithful make a pilgrimage to Rome to obtain a plenary Jubilee indulgence, although promising admission to heaven to any who died on the way; but by the following year cash payment, equivalent to the cost of the journey, was being accepted instead. The sale of such indulgences removed the need for people actually to go on pilgrimages and helped to bring about a decline. Prices were sometimes adjusted according to income: in England in 1500 the Jubilee indulgence was sold for 1s. 4d (6½p) for those with an income of £20 a year or less, rising to £3.6s.0 (£3.30) for those with more than £2,000.[4]

The sale of such indulgences became a useful way of raising funds for building and other Church purposes, and since they did not require a visit to a particular church or shrine they could be sold by anyone so authorised, the itinerant salesmen being known as pardoners. At first the pardoners would be high churchmen, such as the cardinal who negotiated the marriage of Richard II and Anne of Bohemia in 1381 and took the opportunity to sell dispensations of pilgrimages to Rome, Santiago and Jerusalem during his visit to England. But there were many who were less eminent who made their way through town and village—and among them were some who were total frauds, without right or licence. Perhaps the most famous, or notorious, of indulgence pedlars was a Dominican friar called John Tetzel, who acted as the agent of the Archbishop of Mainz. The archbishop had borrowed large sums of money to pay the Pope for his appointment, and more to gain a dispensation to retain another archbishopric as well. He hoped by selling indulgences for the rebuilding of St Peter's and for a crusade against the Turks to make enough to repay his loans. Tetzel preached forgiveness (to those who paid for his indulgences) for the most outrageous sins, and it was this abuse—not the practice of granting indulgences itself—which Luther initially attacked.

Today the attitude of the Roman Church is very clear. A penitent must make a sacramental confession, partake of the Eucharistic communion, and pray for 'the Pope's intentions'—that is the whole Church on earth—and must be free from all attachment to any sin, even venial sin, before a plenary indulgence can take effect. Remission is therefore seen to be dependant upon the spiritual state of the sinner, and in consequence, since 1967, the practice of attaching a length of time to partial indulgences has been abolished, since no one on earth can compute the amount of remission gained.

From the days of the Irish penitents through to the present day the attitude to, and practice of, pilgrimage has varied widely and, even during the period between the death of Thomas of Canterbury and the English Reformation, there was a considerable change in the nature of the pilgrimage made to his shrine. At first simple piety and a sense of bargaining with the saint is seen in the records of those who visited the shrine, then the addition of penitential pilgrims and those who found in pilgrimage a means of escaping from the restrictions of their home, later people for whom pilgrimage was something of an outing and a holiday until, in the later days, there seem to have been pilgrims who were like so many of those who visit Canterbury today—sightseers, out to view the architecture and the curiosities.

On the continent there was another kind of pilgrim, the convicted criminal sentenced to pilgrimage by a lay court. The earliest examples came from the Netherlands, where the sentence seems to have been adopted as a convenient way of removing the offender from society without the expense of keeping him in prison. The practice spread through France and Italy but was never adopted in England. Sometimes detailed religious duties were specified —such as climbing the steps of the Lateran basilica in Rome upon the knees and staying so to hear five Masses—but usually the pilgrimage was viewed as a form of banishment. Even the criminal pilgrim could often avoid carrying out the pilgrimage by making a cash payment, either to the state or to the injured party: at Oudenarde, in Flanders, during the fourteenth century, it cost twelve livres to be excused a pilgrimage to Rome or Santiago and eight for one to Rocamadour in southwestern France (Ypres charged only seven livres for this last, and Alost only five).[5]

Sometimes the criminal penitent was ordered to make the pilgrimage in chains, and such overseas penitents sometimes appeared at English shrines; miracles are recounted of their chains having been suddenly broken. It is also probable that many penitents of the eleventh and twelfth centuries wore their chains quite voluntarily, and Jonathan Sumption suggests that many of these miracles may have actually been the pilgrim suddenly feeling himself to be pardoned and free from guilt, and therefore justified in freeing himself from his fetters. Such self-imposed mortification of the flesh would have been considered very worthy. In the middle of the twelfth century a French nobleman arrived in Norwich as a pilgrim wearing a coat of mail next to his bare flesh and with his sword hanging from his fetters. Wearing a murder weapon suspended from the chains to advertise the nature of the crime was not unusual.

Pilgrimage as a judicial penalty was inflicted frequently by the Inquisition for minor offences against the faith. The Inquisition in Languedoc, for instance, recognized nineteen minor pilgrimages within France, and four major ones—Cologne, Santiago, Rome and Canterbury—were given, as well as pilgrimages to the Holy Land.

For everyone who was instructed by Church or civic authority to under-take a pilgrimage, or who was carrying out the performance of a vow, there must have been many who decided upon a pilgrimage quite voluntarily. In the early days this may simply have been out of piety, but even then there were other aspects to make a pilgrimage attractive. In the days when the feudal system was strictly operated it was one of the few ways in which an ordinary man or woman might gain permission to leave his native village. A pilgrim who was not a freeman would have to obtain permission from his lord of the manor before he could leave home, although this would not normally be denied for such a purpose (after all, his possessions and family were left behind as hostages for his return). Even a freeman could not travel freely: a man who could not produce good reason for his journey might find himself thrown into the stocks or into prison. A law of Richard II[6] obliged English pilgrims to have a permit with a special seal affixed by a 'good man', chosen for every district by the justices. Anyone found travelling without a permit, unless obviously infirm or incapable of work, was treated as a vaga-bond and arrested.

There may have been some who rushed into the nearest shrine, hurried off a few *aves* and *paternosters* and dashed out with their measure of salvation, but for most a pilgrimage made when in good health and with no pressing cause would be one of life's experiences to be savoured and enjoyed. There was no hurry: indeed our language has gained such words from the pilgrim's pace as 'roamer', from one who made their way to Rome, 'saunterer', from one who went to the *saint terre* (Holy Land), and 'canter', from the pace of the horses on the way to Canterbury.

After 1220 and the Translation of St Thomas, such pilgrims would not be likely to choose the winter rigours attendant upon the Feast of St Thomas and the martyrdom but would travel to Canterbury in the summer for the July feast or, like Chaucer's pilgrims in the *Canterbury Tales*:

> *Whan that Aprille with his shoures soote*
> *The droghte of March hath perced to the roote,*
> *And bathed every veyne in swich licour*
> *Of which vertu engendred is the flour . . .*[7]

Whether they travelled far or near, this would be an opportunity to see the world, to look at wonders and to store up memories for wintry firesides. It is only since the coming of the railways that most ordinary people have travelled more than a day's journey from their homes, except when forced to leave by famine or war.

A pilgrimage to Jerusalem or elsewhere across the seas was a major undertaking, and for this the help of others would often be called upon, for it would be a much more hazardous undertaking than a visit to an English shrine. Fellow villagers, or members of a craftsman's guild, would often help to finance such a trip, and sometimes a fixed contribution was expected from all of a guild's members—who, by their charity, would win more merit.

How did a potential pilgrim decide upon the place of pilgrimage? A person's name or trade might be the reason for a special devotion. Perhaps the choice would be partly determined by fitting in as many possible shrines within the time which weather and resources made it convenient to be away. Fashion played its part—many minor cults lasted only for a matter of weeks—and novelty had an attraction of its own. Miracle-working, too, seemed to be largely the prerogative of the newly created saint. A French pilgrim who visited St Denis, according to the record of William of Canterbury,[8] found that the saint had 'left to his colleague St Thomas the business of curing the sick . . . so that a new and comparatively unknown martyr might make his reputation'. Sometimes the reputation of a shrine for granting prayers, sometimes the marvels to be seen, would have swayed the choice. Churches who wanted to be enriched with offerings made by pilgrims and to increase the prestige of their particular saints were not slow to spread suitable publicity. Abstracts of the miracles recorded at Canterbury were sent out to churchmen and monasteries all over England and France. Preaching friars would tell of the virtues of a particular shrine; rhymes and jingles were encouraged that would spread its fame and, after the invention of the printing press, pamphlets produced to advertise its attractions. The rising popularity of Canterbury led other churches to particularly publicise miracles granted to those whom St Thomas had failed to favour.

The competition to attract pilgrims led to a proliferation of relics, the authenticity of which we might question today. Several churches claimed to possess the foreskin of Christ and at St John Lateran in Rome the blood from His circumcision was preserved. Like the tomb of Juliet and the balcony where she was wooed by Romeo which are shown in Verona—physical manifestations of Shakespeare's fiction—some seem to have been created, or at least discovered, to meet a pressing need. At various times no less than three heads of St John the Baptist were said to exist. What is one to make of the explanation given to a pilgrim, who remarked at one place showing it, that he had already seen the head of St John at another monastery? The good monk in charge suggested that 'perhaps that was the skull of John the Baptist when a young man, whereas the one we have is his skull when he was fully grown in both years and wisdom'.[9] Not only were churches happy to display a relic which somewhere else claimed to possess, they might even justify the theft of relics because the saint would not allow them to be taken if it were not his wish! The pilgrim would assess and compare the claims of each shrine. If he could still not make up his mind he might try drawing straws to finalize his choice (William of Canterbury refers to this as a common custom in Wales and the West of England). One pilgrim who chose St Cuthbert's shrine in Durham had an attractive variation: he lit candles to three saints and visited the shrine of the one whose candle burned out first.

Before starting out, the pilgrim had first to make confession of his sins, and before the fourteenth century this had to be to his parish priest. If he failed in this it could negate the whole journey, although some churches, mainly in Rome, gained the right to confess pilgrims on the spot. Partly this was a control over who went on pilgrimage (presumably if your parish priest would not grant you absolution you could not make the pilgrimage), but it was also to ensure that the pilgrim would be pure in spirit, for he should deserve the protection which both Church and State were supposed to give him.

A pilgrim had also to clear all debts and settle all outstanding wrongs before departing on his journey, and in earlier centuries might even sell his belongings and give all to the poor, setting out without a penny for himself and relying on charity throughout the journey, although some funds might perhaps be carried to give in alms. The *Liber Sancti Jacobi*, written for the instruction of pilgrims to Santiago de Compostella, reminds the Christian that 'in times past the faithful had but one heart and soul, and they held all property in common, owning nothing of their own; just so, the pilgrims of today must hold everything in common and travel together with one heart and one soul. To do otherwise would be disgraceful . . . Goods shared in common are worth much more than goods owned by individuals. Thus it is that the pilgrim who dies on the road with money in his pocket is permanently excluded from the kingdom of heaven.'[10]

Such communistic ideas would not have suited the travellers of the later Middle Ages, and stem from a much purer kind of faith. Such extreme interpretation of Christian duty was balanced by the help and protection which others were, in theory at least, supposed to offer to the pilgrim. Many, although not parting with all their possessions, would make generous benefactions before leaving and pilgrims were permitted to make a will—not a general right—which often was a means of giving alms, especially to the Church. It might also be used to ensure that property was secure by making a conditional gift to the Church which could be taken up again for the remainder of his life if the pilgrim arrived safe home again. Even without this, property and family left behind were considered to be under the spiritual protection of the Church and, while a pilgrim was away, he was immune from all civil claims and his feudal service was suspended for the duration of the pilgrimage. Those going on a long and dangerous journey or whose vows took them on a crusade had a very obvious need to settle all their affairs before they left, for there was always the possibility that they might not return—some even made arrangements with their wives as to how long they should wait before they might remarry.

Those going on pilgrimage overseas had to gain permission from the crown, taking an oath that they would do nothing contrary to their obedience and fealty to the king or take out more money or bullion than was needed for the expenses of the journey, and there was sometimes even a clause promising not to reveal the 'secrets of the kingdom'. Currency control and official secret acts are not a twentieth-century invention. At various times the ports of embarkation were also strictly limited: one decree of Edward III compelled English pilgrims to set sail from, and return to, Dover 'in relief and comfort of the said town'; under Richard II special permission was required for all except soldiers or merchants to embark from other than Dover and Plymouth. Ships which carried pilgrims had to have a special licence to engage in the trade.

Whether sailing to St James, taking the overland route to Rome, or to

Woodcut from William Wey's *Informacion for Pylgrymes* (1498) showing a pilgrim, dressed in traditional garb (see page 113), leaving a town.

Venice for a ship to the Holy Land, the pilgrim's voyage was not likely to be very comfortable. A number of traveller's guides were produced to help the pilgrim cope with the problems of the journey, giving advice on everything from what to take to what to eat. A famous one catalogued the dangers of the route to Santiago, giving information on the towns and hospices on the way, places where food and fodder might be got, a list of useful words in Basque and a description of the cathedral at Santiago de Compostella. William Wey's *Informacion for Pylgrymes*, printed by Wynkyn de Worde (Caxton's assistant and successor) in 1498, is not quite the first printed travel guide—that was Bernard von Breydenbach's *Peregrinationes in Terram Sanctam*, an account of a pilgrimage to Jerusalem and Mount Sinai which appeared in Mainz in 1486—but it is the first in English. It gives advice on choosing a cabin ('as nyghe the myddes of the shippe as ye may, for theere is leest rollynge or tombline'); stocking up with provisions, such as buying a cage for hens and seed for them to ensure fresh meat; buying a feather bed in Venice (with a fifty-per-cent refund when you return it on the way back, provided you make a careful note of where you got it); and warnings against foreign foods such as 'melons and suche colde fruytes, for they be not ac-cordynge to our complexyon and they gendre a blody fluxe.' Careful guide-lines are laid down on the fair prices to pay for things, rates of exchange, and there is a list of useful phrases in Greek (almost as inaccurate as are some modern phrase books!). Speed is advised in getting ashore to get the best accommodation on land and to avoid being left with the poorest donkeys; indulgences are listed, sights pointed out and a careful programme devised to enable the traveller to see all the sights of the Holy Land in 'thirteen or fourteen days'. Even for those making a pilgrimage in Britain the going was not easy. Steep hills, rough tracks and bad weather could be as wearying as heaving waves; English innkeepers as rapacious as any in Venice or Aleppo; and if there was no danger of pirates or saracens there were plenty of brigands up and down the country waiting to waylay the unwary traveller, and at many times during the Middle Ages England was riven by rebellion or civil war.

Villeins who fled their home manor and labourers uprooted by the plague and the unrest of the peasant's revolt joined those who fled the harshness of the law to become outlaws in the wild tracts and dense forests that still covered much of the country. Even noblemen were known to organise bands of their retainers operating what today we would call a protection racket and ready to set upon merchants and travellers to steal their goods. Life and property might always be in danger, even on the highway, and for this reason pilgrims and other travellers preferred to travel in groups.

An ordinance of Edward I dated 1285[11] required landowners to clear a space for 200 feet on each side of the road so that neither coppice, brushwood, hollow or ditch would offer a hiding place for robbers. Only large trees such as oaks were allowed to remain. If a road passed through a nobleman's park he had the alternative of closing it off by a wall or hedge too thick to be penetrated or a ditch so wide and deep that robbers could not cross it. Those who failed to carry out these duties were liable for any robberies or murders that occurred and would have to pay a fine to the king. The situation did not improve, however, and, if anything, got worse, so that there are numerous petitions asking for something to be done to make travel safer.

Except where an ancient Roman road might have a solid paving, giving regularity to the earth that covered it by the Middle Ages, roads were usually no more than dirt tracks made firm by traffic but turned into a morass of mud after heavy rain and churned up by cart wheels and horses' hooves.

People travelled either on foot or on horse or donkey, goods were carried by pack animal or in simple carts. A few of the greatest nobles might have a carriage, but it was not the kind of vehicle the word calls up today. Heavy and lumbering, it would have been no more than a box mounted on solid beams above the axles of two pairs of sturdy wheels, and covered by an arched, tunnel-like canopy. The worst jolts were softened by filling the interior with cushions, and the canopy kept out the elements. This would not be a comfortable ride, although the wheels might be carved and gilded and the canopy and hangings the richest of tapestries and embroideries. Such carriages were drawn by two or three horses, one behind the other, and cost a fortune. One made for Edward III's sister cost £1000—and that when a cow cost only 9s.6d and a chicken 1d.

Ordinary carts might be a square-shaped tumbril of heavy planks or a lighter box of latticed willow on two wheels and it would probably be quicker, and certainly more comfortable, to walk than to ride in them. For the rich who, because of sickness or infirmity, could not or did not wish to ride, the most pleasant form of travel was a horse litter, carried on shafts balanced between two horses, one in front and one behind, but both men and women would be more likely to ride and both would ride astride. Women did not commonly ride sidesaddle in England until well into the fourteenth century—one of the earliest illustrations showing an English woman riding sidesaddle is in the Ellesmere manuscript of the *Canterbury Tales*, where the Prioress is riding in the new way, although the Wife of Bath is clearly sitting astride.

Chaucer's pilgrims all rode on horseback and in his time it was easy to hire a horse to make the journey to Canterbury, for the route was the main road from Dover to London and carried much of the traffic to and from the continent. From London to Rochester the hire of a horse cost twelve pence, and from Rochester to Canterbury the same again with a further sixpence if the traveller wished to carry on to Dover. The horses were branded prominently so that there was no temptation to ride off and steal the horse.

Even in the early days of the pilgrimage some people rode—they are depicted in the stained glass of Canterbury, although the same panel shows a cripple making his way on his knees—but the more devout would, if fit enough, have felt it more appropriate to walk. King John found his horse getting restless on the way to Canterbury and took it as a divine warning to dismount. Barefooted pilgrims were thought of particularly highly and Henry VIII once walked barefoot from Barsham to Walsingham on one of his numerous pilgrimages to the Shrine of Our Lady there. In his sermon at the end of the *Canterbury Tales* Chaucer's Parson speaks not only of going barefoot on pilgrimage but of going naked, although in a medieval context this probably meant not totally nude but lightly clad in only a shirt or smock.

The London and Kentish port roads had been continually in use for centuries and one might expect such major highways to be in good repair and provide easy journeys, but that is not very likely. In 1353 even the road from London to the Palace of Westminster, which had been partly paved, became 'so full of holes and bogs' that it had become dangerous to both men and carts.

Bridges were often in poor order—the ancient rhyme 'London Bridge is falling down' commemorates the state into which it got when those responsible for its upkeep spent the income from its endowments on other things. When country authorities tried to force people to do the road repairs which were their responsibility they often found that the protests that the roads were already good enough were upheld in court. Today roads are drained and streams channelled in a culvert underneath, surfaces are smooth and major routes well lit. In the Middle Ages seasonal springlets might gush out and flood the road, making it easy to wander off into boggy stretches on either side, heavy rains would turn the surface into a quagmire and the way could be so uneven that it was easy to stumble. Archbishop Arundel declared in 1407 that 'Pilgrims have with them singers and also pipers, that when one of them which goeth barefoot striketh his tow upon a stone, and maketh it to bleed, it is well done that he and his fellows begin then a song . . . to drive away with such mirthe the hurte'.[12]

For the ill-clad poor or penitential pilgrim, bad weather must have brought the journey to a standstill, but it would delay the wealthy and well-equipped as well. To take one instance, noted by J. J. Jusserand, the parliament of 1339 had to be delayed because 'the prelates, earls, barons and knights of the shires could not battle their way through the weather'. Yet, as Jusserand remarks, 'these members were not poor folks, they had good horses, good coats, thick cloaks covering their necks up to their hats, with large hanging sleeves falling over their knees; no matter: . . . prelates, barons, or knights, halted their steeds at some roadside inn . . . awaiting the subsidence of the waters . . .'[13]

Roadside inns were not the more usual stopping place for members of the nobility, for few such hostelries would offer the traveller much comfort, and in the earlier years of the pilgrimage to Canterbury they would have been few and far between: William fitzStephen does not mention a single inn offering accommodation in his description of London. Men would receive their equals in rank both by way of charity and for their own pleasure. A travelling knight calling at a manor house or castle was rarely refused. Some great houses would have a special room for guests, or an important visitor might be invited to share the master's room. The lesser sort would be offered a mattress on the rushes in the great hall along with the rest of the household. Privacy was not something people expected, although the great might have bed curtains to keep out draughts and watchful eyes, and it would be quite usual to share a bed. It was not until towards the end of the fourteenth century that private withdrawing-rooms began to become the fashion and the hall began its slow decline from the centre of all activity to the entranceway it signifies in most modern homes.

In theory, every Christian had a duty of hospitality towards pilgrims and many householders would be glad to offer a place by the hearth to a traveller with tales to tell. The main burden of providing shelter for pilgrims, however, fell upon the religious houses. Hospitality was the first duty of the Order of Knights Hospitaller of St John of Jerusalem and the seal of the Knights Templar bore the figure of a knight aiding a *'pauper et peregrinus'*. Special hostels were founded for the care of pilgrims: one for English pilgrims was founded in Rome in the eighth century and one of the most famous was at Roncevalles, the high pass which forms the gateway from France to Spain on the route to Santiago de Compostella. At Roncevalles pilgrims might expect the highest standards of hospitality with proper beds instead of straw upon the floor, good food, even baths—and relics of saints and heroes to venerate as well.

Long before it gained its modern meaning, the word hospital meant a place of hospitality (hospice and hotel have exactly the same origin) and there were many foundations which offered shelter to all kinds of people. Today their original purpose is sometimes obscure, but sometimes there are extant documents to make it clear. At Flixton, in Holderness, for instance, was a house of refuge 'to preserve travellers from being devoured by the wolves and other voracious beasts'.[14] St John's at Winchester was refounded in 1275 'for the relief of sick and lame soldiers, poor pilgrims and necessitous wayfaring men to have their lodging and diet gratis free, for one night or longer, as their inability to travel might require'.[15] In 1393 the Bishop of Ely offered an indulgence in return for contributions to a hospital at Brentford 'for the entertainment of poor travellers'. Of more than 700 hospitals known to exist some 200 appear to have been first established as leper houses, and many would have offered hospitality to strangers. Although those that survive today are mainly almshouses, their original purpose may be guessed at, for town establishments at least. Outside the walls they were probably set up for lepers, near a gate for wayfarers and in a main street for the sick and helpless.[16]

At ports such as Southampton, Dover and Sandwich, at Maidstone, Ospringe and other places on the way to Canterbury, were such establishments, sometimes known, as at Ospringe and Dover, as Maisons Dieu. Such independent foundations became common from the twelfth century onwards but, long before, the monasteries had provided shelter and it was a specific item of the Benedictine rule that 'guests are to be received as though they were Christ himself'.

People of high rank were usually received in the monastery proper, but most travellers and pilgrims would be housed and fed in accommodation specially built. This guest house might be in or outside the precincts, as at Battle where the guest house can still be seen outside the entrance gate. Accommodation was usually in a long dormitory—the shape of the building is often a guide to identification—which would be hall by day, sleeping room by night, or there might be a long hall with doors along each side opening on to sleeping rooms. Old inventories for the Maison Dieu at Dover suggest that there were beds set up permanently in the hall.

The king had the right to requisition accommodation and billet his soldiers and his train on anybody (and to commandeer carts to carry his goods). Although some payment would usually be made, unscrupulous officers would often abuse these rights. In the same way many of the nobility abused their right to hospitality in religious houses. Even if the great man did not stay there himself he might send his retainers. Monasteries would attempt to entertain a guest according to his rank, and their coffers were soon depleted by some lordly demands. The monks did not try to avoid their duties but they had cause for complaint. The accounts of the Priory of Clerkenwell, for instance, refer to 'much expenditure which cannot be given in detail, caused by the hospitality offered to strangers, members of the royal family, and to other grandees of the realm who stay at Clerkenwell and remain there at the cost of the house'. They left the priory in the red with an expenditure of £21.11s.4d greater than their receipts.

There was some justification in the nobility making these demands—most religious houses had been founded or endowed by nobles—but Edward I decided that they had gone too far. While 'the king intendeth not that the grace of hospitality should be withdrawn from the destitute', and the poor were to continue to be lodged for nothing, he forbade anyone to demand food or lodging of a religious house unless he had been expressly invited by the superior or were himself the founder of the establishment—and even then his consumption should be in moderation. The decree does not seem to have had any lasting effect, for in 1309 Edward II reconfirmed it and in 1315 was specifically promising that neither he nor his family would abuse the hospitality of the monks, as an example to his court. It still did not solve the problem. Sixty years later the clergy were still complaining that the sheriffs 'with their wives and other excessive number of people on horseback as well as on foot' came to stay in monasteries under the pretext of collecting monies for the king.[17]

The picture should not be painted too darkly, for there were many generous benefactions made by those who enjoyed the monks' hospitality—

and there were complaints against the clergy too, for when livings and benefices were given to people who continued to live elsewhere they often neglected their duties. The English Commons protested that foreigners who had been given priories 'suffer the noble edifices . . . to fall quite to ruin' and neglected 'to keep hospitality', and asked the king to ensure 'that all other persons advanced to the benefices of Holy Church, should remain on their said benefices in order to keep hospitality there . . . exception being made for the king's clerks and the clerks of the great of the realm' (who, of course, required the income from their clerical posts to enable them to get on with their secular jobs).

Inns and private hostelries appeared to meet the demand for places to stay. Some of them, perhaps, developed from the hostels set up by the monasteries: the famous Chequer of Hope at Canterbury, for instance, was actually owned by Christ Church Priory. The monks received the very poor out of charity and the very rich out of necessity—the common inns charged too much for the former and were too miserable for the latter, but they met the needs of merchants, packmen, and pilgrims of the middle sort. Sleeping arrangements were usually two or three to a bed and several beds to a room. Beds might be a simple straw-filled palliasse or, later, might be mounted on a simple frame. Beds were valuable commodities, noblemen might travel with their own and, even in the seventeenth century, William Shakespeare made a point of making sure that his widow should inherit his second-best bed. If the straw scratched through its covering it was less troublesome than the

Pilgrims arriving at an inn and being served a meal. From the early fifteenth-century manuscript of an allegorical poem called *Pilgrimage of the Life of Man*. (*British Library*.)

creatures living in it. A *Manual of French Conversation* written by an Englishman at the end of the fourteenth century[18] quotes a discussion between two travellers about the bugs in the room where they have been sleeping: 'William, undress and wash your legs, then dry them with a cloth and rub them well . . . that the fleas may not leap on your legs, for there is a peck of them in the dust under the rushes . . . Hi! The fleas bite me so! . . . I have scratched my shoulders till the blood flows.' Elsewhere in the book an inkeeper assures a traveller that there are no fleas, or bugs or other vermin and promises that he 'will be well and comfortably lodged—save that there is a great peck of rats and mice'—which presumably would worry no one!

If the comforts offered would not have satisfied travellers today they would at least have found complaints about overcharging very familiar. Two statutes of Edward III's reign[19] attempted to control 'the outrageous cost of victuals kept up . . . by inkeepers . . . to the detriment of travellers' and Chaucer's Parson refers to 'thilke that holden hostelries [and] sustenen the thefte of hire hostilers'.[20] William Thorpe, the Lollard whose defence before the Bishop of Arundel was quoted earlier, arraigns the pilgrims for 'spending their goods upon vitious hostelars, which are oft uncleane women of their bodies'. No doubt some hosts did sting travellers for all they could, and no doubt some ran a bawdy house, but there must also have been others like the Host of the Tabard, who joined Chaucer's pilgrims, who ran a 'gentil hostelrye' where 'the chambres and the stables weren wyde, And wel we weren esed atte best'.

How much did bed and board cost? Money values have changed so greatly from century to century that comparisons are difficult, but two fellows of Merton College, Oxford, who travelled north with four of their servants in 1331 kept a note of their expenses which has survived. The costs for all six on one particular day came out at:

Bread	4d	Candles	$\frac{1}{4}$d
Beer	2d	Fuel	2d
Wine	1$\frac{1}{4}$d	Beds	2d
Meat	5$\frac{1}{2}$d	Fodder for	
Soup	$\frac{1}{4}$d	horses	10d

Accommodation in London was more expensive, probably about a penny a night. Sometimes they treated themselves to a luxury. Sugar, for instance, cost them 4d and a salmon 'bought for the journey' cost 1s.6d—they had to pay another 8d to have it cooked! They also had to pay 8d to be ferried across the Humber, but this was a wide river and the charge presumably included their six horses and must have saved a very long journey upstream to a bridge.

For refreshment along the road there were alehouses, or alestakes, at the more important crossroads, and along frequented ways. They were easily recognized by their sign, a pole with a branch or bundle of twigs tied on the end—it became the fashion to have such long poles that the law had to regulate their length. The beer was usually brewed by the alewife herself (that was considered women's work). Getting drunk was a popular way of easing one's cares if William Langland's picture of a tavern in his *Vision of Piers the Plowman* is anything to go by:[21]

> *There was laughyng and louryng . and "let go the cuppe"*
> *And seten so til evensong . and congen umwhile,*
> *Tyl Glouton had y-globbed [downed] . a galoun un a jille.*
> *His guttis gun to gothely [rumble] . as two gredy sowes;*
> *He pissed a potel . in a pater-noster while,*
> *And blew his rounde ruwet [trumpet] . at his rigge-bon ende [rump]*
> *That alle that herde that horne . held her [their] nose hereafter . . .*

It would be fitting to think that pilgrims would not behave so coarsely, but the continuation of the *Canterbury Tales* shows some of Chaucer's party lusting, and Erasmus describes sham pilgrims stealing from the collection plate at Walsingham. We must imagine all manner of people from devout spinsters to thieves and rogues among the throngs making their way to Canterbury.

By Chaucer's time the pilgrimage had become a pleasant holiday excursion for many people. His motley crew included no obvious penitents or cure seekers, nor are any of them very poor—all could afford a mount of some kind and to stay at a good tavern. If these seem rather different from the pilgrims whom monks William and Benedict recorded at the shrine, it does not mean that it was not still a profound religious experience for many. True, the shrine now seemed to produce few miracles, but fourteenth century wills contain numerous bequests for hirelings to fulfil pilgrimage vows by proxy, and the success of the pardoner in selling his wares is proof enough of the attraction of indulgences.

Let us take a look at Chaucer's band. First there is the poet himself: a civil servant well thought of by the court. Then there are a number of ecclesiastics. The prioress, fine mannered and tender hearted, is dressed in a pleated wimple and coral trinkets with green beads and a gold brooch on her rosary. She is used to elegant living, even 'small hounds had she that she fedde / with rosted flessh, or milk or wastel-breed [white bread]'. With her travel a nun and three priests. There is also a rather lordly monk, dressed in a fur-trimmed robe, mounted on a palfrey and more inclined to riding, hunting and coursing than to sitting meditating in a monastic cell. Less grand, but also very worldly, is a friar, but his eye is for girls and drink rather than the hounds, and he makes a good living out of alms and absolutions and settling disputes. Not for him the threadbare habit of the cloisterer, 'But he was lyk a maister or a pope. Of double worstede was his semycope.' There is a scholar, nevertheless, the 'clerk of Oxenford', who spends all his money on books. There is even a pardoner, a seller of indulgences, among the company —is he genuine? He wears a badge of the handkerchief of St Veronica in his cap, which pilgrims who have been to Rome would do, and he says he has come from there. He has a bag full of dubious relics, which he freely admits make him an excellent living from the gullible. With him is a summoner, employed by the ecclesiastical courts, a lecherous wine bibber with a fiery pustule-covered face, who runs a line in petty blackmail of those who want to avoid prosecution. He has not much hope of a cure from St Thomas unless he suddenly reforms.

Another pilgrim, the skilful cook, has a nasty sore upon his shin—perhaps he *does* hope that St Thomas' water will clear it up. He comes with a group of tradesmen dressed in the fine livery of a guild to which they all belong: a haberdasher, a dyer, a carpenter, a weaver and a tapestry maker. There is a miller too, a big brawny man who plays the bagpipes and has brought them with him to liven up the journey, and a doctor who seems rather a quack.

With medicine as it was, it is not surprising that people put their faith in miracles. In fact, since sickness was thought to come from sin, religious discipline was a logical way to cure. In the thirteenth century the Lateran Council of 1215 actually forbade doctors to pay a second visit to a patient unless a priest had seen him beforehand, and a synod which met in Paris in 1429 forbade doctors to treat any patient who was in a state of mortal sin. The actual pilgrimage may have acted as good natural medicine for many who sought (and probably thought that they received) miraculous aid. Fresh air, exercise and a conviction that they were doing the right thing would ease the troubles of those suffering from melancholia (considered a form of madness in twelfth-century England according to the Canterbury records) and help with all kinds of psychosomatic disorders. A change of food might also have given a range of vitamins lacking in the usual medieval diet.

If the doctor was a charlatan, Chaucer makes it clear that the poor parson among the pilgrims was a truly devout and sincere man: '. . . Christe's love and his apostles twelve/ He taught, but first folwed it hymselve.' His brother, travelling with him, was a ploughman and tried equally to live according to the faith. He is perhaps the simplest of the party, wearing a country smock and riding his farm mare.

Not so kindly, but very proper, is the reeve, a manor overseer; and the careful-living maunciple, a servant at the Inns-of-Court, is another honest man. The third representative of the law is an eminent Justice sporting a particoloured outfit and a fine ribbed-silk girdle. With him is travelling the frankeleyn, a substantial landowner, with delicate taste: 'Epicurus owene sone.'

The merchant, also sporting the particoloured fashion, together with a beaver hat and fine buckled boots, may have a private reason for his pilgrimage. Chaucer ambiguously tells us that 'ther wiste no wight that he was in dette', and going on a pilgrimage would (if he were trying to hide the fact) prevent any of his creditors taking action against him. By his return perhaps his fortunes will be better. A ship's captain is another member of the party. A tough-sounding character, he comes from Dartmouth and rides a farm horse: he obviously is not used to being in the saddle.

Apart from the prioress and her nun the only other woman in the party is a cheerful, garrulous, middle-aged widow from Bath who has seen out five husbands and who makes a hobby of pilgrimage. The pardoner may never have been to Rome, but she has—and to Boulogne, St James of Compostella and the shrine of the Magi at Cologne—and three times she has made the pilgrimage to Jerusalem.

The three remaining members of the original party include 'a verray parfit gentil knyght' who has fought in many battles but keeps a mild demeanour and is as wise as he is important; he rides a good horse and wears a tunic of fustian (twill or corduroy) marked by where his armour has rubbed, for he has just got home from service and is making the pilgrimage in thanks for his return. He is travelling with his son, a lively young squire in a fashionable

The 'parfit gentil knyght' from Caxton's edition of the *Canterbury Tales*.

One of the types of lead pilgrim's badges sold in Canterbury and worn to show that a pilgrimage had been completed. (*Museum of London*)

embroidered short gown with long wide sleeves. With them, as servant, goes a yeoman, a forester dressed (like Robin Hood) in green with a horn about his neck, a bow in his hand, and quiver, sword and shield at his side. He wears a St Christopher medal about his neck to give him a safe journey, but his weapons would stand him in good stead. The knight and his son also carry arms, and Chaucer describes the frankelyne as carrying a dagger and the miller as having a sword and buckler, and perhaps some of the others also carried weapons. Under the knight's command they will be able to cope with small bands of robbers.

Against this colourful holiday company we should compare the traditional pilgrims, both the devout and those who made a life of it, perhaps as proxy men for others. However differently some pilgrims might travel, a characteristic mode of dress had long been established as the popular image of a pilgrim. A long staff and a scrip, a small pouch, were the accoutrements of any traveller on foot, but became particularly associated with the pilgrim— King Cnut had them when he set off for Rome in 1027—, and a century later one writer describes pilgrims as habitually going unshaven. Later, it is not clear when, a long coarse tunic, known as a sclavein, became the accepted garment. It was sometimes embellished with cross-shaped patches, especially if the pilgrim were going to the Holy Land or was a 'professional'. About the middle of the thirteenth century many pilgrims adopted a broad-brimmed hat which was worn with the brim turned up at the front and with a long scarf attached to the back which was wound around the body. The staff usually had a knob at the top, sometimes decorated, and an iron spike at the bottom. It served as a defensive weapon and as an aid to leaping streams and boggy patches as well as being a walking stick. These pilgrim attributes came to be given symbolic meaning: the pouch stood for the Christian alms, because it was too small to hold much and the pilgrim carrying it had to depend upon charity; the staff, which forms the third leg of the pilgrim, stands for the Trinity and, since it is used for driving off wolves and wild dogs and other evils that beset the traveller, it represents the Trinity in conflict with the powers of evil. Others described the staff as standing for faith (it represents the cross), the pouch for hope, and the sclavein for charity.

On their return, pilgrims would decorate their clothing with badges to show where they had been, just as the modern globetrotter sews patches on his backpack or his anorak to show how far he has travelled, or automobiles flourish stickers. Most famous, and the first perhaps, were the palms of Jericho (from which the English word 'palmer', meaning pilgrim, is derived), while, as already mentioned, pilgrims who had been to St James of Compostella wore a cockleshell—at first picked up from the beach and later made of lead; the sacred vernicle was one of several badges that might be bought in Rome and at Canterbury there was a considerable choice from depictions of St Thomas riding on a horse to portrait heads, small bells or ampulla which could hold the sacred water of St Thomas. The manufacture of these badges was usually localized and licensed by the Church, which collected a commission from their sale. Sometimes badges were sold elsewhere—fake souvenirs for phoney pilgrims—which led to complaints from the churches because of their lost income as much as because of the deception that was involved.

The places with important shrines gained a great influx of trade from pilgrims so there cannot have been that many who took the idea of travelling in poverty entirely seriously. Indeed, if they had given everything away and not kept back some thankoffering for the shrine, the Church would be the loser—in 1320, the year of the first Jubilee, Canterbury had a deficit of £83 and there were often losses on the balance sheet in years when pilgrim numbers were at their greatest. Fortunately the monastery had a large income from land.

It was offerings which paid for the building of the magnificent churches which housed the relics of saints, and they were often thought of as a kind of tribute money like that which a vassal might pay to his liege lord. They were not considered an essential part of pilgrimage until the development of the cash purchase of indulgences. Jewellery, as well as coin, was often given, and the finest gems might be used to decorate the shrine itself. People expected a famous shrine to have a rich display and took its wealth almost as an indication of the degree of holiness—it was certainly an indication of its popularity with the pious. The plate and precious stones in the treasure house also constituted the reserves of the Church at a time when a money economy was not properly established. They could always be sold or melted down and sometimes were—as for instance when Reading Abbey stripped the gold leaf from its hand of St James to settle a debt to Richard I. These riches could also be a spur to piety in themselves. A Greyfriar preaching in 1535, when the heyday of pilgrimage was passed, spoke of those going to Canterbury who 'when they see the goodly jewels that be there . . . think in their hearts "I would to God and that good saint that I were able to offer such a gift".'

Not only gold and jewels were given to the shrine, many *ex voto* offerings were left behind, sometimes fashioned in silver, sometimes in wax, and often in the shape of the affected limbs of those who sought or wished to give thanks for a cure, or as a kind of sympathetic magic that goes back long before Christianity. One shepherd cut off a withered finger and laid it on the altar at Durham in the hope that another one would grow. A tapeworm removed from Henry of Maldon hung as an *ex voto* at Canterbury;[22] and the Christ Church monks were most upset when an archdeacon, at last relieved of a cherry stone that had stuck in his nostril, persisted in taking it home with him. Such offerings can still be seen in many Catholic churches and must once have been left in great quantity at Canterbury.

It is difficult to recapture the mood and atmosphere that surrounded the pilgrim of the Middle Ages. But at Lourdes we can still see thousands with an undying faith in miracles, barefoot penitents at Lough Derg in Donegal, and the ecstatic devotion of thousands climbing the rough slopes of Croagh Patrick in County Mayo. Whether on their knees on the Scala Sancta in Rome, at the Shrine of Our Lady of Guadalupe in Mexico, the Oratory of St Joseph at Montreal, or whether they are the millions who each year visit the Shrine of the Immaculate Conception in Washington, DC, there is abundant evidence of the appeal of pilgrimage at all its levels. Although modern transport has taken the penitential element from the journey for most contemporary pilgrims, and the papacy has given a stricter interpretation of the benefits to be gained in our time, pilgrimage still has a great meaning to many Christians. Christians outside the Roman Church may also gain spiritual value from a devotional journey and Moslems and Hindus still hold it as a vital item of their faiths. And for those without a god? The free modern usage of the word is answer enough. A journey of spiritual refreshment, of cultural richness, of separation from the world around—for each it may mean something different, but it still seems to have a contemporary role.

PART THREE: THE PILGRIMAGE TO CANTERBURY

8 The Pilgrims' Way I

HENRY II MADE a penitential pilgrimage in 1174; we do not know what route he took to get to Canterbury except that from Southampton he made his way to Winchester and thence to Thomas' tomb. There was a road he might have taken, an ancient route that is known today as the Pilgrims' Way. But, despite the clear identification of it by that name on Ordnance Survey maps and name markers erected along part of the path, especially in Kent, there is no evidence that this was the way in which a single pilgrim came to offer prayers at St Thomas' shrine; indeed, the name does not appear to have been used for any of the route before the eighteenth century, and the romantic tradition that the pilgrims of the Middle Ages all came along this particular track is a comparatively modern one. In 1936 C. G. Crump wrote an article[1] demolishing the idea, but many other writers from Hilaire Belloc in 1904[2] right up to the present day have encouraged the tradition. There is insufficient evidence to prove a case either way, and it is indisputable that the track, the Old Road as Belloc calls it, was ancient long before the days of pilgrimage.

From the plateau of Salisbury Plain in southern England, ridges of high land stretch out in six directions: southwest the Dorset Downs, west the Mendips, north the Cotswolds, northeast the Chilterns, east the North Downs and southeast the South Downs. These highlands would form the most convenient routes for prehistoric travellers, and along them may be found evidence of ancient ways radiating from the heartland where such major monuments as Stonehenge and Avebury suggest the concentration point of a widespread society. These ancient ways, first trodden out by neolithic man, enabled the men of the Bronze Age and the Iron Age to take the tin and iron of the west country across to Kent and thence, by the shortest crossing of the channel, to the continent. The ancient road did not pass through Winchester, but from Farnham struck out towards Stonehenge and in the east it has been suggested that it bypassed Canterbury and bent south to Folkestone or Dover. There is no evidence of there having been a Roman road between Winchester and Canterbury, and even today there is no major through route, only a succession of minor roads provide the link. Yet, in Saxon times, Winchester became the capital and administrative centre of the kingdom while Canterbury became its religious centre. It would be strange if there were no regular traffic between the two.

By the time of Thomas' death London, England's leading commercial centre, was already beginning to establish claims for its supremacy, and for most of the centuries of pilgrimage the road from London would have carried many times more travellers but, for those coming from Winchester and the west, the ancient trackway could have provided the most convenient direct route.

The Way is older than the settlements that line it, and there is no significance to be drawn from the fact that most are slightly off its path. The position of the track was determined by the ease with which it could be traversed: avoidance of the damp valleys, the exposed north faces of the downs and difficult gradients; following well-drained slopes, firmer going underfoot, easy fords and sheltered, sun-warmed southern hillsides, and trying to follow a route where the way ahead can be clearly seen. Sometimes it can be identified as a terraced ledge, at others as a 'hollow-way' cut deep into the ground by millenia of use. Sometimes its track is lost and is the subject of conjecture and the possible changes in landscape features such as the depth and meander patterns of waterways make identification of some river crossings difficult, but these are problems connected with the exact location of the ancient way and not its general line. The villages and habitations along the route chose locations for different reasons—a fresh water supply for instance, which is infrequent along the Way—and they were sometimes linked by later roads lower down the slopes.

Those who now walk the Way may gain added pleasure from the thought that they may be treading on the very ground that medieval pilgrims trod—which prehistoric forebears trod before them and more recent countrymen too, drovers and traders who took these paths rather than pay the tolls required for the eighteenth-century turnpike roads—but there is no reason to suppose that the pilgrim stuck entirely to the Way. Like modern travellers he would have turned aside to seek shelter or to visit a particular place, making a detour or choosing an alternative route.

If you wish to walk the Winchester–Canterbury Pilgrims' Way today you must be prepared to have to make the occasional detour, because the path crosses private land and no right-of-way survives, or where the Way becomes almost impassable because of undergrowth. As Christopher John Wright remarks in his pocket route guide to the Way[3] 'the modern pilgrim should be a dedicated footpath preservationist and carry pruning saw, shears and wire cutter, to deal suitably with the natural and man-made constructions across his route'. In winter the undergrowth will be less, but be warned that wet chalk can be unbelievably slippery and those stretches where you have to negotiate wet clay, sandy mud or flooded hollows will make it quite clear why the original users of the path tried to keep clear of the valley clays. Such conditions can slow your slithering pace to that of a snail.

In the early days of the cult of St Thomas the main celebration was the

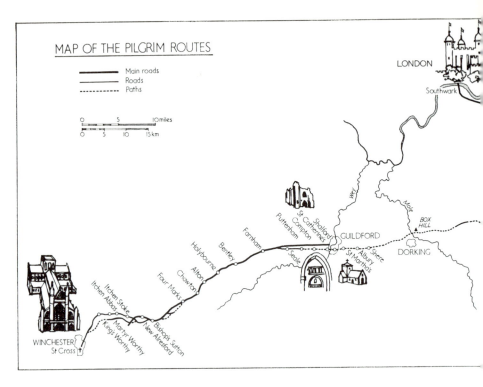

The Pilgrims' Way, Winchester to Canterbury, and the London Road.

anniversary of the murder, so that pilgrims were making their way to Canterbury at Christmastide. Perhaps winter cold made the ground hard and firm, but against that must be set the possible hazards of snow and ice. The Festival of the Translation was in July: high summer brings flies as well as luxuriant growth. The summer brambles will still be there in autumn so for those who want to walk the entire route the months of late April and May are preferable, and hotels and hostels are also less likely to be full at that time of year.

For two hundred years before the canonisation of St Thomas the shrine of St Swithin at Winchester had been a major centre of pilgrimage—some of the pilgrims no doubt coming along the Old Road from the east. With the popularisation of the cult of Thomas it is reasonable to speculate that many would wish to gain the benefits brought by a visit to both these great shrines, and such lesser ones as they might pass on the way. Perhaps they went one way *via* London, the other along this route; visitors from the continent perhaps made one crossing to Southampton and Winchester, and the other from one of the Thanet ports across the Straits of Dover.

Imagine a countryside much more heavily wooded than today, before the great forests had been cut down for fuel or to build houses and the wooden walls of England's fleets. A countryside of sparse population, half that of

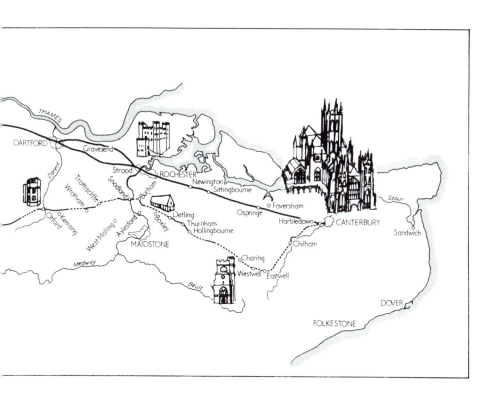

modern London, settled across the land with long stretches without any habitation, where wild animals were still a danger and brigands and outlaws might be lurking beneath the trees. Inns, even wells, are infrequent; protection from the weather is provided only by the branches above, the lee of a bank and the cloak you wrap around you.

Let us begin outside the walls of Winchester where, about a mile south of the city, as travellers made their way up the valley of the river Itchen from Southampton and the coast, they reached the Hospital of St Cross. Founded in 1136 by King Stephen's brother Henry of Blois, Bishop of Winchester, it was set up for the support of thirteen poor men, 'feeble and so reduced in strength that they can hardly, or with difficulty, support themselves without another's aid'. If any of the inmates recovered his strength he was 'to be sent abroad with honour and reverence and another put in his place'.[4] In addition the hospital was to give dinner daily to one hundred additional poor and provide other charity. Here for two decades before Thomas' death travellers might have received help, and here pilgrims might call for shelter and for sustenance on their way to Canterbury. In the ornate chapel a thirteenth-century artist painted the murder of St Thomas; this is still discernable. The modern pilgrim can start his journey with a taste of medieval charity for St Cross still offers travellers the 'wayfarers dole', a horn of beer and a piece of white bread—although the quantity for each day is restricted and if you call too late it may have been exhausted.

The Hospital of St Cross. The wayfarer's dole is still dispensed from the archway beneath the tower. Two of these three brethren wear the black gowns and cross-potent badge of Henry of Blois' foundation, while the centre man is wearing the claret gown and cardinal's hat badge of Beaufort's almshouses. (*British Tourist Authority*.)

Cardinal Beaufort, Bishop of Winchester 1405–47, set up a new foundation at St Cross to provide for 'noblemen or members of our family (those who had been in his employment)'—reduced gentlefolk, in fact, rather than the wretchedly poor. Unfortunately the Wars of the Roses interfered with the endowment of this 'Almshouse of Noble Poverty', as Beaufort called it, and in 1487 its permanent incumbents were reduced to one chaplain and two brethren. Today both foundations still survive, each with its distinctive gown.

A short way further up the straight Roman road the pilgrim reached the walls of Winchester. A settlement long before the time of Christ, this became the Roman market town of Venta Belgarum. The Saxons found protection behind the Roman fortifications and the location a convenient centre for communications, and Witanceaster became the capital of Wessex.

Swithin, bishop 852–862, probably enlarged the cathedral, rebuilt the city bridge and added to the city's fortifications, but little is really known about him, though he seems to have been very popular with the ordinary people. On his death he asked not to be buried in a place of honour in the church but, according to a twelfth-century account by William of Malmesbury, where 'he would be exposed to the feet of passers-by and the raindrops falling from the heavens'. He was indeed buried outside the church, but popular feeling for his memory and the reports of miracles associated with him led to his generally being thought a saint and, on July 15th, 971, his remains were transferred to a shrine behind the high altar and his name added to those of Saints Peter and Paul in the dedication of the church.

Tradition says that when the body was transferred the skies opened and it rained for forty days—the saint's attempt to prevent his relics being moved. There is no historical evidence for this, and it is probably a later invention, but it has given rise to a weather lore which says that if it rains on St Swithin's Day (July 15th, the day of the Translation) forty days of rain will follow.

Winchester's defences did not prevent the city from being sacked by the Danes but, like the Saxon kings, the Danish King Cnut (1017–35) made it his capital and, after the Norman conquest, it was William I's capital too. The Saxon and early Norman kings were crowned here as well as at Westminster; here was the royal treasury and here the Conqueror kept the Domesday Book. Winchester was of equal importance with London up to Thomas' own times. The pilgrims of the early Middle Ages were not approaching the comparatively small, historic cathedral city and market town which Winchester seems today, but one of the major cities of the kingdom.

Tenth- and eleventh-century pilgrims to St Swithin's shrine would have found two churches side by side, so close—in places only a third of a metre apart—that the singing in one interfered with services in the other. The Old Minster was the cathedral church and the New Minster was the church of a monastery founded by King Alfred, who was buried there, and his son Edward. The Old Minster was rebuilt, and in 1079 Wakelin, the first Norman bishop of Winchester, began the present building, to which St Swithin's relics and golden shrine were transfered in 1093. Eventually, in 1110, the monks of the New Minster, tiring of the problems raised by being so close to another monastery, built a new foundation outside the city walls at Hyde, to which they removed the remains of their founders, and all the saintly relics in their possession.

On arriving in the city the pilgrims would seek out lodging. The very noble might be guests in the royal palace, important ecclesiastics might be received at Wolvesley Castle, the bishop's residence, and there would be inns and shelter in the monasteries for lesser men. God Begot House, much rebuilt and 'restored' but still to be seen at 101 High Street, was once a hospice for pilgrims and strangers. It was given to the cathedral by Queen Emma, wife first of King Ethelred and then of Cnut, and herself the mother of a saint: Edward the Confessor. Women pilgrims might find shelter at the Nunnaminster, a nunnery founded by King Alfred. The Strangers' Hall, of which a few fragments remain in the cathedral close, and the Pilgrims' Hall, built in the fourteenth century near St Swithin's Gate, which has the earliest known hammerbeam roof, also provided shelter, as did the guest hall of Hyde Abbey outside the city.

Right through the Middle Ages, when so many of Europe's great churches were being extended and reshaped, the Old Minster must have echoed with the sound of chisel on stone, and the modern visitor is not alone in having his view marred by the restorer's scaffolding. We can raise our eyes in wonder at the achievement of the past but can only imagine the excitement of the men and women who originally watched these soaring glories taking shape. They could share, more than most visitors today, the aspiration of the builders in reaching up to heaven.

In Winchester the pilgrims entered the longest cathedral in England. From 1300 they might first visit a chapel built over the saint's original resting place. Then they might join the queue of pilgrims at a door, now blocked, in the north transept, to be guided through the Minster by some of the monks who would display and explain the relics, perhaps allowing them to kiss or touch the elaborate caskets and reliquaries in which they were placed, eventually reaching the glittering shrine of Swithin himself. The pilgrims, unless especially privileged, were not permitted in the south transept, which connected with the monastic buildings, or the choir, reserved for the monks' own use. A wrought-iron screen across the transept kept out visitors who passed around the east end of the church.

The modern pilgrim can pass through the whole church, seeing everything from the twelfth-century Norman font of black Tournai (slatestone) carved with scenes from the life of St Nicholas, perhaps better known today as Santa Claus, to the elaborate fan-like vaulting of the Lady Chapel. There is still a shrine to St Swithin—a modern one placed where the old shrine once stood in the retrochoir. Placed over the side screens of the choir are mortuary chests which contain the bones of Saxon and Norman kings, including Edmund, Edred, Egbert, Kingelis, Ethelwulf and William Rufus, and Danish Cnut with Emma his queen, collected at various times in the twelfth, sixteenth and seventeenth centuries when they had been disturbed by changes to the building.

Not many of the medieval pilgrims would have gained access to the royal castle and palace, but today the Great Hall is open to all (apply at the tower gateway). Here the parliaments of England sat for 400 years. The fine Early English architecture is still impressive with its double arcade of Purbeck marble columns. Above the remains of the dais at the west end is a pethisis, or 'king's ear', an aperture in the wall connecting with the royal solar through which he could hear the deliberations of his parliament or give orders.

More famous than the hall itself is the Round Table which has hung on the west wall since the 1460s. Long viewed as a curiosity, and often claimed to be the original Round Table of King Arthur, it is divided into segments, each inscribed with the name of a knight, with an enthroned king in one portion and a Tudor rose in the centre. Those pilgrims who saw the table would have been reminded of another kind of pilgrimage: the quest for the Holy Grail.

Geoffrey of Monmouth began the medieval cult of the chivalric Arthur, who was actually a British leader in post-Roman times, with his account of the legends in about 1136. He regarded Winchester as one of Arthur's cities, but the idea of a Round Table is later than his version of the stories. In 1967 the table was taken down from the wall and x-ray, radiocarbon and tree-ring studies show it definitely to have been a table and probably made in the early years of the reign of Edward III, who actually founded an Order of Knights of the Round Table in the 1340s. Froissart, who was in England around 1390, mentions the table in his *Chronicle*. The Tudor rose (not an overpainting) cannot have been added before 1485, while the figure of the king is considered by the experts to be a representation of Henry VIII, painted about 1518.

As the pilgrims set out from Winchester they would probably stop at the abbey built by the monks of the New Minster at Hyde, just outside the walls. The new monastery of St Peter and St Frimbald was burned down in 1140 but soon rebuilt. The gateway to the abbot's lodging is all that remains today, except for some masonry built into an adjoining shed and a few fragments in nearby St Bartholomew's Church, which was originally the church for the abbey's tenants and servants. To the pilgrim this was a place of some importance. Here were the remains of King Alfred and his son, the head of St Valentine, given by Queen Emma, relics of St Grimbald, once abbot of the monastery, and St Josse, and a great silver rood given by King Cnut. The cathedral library at Winchester contains a life of St Thomas in medieval Latin into which has been inserted the tale of a monk imprisoned at Hyde monastery who, having been released by the aid of St Thomas, immediately made his way to Canterbury where 'he offered up the reins of his fetters with a suitable inscription'.

From Hyde, the first part of a Roman road leading north-east would take the pilgrim on to Headbourne Worthy, where a Saxon church dedicated to St Swithin may have been a stopping place for pilgrims to his shrine. Before the Reformation it had a huge rood carved on the west wall where it could be seen by travellers. The road then passes through Kings Worthy and, turning east to Martyr Worthy and Itchen Abbas, follows the north bank of the river. Alternatively, the pilgrim might have passed by the Church of St Bartholomew at Hyde and crossed the river to take the route variously known as the Nun's of Monk's Walk, joining the other road at Kings Worthy or keeping south of the river and following through the villages of Easten, Avington and Ovington and Bishop's Sutton. At Itchen Soke the northern route turns south and the old road crosses the river to Ovington, but the modern road goes *via* New Alresford, and an ancient way may also have followed that route. Choices and variations in the possible route occur from time to time along the way to Canterbury, and arguments can be put forward for the choice of each, but this was not a ritual path or processional way to which travellers had to adhere. Strength (many pilgrims were sick people), age, season and weather would determine progress and dictate when they must look for shelter—as it will for the contemporary walker—and cause individual deviations.

At Bishop' Sutton there was once a manor house of the Bishop of Winchester and perhaps here, about ten miles from Winchester, the infirm might find their first resting place and others call in hope of charity. On through Four Marks, Chawton, Alton, Holybourne and Bentley to Farnham the Way uncharacteristically does not keep to dryer levels but follows the river Wey close to the water. Hilaire Belloc considered that the route was dictated by the deep indentations in the hills which would considerably increase the distance to be covered if it followed a higher contour. In most cases the Way skirts the edges of villages but here it passes right down the main streets of Alton, Bentley and Farnham.

It is at Farnham that the pilgrim route joins the ancient Hoar Way from Salisbury Plain. The town's name is Saxon, and means a settlement among the bracken—but there was a settlement here six thousand years before the Saxons came. Farnham was a manor in the possession of the Bishop of Winchester from 803, and in the twelfth century Henry of Blois, the bishop who founded St Cross, built a castle here. It was one of those demolished by Henry II on coming to the throne, but was soon rebuilt. Until 1929, when the see was divided and Farnham went to the Bishop of Guildford, this was the official palace of the Bishops of Winchester, and many great prelates, monarchs and famous men rested within its walls. Here, perhaps, some pilgrims would have stayed, but in the town the bishop provided at least one hostel for pilgrims which still stands, a medieval building hiding behind later alterations and now known as the Old Vicarage in Church Lane. Farnham was a thriving market town all through the Middle Ages, a leading centre for wheat, and there were many inns and hostelries. The 'Lion and the Lamb' dates from 1537, just within the times of the pilgrimage, and there are other houses in the town in which a Georgian facade hides older work.

From Farnham the modern road follows the ridge of the high chalk down known as the Hog's Back which, though often having no place for walkers unprepared to risk life and limb against the heavy traffic, can offer fine views, especially to the north. Perhaps some pilgrims came this way, especially if mounted, for the route along the ridge would be easy to follow although bleak and exposed in winter. However, it is generally considered that travellers would have followed the lower road, keeping to the south flank of the downs (as the Pilgrims' Way does now for almost all the way to Canterbury) through the villages of Seale and Puttenham. Just outside Puttenham the modern pilgrim takes to the lanes and paths which follow the ancient Way, striking out across Puttenham Heath.

Compton, south of the Old Road, is generally thought to have been a pilgrim port of call because the Church of St Nicholas, which has a Saxon tower, exhibits a very curious feature. About a century after the chancel itself was built, a second storey was built above the sanctuary, open to the nave save for a nine-arched screen—itself a rare survival of Norman woodworking—and carried upon a low vault. On both levels was an altar, for a piscina can still be seen in the upper part, and outside steps once led up to a now-blocked access doorway. Why was this unique arrangement made? It has been suggested that the upper sanctuary was a pilgrim chapel or that it was built to display some important relic—but there is no record to enlighten us. Today the church is worth a visit for itself.

Beyond Compton the Pilgrims' Way continues as a sandy, tree-lined bridle path which is often a deep-cut hollow way. After about two miles it comes out on a road which leads on to join the Guildford–Godalming road a few yards away from a grassy knoll on which stand the remains of St Catherine's Chapel. This, according to some sources, was built by Henry II, but the ruined shell that remains today is in the Early English style and was completed in 1317. For some reason that early fourteenth-century building did not serve its purpose and, in addition to the usual west door, new doorways were pierced in both north and south walls and, even more surprisingly, the windows above them were also converted into doors which must have been reached by external stairs, now gone. As at Compton we do not know the reason for this unusual arrangement. Again it seems likely that here there was some object for special veneration which drew the devout in great numbers. On two levels they could pass in at one side of the church and out the other (like the crowds which today attend a lying-in-state or visit the tomb of Lenin, or go to see the crown jewels in the Tower of London), kneeling to say a prayer and perhaps to kiss some sacred object. Did such large crowds come only for some special feast or festival or were they frequent through the year? Can St Catherine's and Compton Church be used as evidence that large numbers of pilgrims did actually follow the route from Winchester to Canterbury?

9 The Pilgrims' Way II

FROM ST CATHERINE'S CHAPEL the medieval pilgrim could see the way ahead on the other side of the river Wey up the hill to Chantries Wood and on to where St Martha's Church stands on the top of the downs. Photographs taken earlier in this century show the church clearly against the skyline, not hidden by the wood as it is today, but in the Middle Ages this was probably a well forested countryside.

How did the medieval traveller reach the other bank? There is no bridge here, although about a mile upstream the name of the village of Shalford, on the other side, draws attention to the fact that there was a shallow ford there by which the river could be crossed. But the Old Road rarely makes such a deviation from its path and there is no sign of an ancient way climbing up the hill from Shalford to where the road continues. Since the prehistoric times when the road was first trodden there may have been changes in the course of the river, as it meanders in many channels after flooding the low-water meadows. It has been deepened and cleared to ease navigation and the physical evidence suggests that the river once flowed in a rather wide channel of little depth through what can still be quite marshy ground. By the Middle Ages, however, there may have been a ferry at this point to take travellers across the water to where the path continues. There certainly was one in more recent times, although it is not operating now. On the slope of St Catherine's Hill a line of ancient cottages mark what seems a very ancient track that carries the name Ferry Lane and leads (over a railway line) down to the water's edge.

The traveller may, of course, have chosen to make his way downstream to Guildford. In the absence of a ferry a three-quarter mile walk along the riverside path will bring the modern pilgrim to the town and a bridge, from which he can retrace his steps along the other bank. However, he would be well advised to stop and take a look at this ancient town, as his pilgrim predecessors probably did, perhaps going there to seek shelter for the night.

In the Domesday Book Guildford is recorded as having 75 households, and a street plan of 1617 shows scarcely more than that number of houses, so we should not imagine a very large town during the Middle Ages. However, it was quite an important one. Here, shortly after Thomas' death,

Henry II built, or rebuilt, a strong Norman castle and, being a day's ride from London and from the south coast, it became a useful staging point with many inns. The Georgian-fronted Angel Hotel in the High Street hides an earlier timbered building, and its name suggests that it was probably originally called the 'Salutation of the Virgin', a popular name for inns, with a sign showing an angel and the annunciation; at the Reformation this popular name was usually changed to the 'Angel' or the 'Salutation'. Beneath the Angel is a late thirteenth-century undercroft, now used as a bistro bar, and on the opposite side of the High Street is another which is somewhat finer. Experts consider both were the shops of merchants, set beneath their houses and entered by a few steps from street level—which was somewhat lower than it is today—but perhaps even in those days the Angel was an inn.

The Hospice of the Holy Trinity at the top of the High Street was not founded until the seventeenth century—by George Abbot, an Archbishop of Canterbury who was a Guildford man—but it is well worth a visit. A Dominican Friary, long gone but remembered in the name of Friary Street and Friary Ales which were brewed on the site, may have sheltered some for it had a guest hall, but although it once gave lodging to half the royal retinue its accommodation was not great and would probably be mainly used for visiting ecclasiastics and friars. The Friary was founded by Eleanor of Provence, wife of Henry III, in memory either of her husband, who died in 1272, or of her grandson the little Prince Henry, who died at Guildford in 1273 and whose heart was given to the house for safe keeping. Records show that there were never more than 24 friars in residence, and usually many of them would have been away on preaching tours, but excavations since the demolition of the brewery have revealed a large church and much of the ground plan of the brethren's quarters.

After the crossing of the river Wey the path continues up the hillside into Chantries Wood and across a patch of heath (now used as a car park) up the steep, wooded slope to St Martha's. The present church is largely a rebuilding from 1850, for the Norman church was seriously damaged by an explosion at the gunpowder factory in the village below and had fallen into a ruinous state. The diocesan architect and others in the parish have calculated from the foundations and other remains that the original church tower must have been exceptionally high, perhaps 30 metres or more, and it would have been a clear landmark, easily recognizable from across the river. Today, looking back across the river, St Catherine's can be seen above a great scar of exposed red sand which seems to bleed down to the riverside.

Although it has been rebuilt, St Martha's retains the massive walls and small windows of the Norman style and incorporates much of the old stone, including the west door arch which is original. Unfortunately the 'restorers' thought fit to recut some of the capitals and totally recarved a Norman font. The original high tower was at the west end of the church, but today's squat tower is built at the transept crossing.

Visitors to St Martha's are shown pieces of stone carved with single and double crosses which, it is claimed, were cut by pilgrims on their journey, and the uncoffined skeletons discovered in shallow graves when new interments take place in the churchyard are thought to be those of pilgrims, cheaply buried, who did not complete their journey—a reminder that many of them were sick and hoping for a cure. A modern stained-glass window in the church shows St Thomas, and during the Middle Ages there was a chapel dedicated to him. Although such a dedication was common throughout England this was one built in the twelfth century: it has been claimed that it was expressly for the use of pilgrims to his shrine.[1] Certainly, in 1463, Bishop Waynefleet of Winchester granted an indulgence of forty days to any penitent who came here on pilgrimage and gave money for the upkeep of the church. His announcement describes the church as 'the chapel dedicated to St Martha the Virgin and all the Holy Martyrs commonly called Martirhill' and it is disputable whether this was originally a dedication to St Martha at all. It is a very rare dedication and there is no reason to expect it here. It may well be the result of a corruption of 'Saint martyrs', for there is an old tradition that six hundred Christians were martyred on this spot about the beginning of the seventh century.

On the other side of St Martha's the ancient road can be seen again as a hollow way, though overgrown (it is necessary to take the path that runs alongside); and a few fields further on, at the edge of Weston Wood, features of both hollow way and terraced road can be clearly seen. The Way leads eventually to Shere, where the Norman church has a large chest of the type which was placed in churches at the order of Pope Innocent III to collect offerings for the crusades. There are medieval houses in the village too, including the White Horse Inn, parts of which date back to the fourteenth century. The original path both in and out of Shere is uncertain—it may not have passed through the village at all—but on the hillside above Gomshall some authorities claim an apparent terraceway as the continuation of the road, although others prefer not to commit themselves until a point on the hillside above Wescott. The upper road is quieter but the metalled route through Gomshall, Abinger Hammer and Wotton gives a glimpse of the extensive ponds created to provide water power for the hammers of the early Wealden iron industry. At Wotton's Norman church one can see not only memorials of the Evelyn family but a set of thirteenth-century portrait heads around the porch arch representing the protagonists in the clash between Church and State in the reign of Henry II's son John. The king, the queen, Pope Innocent III, Archbishop Stephen Langton, a cardinal, a pilgrim, a nobleman and a priest can all be identified.

From Wotton the traveller on the lower road can strike up towards Ranmore Common and join the road as it continues through Ranmore Woods and down into the valley of the Mole, above Dorking. Dorking is not on the line of the Old Road but the town is of Saxon origin and was thriving in the Middle Ages, with a weekly market granted in the reign of Edward I, and would have been a convenient stopping place for pilgrims.

The Mole may have been crossed at many places. Burford indicates by its name that it is a ford, although today the traveller can keep his feet dry by using a set of stepping stones, but the River Mole gets its name from a tendency to 'burrow underground' and at the places where it goes beneath the earth the level of the surface water drops, making it relatively easy to ford.

The Ordnance Survey map places the Pilgrims' Way on the slopes of Box Hill, but the slope is very steep and travellers may have found it easier to climb over the top of the hill. It is usual for the Old Road to avoid the wetter land of the valleys and, where these hillsides are too precipitous to support a terrace, it may have taken to the crest.

It certainly passed to the north of Reigate, although the modern town now spreads out towards it. Reigate appears in the Domesday Book as Cherchefell and was well established in the Middle Ages. Some of its houses date back to the fourteenth century, and there are Norman columns in the parish church. In 1235 an Augustinian Priory was founded here and, before the Reformation, in the very centre of the main street a chapel dedicated to St Thomas stood where the eighteenth-century old town hall now interrupts the traffic. There would be shelter here for travellers coming down the Old Road, and St Thomas' was an added attraction for the pilgrim.

From Reigate the road proceeds by way of Gatton Park (where the walker must take another route to avoid private land) to Merstham, famous in the Middle Ages for its sandstone, which was used in the building of Westminster Abbey and Old St Paul's. The parish church of St Katherine dates from 1220 and until 'restored' a century ago is said to have had a series of frescoes on the south wall showing the life of St Thomas. The manor of Merstham was given to the monks of Christ Church by Athelstan in the tenth century and therefore might feel a special link with St Thomas.

From Merstham to Titsey the route is ill-defined and sometimes lost completely as it traverses the downs, but from there on it can be more easily identified and, especially where metalled, is easier to follow. The boundary between Surrey and Kent is about a mile and a half past Titsey where, at a crossroads, the Kent County Council have set up a sign identifying the Way by name and bearing the symbol of a cockle shell. Useful though these signs are to the walker they have occasionally been set up in places where the line of the route is disputed.

At Chevening Park, given to the nation in 1967 and now the country home of Prince Charles, the Way crosses private grounds and the walker must again make a detour to rejoin the route beside the parish church of Chevening village.

The Way now drops down into the Darent valley to Otford, where it coincides with the main village street. At Otford was one of the 'palaces' of Archbishop Thomas. The land here was given to Christ Church by King

Offa in 790, and when Christ Church properties were divided between the monastery and the archbishopric Otford went to the latter. This seems to have been a favourite place of Thomas who, there being no well or spring to supply fresh water for his manor, is said, Moses-like, to have struck the earth with his staff and caused water to flow in what is known as St Thomas' Well. All that is to be seen today is the roofless, floorless shell of a once elegant tower in which the fireplaces are the nesting places of white doves that fill the emptiness with their gentle cooing, and the walls of a long gallery, now divided into a row of cottages. Thomas would probably not have liked the doves for it was here (as the Kentish historian Lambarde tells it) that being 'busie at his prayers in the garden at Otford' Thomas 'was much disturbed by the sweet note and melodie of a nightingale that sang in a bush beside him, and in the might of his holinesse commanded all birds of this kind to be henceforth silent'.[2]

Today's remnants are not from the manor house of Thomas' time but from a fine mansion raised at the beginning of the sixteenth century. Two stories high, with taller towers at each corner, it covered an area 67 metres by 134 metres. Henry VIII stayed at the Palace a number of times: once was on his way to France for the great meeting with Francis IV at the Field of Cloth of Gold; he brought a retinue of 3,400—plus 1,200 waiting upon Queen Katherine. They had come from London first by river and then up the Darent valley. It was perhaps a route that was often used.

At the Dissolution of the Monasteries Cranmer made a present of the

The archbishops' palace at Otford. The row of cottages incorporates parts of the long gallery.

archbishop's palaces at Otford, Wrotham and Charing (we reach the others later in our journey) to the king, who had perhaps dropped some rather heavy hints; although he later complained that this house was 'rheumatik'. Princess Mary came to live here but, during her half-brother Edward VI's reign, the lead was stripped from the roofs, leading to rapid dereliction; and eventually Elizabeth I sold Otford to raise money for the Irish expedition of 1601.

The stream that brought the dampness that plagued the royal rheumatism runs behind the little row of cottages and flows down from St Thomas' Well, which can be reached by walking through the churchyard and following the path beyond past gardens and a tennis court to where a square of high railings can be seen across a field. There seems to be no access except by climbing through the wire fence, and the railings prevent a close inspection of the 'well', which is an oblong, stone-lined basin, about six by eleven metres, which excavations suggest was once covered by a timber roof. It may have originally been connected with a nearby Roman villa and, although it was almost certainly the original source of water for the 'palace', it is thought by some writers to have been used as a bathing place and that, because of its connection with the saint, pilgrims would have bathed in it to share some of his virtue.

The palace remains close the vista across Otford's village green, to the left of which stands the parish church of St Bartholomew, originally Saxon with a Norman tower, though much 'restored' a century ago. A duckpond adds to the rural charm, and even the busy main road beside it does not destroy the peace.

The Way now follows the same road as the juggernauts along Otford's main street, but across the railway bridge takes the by-road on to Kemsing, leaving the worst of the traffic behind.

The village of Kemsing lies a little below the Way. In the centre of the village is St Edith's Well, now hidden below a war memorial cross. Named after a daughter of the Saxon King Edgar, it is actually a spring and was reputed to cure sore eyes. St Edith was born at Kemsing and, during the Middle Ages, the Church of St Mary the Virgin, only a few yards from the Way, had a shrine to her in the churchyard which attracted pilgrims and was especially revered by local people. She seems to have taken over the role of some earlier fertility goddess. Lambarde, writing in the reign of Elizabeth I, after the Reformation had suppressed its practice, describes the ritual at the shrine which

> was religiously frequented . . . for the preservation of Corne and Graine, from Blasting, Myldew, Brandeare, and such other harmes as commonly do annoy it. The manner of the whiche sacrifice was this: Some seelie bodie brought a pecke, or two, or a Bushell of Corne, to the Church: and (after praiers made) offered it to the Image of the Saint: Of this offering,

the Priest used to toll the greatest portion, and then to take one handful, or a little more of the residue (for which you must consider he woulde be sure to gaine by the bargaine) the which after aspersion of holy water, and mumbling of a few woordes of conjuration, he first dedicated to the Image of Saint Edith, and then delivered it back, to the partie that brought it: who then departed with full persuasion, that if he mingled that hallowed handfull with his seede Corne, it woulde preserve from harme, and prosper in growthe, the whole heape that he should sowe, were it never so great a Stacke, or mowgh.

A medallion showing the Virgin and Child in the lancet window in the east wall of the church dates from 1220, and is among the oldest stained glass in the country. Other glass from the fourteenth century, fine carving and colourful decoration make this church well worth a visit despite its enlargement and restoration in the 1890s.

Three miles from Kemsing the Way reaches Wrotham, though again the village lies slightly lower than the road. The Church of St George dates largely from the thirteenth century, replacing a Saxon building, and has a fifteenth-century tower built over an open passageway, supposedly so that processions could circle the outside of the church without leaving the churchyard. There is also a strange gallery reached by an extension of the stair which once gave access to the rood. Known as the 'Nun's Gallery', it was perhaps a watching chamber from which guard could be kept over treasures on display in the church—suggesting that here, as at Compton and St Catherine's, there may have once been a particularly popular relic for pilgrims to visit.

Wrotham has some old houses and inns, but there is very little left of the palace or manor house of the Archbishops of Canterbury, which was largely demolished in the middle of the fourteenth century to provide building materials for the palace at Maidstone. Before then it perhaps provided shelter for pilgrims.

The metalled road continues for about a mile beyond Wrotham, then turns sharply right while the Old Way continues as a track until it meets a road running down to Trottiscliffe village (pronounced locally as 'Trosley'). To the east of the village stood a 'palace' of the Bishops of Rochester which may also have offered pilgrims succour. The land belonged to the see from 774 but was sold in 1648. An old gateway is probably all that survives of the medieval buildings, but most of the Norman church dates from the middle of the twelfth century, although the tower is two hundred years later. Once the village clustered around the church but the population moved westward in the fourteenth century at the time of the Black Death, which killed thirty-two of the palace staff.

Yet further east, and still 30 metres or so below the level of the Way, from which they can be reached by a bridge path, lie the Coldrum Stones. These stones, now standing on the edge of a slight terracing of the slope, are the remains of a prehistoric burial chamber. Four massive sarsen stones about four metres high still stand from the central chamber, and nearby can be seen the scattered stones which probably once formed a circle around them, near the edge of the mound of earth which once covered them all. They have no pilgrim connection but are a reminder of the antiquity of the route. The Old Road is now approaching the Medway valley and, although it can be traced a little further along the downs and picked up again along the hillside on the other side of the river, it is uncertain how it crossed the broad flat valley. Kent County Council have chosen a road through Upper Halling and a crossing at Cuxton, well downstream, and erected their Pilgrims' Way signs to mark it; but there is no evidence that the river was ever fordable here and it adds several miles to the journey.

Halling, a little further upstream, gives a route which is clear of the clay which the Old Way seeks to avoid. Snodland lies in a direct line between the known traces of the Old Road; the crossing would be less deep here—at low tide riders could ford it easily—and there is an apparently permanent outcrop of greensand. There was a ferry here in recent times and there may have been one in the Middle Ages. At Snodland a Norman church stands very close to the river and on the other side there is a clear road up to Burnham,[3] while on the eastern side there are further prehistoric remains which echo the Coldrum Stones. Today, however, it is impossible to cross the Medway here. To find a bridge we must either go downstream to Rochester or upstream to Aylesford—and it is quite likely that in the Middle Ages travellers did the same if they were fit enough not to find the extra distance a heavy burden.

At Rochester they could join up with travellers on the London–Canterbury road—and visit the shrine of William of Perth. At Strood, still on the west bank of the river, they would pass the Hall of the Knights Templar and it is sometimes suggested that this would be a stopping place. Strood was a royal manor, given to the Knights Templar by Henry II in the early years of his reign. The surviving building, now surrounded by the warehouses and factories of an industrial estate, was put up about seventy years later, perhaps to provide lodging for Temple dignitaries travelling between London and Dover. When the Order was dissolved in 1312, following prosecution for black magic, sexual offences and compromising with Islam, it was supposed to have been handed over to the Knights Hospitallers, but the crown had been enjoying its revenues since the imprisonment of the English Templars in 1308 and it seems never to have been fully relinquished. Edward III granted it to the Countess of Pembroke to endow any religious order she pleased, and from 1344 until the dissolution of the monasteries its revenues went to the Franciscan nunnery at Denny. The manor house was probably used only as a home by the families who held the land to farm on a money rent. Even in the century when the hall was in Templar hands it is unlikely that they would have offered pilgrims hospitality there.

Taking the road south, upstream to Aylesford, travellers might decide not to cross the river but to press on to Maidstone. Indeed, they may have chosen to diverge from the Old Road much earlier, heading from Wrotham or elsewhere along the Way for West Malling, where there was an abbey of Benedictine nuns founded in about 1100 by Bishop Gundulph of Rochester. Here women pilgrims, in particular, might have found rest and refreshment. In his *Peregrination of Kent*, Lambarde (writing after the nunnery had been dissolved) suggested that the nuns offered more than hospitality to visiting monks who there 'might quench their heats . . . a very common practice in Papistry'. Of the ancient buildings a ruined tower, the guesthouse and parts of the cloister still stand and new buildings have joined them, for at the turn of the century this became a nunnery again—albeit with Anglican Benedictines who no longer keep a guesthall.

At Aylesford, however, the modern pilgrim can still find hospitality at the Carmelite Friary which was bought back by the Order, after four centuries in private hands, and re-established in 1949. A serious fire in 1930 damaged much of the surviving medieval buildings, but the ancient Pilgrims' Hall still stands, now used as a dining hall for visitors, together with part of the cloister, the lower part of the gatehouse and the original prior's house. Most of the buildings in the main courtyard date from the middle of the fifteenth century, when the priory was being expanded and rebuilt, but the dormer windows in the roofs and most of the other windows are late seventeenth-century, added when the Friary was in private ownership.

The foundations of the Friary church are marked out by darker paving stones, and the area where it once stood is now a great open-air church facing the shrine of Our Lady, from which radiate several chapels, including ones dedicated to St Joseph and St Anne and a relic chapel of St Simon Stock, Prior General of the Order in the thirteenth century. His remains are displayed behind the altar in a towering reliquary which, in its design, symbolizes Mount Carmel and its hermits' cells, where the Carmelites originated.

It was at a chapter meeting of the Order, held at Aylesford in 1247, that the character of the Carmelite life was changed from that of a hermit to that of a friar, following the new form of monastic life begun by St Francis and St Dominic in which, while continuing to live in a monastic community, friars went out into the world to serve and to preach. Among medieval pilgrims visiting the Friary was Edward II who, in 1326, gave fourpence to each member of the house.

The Friars, as the friary has been known for centuries, is now a centre of pilgrimage for many thousands every year and vast congregations gather in the open-air church. Not only Roman Catholics attend—the Anglican Church has an annual pilgrimage to Aylesford—and the attitude at the Friars is more than ecumenical: moslems, hindus, jews and nonbelievers are equally welcome if they seek peace. Many come here to go into retreat or to attend study conferences and, despite the aggressively mid-twentieth-century nature of

Inside the Pilgrims' Hall at the Friars, Aylesford. The galleries are a modern addition to provide extra accommodation. (*British Tourist Authority.*)

the ceramics and other works of art with which the shrine and chapels are decorated, there is a real sense of calm and a friendly welcome for every visitor.

Aylesford itself is an attractive place with a fine parish church high on the hill above the Friars and a medieval bridge with refuges on each side for pedestrians, which replaced the ford that gave the town its name.

Going still further upstream along the Medway the pilgrim would reach Maidstone, where a hostel for travellers and almshouse for ten of the poor was founded about 1260. Known as the Hospital of the Newark, or New Work, it lies on the west bank of the river a stone's throw away from the foot of the bridge. Only the chapel remains today. Transepts and a new west end were added in 1836, and the church rededicated to Saints Peter and Paul. Here poor pilgrims would have stayed. Ecclesiastics of the grander sort and other important travellers may have been given hospitality on the other side of the river in the archbishops' palace. Built in the fourteenth century—partly of stone brought from the Wrotham 'palace', it replaced or supplemented a house given to the Archbishop of Canterbury by the rector here in 1205. Archbishop Thomas did not know this building, but the manor of Maidstone was already in the possession of the archbishops when the town is first mentioned in a document of 975.

The archbishops controlled life here during the Middle Ages, and there was considerable friction between them and the townsfolk. Between the palace and the church are buildings known as the guard room and the dungeon and it was here, perhaps, that Archbishop Sudbury imprisoned John Ball, the demagogic priest who helped to lead the Peasant's Revolt. In 1381 Wat Tyler and his followers overran Maidstone and rescued Ball.

The Church of All Saints, a fine example of perpendicular architecture, was begun in 1395 as a collegiate church, replacing the former church dedicated to the Virgin. Today it lacks its spire (burned when it was struck by lightning in 1731), which must have given it an even more soaring line. Inside, a wall-painting still survives showing St Thomas being presented to the Virgin. The buildings of the college, with a fine gatehouse, still stand on the other side of the church, making a fine group along the bank of the river.

Facing the main block of the palace is a massive building known as the archbishop's stables. There was originally stabling in the lower part and above it accommodation for the retainers of noble visitors such as Henry VI and Henry VIII; the latter stayed here on his way to the Field of Cloth of Gold, the next stage of the journey after Otford.

From Maidstone travellers could join the Way six miles or more past the Snodland crossing of the Medway, but they would have missed one of the most famous of the relics to be seen between Winchester and Canterbury. And the modern traveller would miss a famous group of prehistoric monuments.

If a ferry were available at Snodland directly across the river it would leave the traveller with a patch of soggy marshland to negotiate on the other side along a meander loop, so perhaps it would have followed the river along the bend and dropped its passengers at the foot of a short lane leading to Burnham old church. Thence, passing below the new church and village of Burnham and above Eccles, the Way regains the slopes of the downs. Past the road leading down to Eccles it becomes a dual carriageway until it reaches

Wood Road, coming up from Aylesford, by which travellers taking the Aylesford crossing could rejoin the route. To the southwest of this junction lies the Coffin Stone and its surrounding circle of stones, which can be reached by a path off the Aylesford road. Not so far down on the other side of Wood Road, and marked by a clump of elms (and a signpost labelled Little Kit's Coty) are the Countless Stones, so called because the overlapping jumble of rock around the tree trunks makes it impossible to be sure whether one is counting two pieces of the same stone. These are the tumbled remains of a neolithic tomb used for collective burial c.2000BC. They were demolished c.AD1690 by a farmer who hoped to sell the stones for road-making. The tomb originally consisted of a chamber constructed of large sarsen stones with a roughly square curb of smaller stones, all covered by a mound, as at Coldrum.

Up a steep path beneath a tunnel of high, overhanging hedges, which leads northward from the road junction, another neolithic tomb can be found in an open field to the left. This is Kit's Coty House—the name has many interpretations but none bear much relevance to its origin. Once again these are the central stones of an ancient burial chamber which originally lay beneath the east end of a barrow similar to those in Western Europe known as 'Hun's Beds'.

Back at the crossroads a track leads off, between Wood Road and the continuation of the main road, as a terraceway on the fringes of a wood emerging below a filling station on a main road. A tunnel takes the walker to the other side where the track resumes. Another prehistoric megalith, the White Horse Stone, can be found by a narrow footpath on the left.

After another mile the path joins a sharp bend in a road which, to the right, leads down to the site of Boxley Abbey and to the left forms a continuation of the Way. Boxley Abbey, which in the Middle Ages could probably have been reached by a direct route from Aylesford (though today this involves negotiating main roads and a motorway), provided sights no traveller would want to miss. A hugh barn, 57 metres long and built of stone, still stands. It was possibly the guest house of the monastery, and its very scale is an indication of the number of pilgrims and other travellers it could offer shelter. (The coupled roof trusses and slates date from the eighteenth century.) The remnants of a gateway and numerous stone walls indicate the area the abbey must have covered, a total of some six hectares altogether. The walls of a garden are, in fact, the lower courses of the abbey church, but the private house was built after the Dissolution.

Boxley was founded in 1146 by William of Ypres, Earl of Kent, who presumably hoped thereby to gain remission for his manifold sins. It was a Cistercian house, only the second in England, and despite its great extent seems to have had only a small number of brethren: the records show only 18 in 1381 and only ten monks in 1538, at the Dissolution. (The Abbot of Boxley was at Christ Church at the time of St Thomas' martyrdom and helped to disrobe the body of the saint ready for burial.) There were two marvels for the pilgrim visitor to wonder at. The first was a small statue of a child, St Rumbold, the son of a pagan king of Northumberland and his Christian wife, a baby so precious that at birth he could speak—and in Latin, too—and three times announced that he was a Christian, repeating the Paternoster and the Credo. For the three days of his life he lectured all the learned men of the court and neighbourhood on the tenets of the Christian faith and—equally precociously—passed on to Paradise. His relics were taken to Buckingham where a shrine was erected in an aisle of the church dedicated to him. This Boxley statue, though small in size and easily carried, appeared to be immovable when many persons tried to lift it. According to tradition, only the pure and virtuous could lift the statue, and only those who lifted it could pass on to venerate the next of Boxley's marvels. Before they tried to lift this infant saint the pilgrims would make their confession— perhaps enabling the monk confessor to assess whether they had in fact made full confession of their sins, and certainly enabling him to count the value of the offering which they then made; this had an effect upon their lifting power, for the monks had some kind of catch or controlling mechanism which could be used to root the statue to the floor. As the Kentish chronicler Lambarde declared, 'Many time it mooved more laughter than devocion to beholde a great lubber to lift at that in vaine, which a young boy (or wench) had easily taken up before him. I omit, that chaste Virgins, and honest married matrones, went oftentimes away with blushing faces, leaving (without cause) in the mindes of the lookers on, great suspicion of uncleane life, and wanton behaviour.'

If they had managed to lift St Rumbold the devout might then go on to offer their prayers before the Rood of Grace, a crucifix with a figure of Christ which seemed miraculous. We do not know when the Rood was first erected at Boxley but its appearance there was reported to be a miracle itself. Again, Lambarde tells the story.

It chaunced (as the tale is) that upon a time a cunning Carpenter of our country was taken prisoner in the warres betweene us and Fraunce, who (wanting otherwise to satisfie for his raunsome), and having good leysure to devise for his deliverance, thought it best to attempt some curious enterprise, within the compasse of his own Arte and skill, to make himselfe some monay withall: And therefore, getting togither fit matter for his purpose, he compacted of wood, wyer and paper, a Roode of such exquisite Art and excellencie, that it not onely matched in comelynesse and due proportion of the partes the best of the common sorte; but in straunge action, variety of gesture, and nimbleness of joints, passed al other that before had been seene; the same being able to bow downe and lifte up it selfe, to shake and stirre the handes and feete, to nod the head, to rolle the eies, to wag the chaps, to bende the browes, and finally to represent to the eie, both the proper action of each member of the body, and also a liveley, expresse, and significant shew of a well contented or displeased mynde; byting the lippe, and gathering a frowning froward, and disdainful face, when it would pretend offence; and shewing a moste milde, amyable, and smyling cheere and countenance, when it woulde seeme to be well pleased.

... This done, he made shifte for his libertie, came over into this Realme, of purpose to utter his merchandize, and laide the Image upon the backe of a Jade [a nag, or horse in poor condition] that he drave before him.

Now when hee was come so farre as to Rochester on his way, hee waxed drie for reason of travaile, and called at an alehouse for drinke to refreshe him, suffering his horse neverthelesse to go forwarde alone along the Citie:

This Jade was no sooner out of sight, but hee missed the streight westerne way that his Maister intended to have gone, and turning Southe, made a great pace toward Boxley, and being driven (as it were) by some divine furie, never ceased jogging tell he came at the Abbay church doore, where he so beat and bounced with his heeles, that divers of the Monkes heard the noise, came to the place to know the cause, and (marvelling at the straungenesse of the thing) called the Abbatt and his Convent to beholde it.

These good men seeing the horse so earnest, and discerning what he had on his backe, for doubt of deadly impietie opened the doore: which they had no sooner done, but the horse rushed in, and ran in great haste to a pillar (which was the verie place where this Image was afterwarde advaunced) and there stopped himselfe, and stoode still.

Now while the Monkes were busie to take off the lode, in commeth the Carpenter (that by great inquisition had followed) and he challenged his owne: the Monkes loth to lose so benificiall a stray, at first made some deniall, but afterward, being assured by all signes that he was the verie Proprietarie, they graunt him to take it with him.

The Carpenter then taketh the horse by the head, and first assayeth to leade him out of the Church, but he would not stirre for him: Then beatheth hee and striketh him, but the Jade was so restie and fast nailed that he would not once remooove his foote from the pillar: at the last he taketh off the Image, thinking to have carried it out by selfe, and then to have led the horse after: but that also cleaved so fast to the place, that notwithstanding all that ever he (and the Monkes also, which at length were contented for pities sake to helpe him) coulde do, it woulde not be mooved one inch from it: So that in the ende partly from weariness in wrestling, and partly by persuasion of the Monkes, which were in love with the Picture, and made him beleeve that it was by God himselfe destinate to their house, the Carpenter was contented for a piece of money to go his way, and leave the Roode behind him.

Again, according to the quality of the person or their further offering at the Rood, the monks would make this automaton bend benevolently or glare displeasure.

At the Reformation the Rood was removed to Maidstone market and there exhibited for the fraud it was. The royal commissioners reported that they 'found therein certayn engyns of old wyer with olde roten stykkes' which worked the movements. John Foxe in this *Book of Martyrs* claimed there were 100 wires and recorded that a piece of silver was received with frowning lips, but a piece of gold caused the 'jaws to wag merrily'. From Maidstone the Rood was taken to London and publicly burned at St Paul's Cross.

Boxley village is another mile along the Way and closer to it. The intriguing narthex attached to the west side of the tower of the parish church has suggested to some people that this may have been a relic chapel and a stopping place for pilgrims, but the discovery of Norman arches beneath the plaster of the north wall in 1921 suggests that this should now be interpreted as the original Norman church which was extended to the east in the thirteenth century, while the tower was built over the original chancel in the fifteenth century.[4]

Detling is the next village the traveller encounters, again set a little below the Way, which has a partly Norman church which possesses a very fine fourteenth-century four-sided lectern carved with pierced roundels and decorated with animals (including what appears to be an elephant) and grotesques. It is thought likely that it came from Boxley Abbey.

The route continues past Thurnham, where there are the earthworks of a Norman castle. Just north of its line are a Coldblow Lane and Coldblow Farm, and a place called Coldharbour, which may have some significance in identifying an ancient road. A cold harbour—and there are many places which carry the name up and down the land—was a shelter where travellers might get some protection from the worst of the weather. It might indicate simply an enclosure without a roof, and some antiquaries have suggested that the name indicates the site of a Roman villa, in the ruins of which the travellers of the Dark Ages would spend the night. Perhaps they were important as recognized camping sites where the company of other travellers might offer some protection from marauders, animal or human, and a fire could be shared and maintained.

After Hollingbourne (the manor belonged to Christ Church, Canterbury' from 980), the path again reverts to being a track. Even in the Middle Ages this bridle path was duplicated by a lower route which linked up the villages of Hollingbourne, Harrietsham, Lenham and Charing.

The great attraction of Charing in the Middle Ages, was, yet again, a relic. The Church of Saints Peter and Paul exhibited the very block on which it was said that John the Baptist was beheaded at the order of Herod Antipas. Richard I brought it to England towards the end of the twelfth century and gave it to Charing Church. The church that housed it was largely destroyed

The entrance gate to the archbishop's palace (left) and the Church of Saints Peter and Paul at Charing.

by a disastrous fire. It was 'burned upon Tuesday the fourth of August, 1590', says a contemporary account, 'and the bells in the steeple melted with the extremity of the fire. Nothing of the church was left but the bare walls, except the floor over the porch, and the floor over the turret where the weather cock doth stand. The fire chanced by means of a birding-piece discharged by one Mr Dios, which fired in the shingels, the day being extreme hot and the same shingels very dry.'[5] If the heading-block was not destroyed at the time of the Reformation but was hidden somewhere, one wonders if it survived the fire.

The manor of Charing was traditionally given to the archdiocese of Canterbury by Vortigern in the fifth century, and a charter of 799 restores it to the Church after it had been in secular hands. The Manor House, like others of the archbishops, is often called a palace, and c.1300 some very palatial rebuilding was carried out. Archbishop John Stratford, who held the see 1333–48, seems to have been the first primate to live at Charing for any length of time, and the building may date from his archiepiscopate. Archbishop Morton (1485–1500) also 'made great building' here. The gatehouse, to the left of the short road leading to the church, gives access to a quadrangle of partly ruined buildings which now forms the yard of Palace Farm. The farmhouse is largely medieval, the date on the porch presumably referring to later reconstruction. The enormous barn was the banqueting hall of the palace and saw many important visitors, among them Henry VII and Henry VIII, and it was another of the estates which Archbishop Cranmer had to surrender to the latter. Since 1724 it has been in private hands but, by courtesy of the occupant of the house, an Archbishop of Canterbury who visits Charing Church still robes at the palace before processing to the West Door.

The very wealthy and the very poor among the pilgrims may have found shelter in these walls but Charing has many old buildings and among them two inns, the Swan and the King's Head, were already in business in the Middle Ages. The Swan is half-timbered but was given a brick face in the seventeenth century and has now been converted into flats, and the King's Head has been rebuilt more than once. Next to the half-timbered and herringbone-bricked Pierce House, which is set back a little from the line of the street, is a rectangular stone building which has been identified as part of a thirteenth-century hostel for travellers. It has a small window on the west side through which alms could be dispensed. Also in the street is an ancient butcher's shop, referred to in a rent roll of 1500 and still in use.

From above Charing the Way continues along the southern slope of the downs. Soon they begin to turn to make way for the wide valley of the Stour and the road turns with them. Westwell was another possession of Christ Church Priory—its revenues supplied the refectory—and at Boughton Aluph the church has a fireplace in the southern of its two porches where, local tradition says, pilgrims found warmth and shelter.

The Way next climbs higher towards Soakham Downs, and here Hilaire Belloc claimed the pilgrim might get his first view of his destination, though it seems unlikely that even those who knew the route would really be able to do so. At Godmersham, another property of Christ Church, the originally Norman church of St Lawrence houses a late twelfth-century relief of an archbishop. Now on the south wall of the choir, it was brought in 1935 from the remains of Court Lodge, once the manor house from which the monks looked after their property. Could this be Thomas? Julia Cartwright saw it in the ruins and thought it represented Prior Henry de Estria, who rebuilt the house in 1290,[6] but if it is Thomas it is the earliest known sculpture of the martyr (though it is not finely executed).

A mile or more past Godmersham it is indeed possible to gain an occasional glimpse of Canterbury through the trees, but it is not always easy to identify the route, and at Chilham Park a detour is necessary to avoid private land, although Chilham Castle and its grounds are open to the public on several afternoons each week during the summer. The Norman castle keep, built by Henry II in 1171-4, still stands but much of the castle was pulled down to provide building materials in the sixteenth century. The hexagonally shaped manor house between the castle and the pretty village was completed in 1616. At the Dissolution of the Monasteries the shrine of St Augustine was brought to Chilham, but it did not escape destruction on the orders of Archbishop Cranmer.

Canterbury is now only six miles away, but the direction of the Way is not clear. One route takes it on a detour to the north through the quaintly named Old Wives Lees—actually a corruption of Oldwood's Lees (meaning clearings or fields within an old wood), but there is evidence of an ancient road at Whitehill.

Beyond Shalmsford Street the route becomes more certain, passing through Chartham Hatch until it cuts right though the earthworks of an Iron Age fort known as Bigbury Camp. This ancient fort encloses an area of 10 hectares, and was probably constructed as a defence against the attacks of the Belgae, who eventually settled in Kent about the time of Christ. Caesar, who in 54BC was here victorious against the native forces, called the Belgae the most civilized peoples of Britain. Excavations have produced large quantities of their pottery and metalwork.

From Bigbury, one route probably went directly into Canterbury, but it is no longer possible to follow its actual way except for short sections; although there is a path marked as the Pilgrims' Way and shown on the Ordnance Survey map, it seems likely that pilgrims would have been attracted by a detour to the north to visit Harbledown, where they would link up with the road from London.

10 The London Road

PERHAPS THE 'Pilgrims' Way' is a misnomer and the Old Road was not a regular route during the Middle Ages, but no such doubts occur about the road from London. The Roman Watling Street, the major highway from London through Rochester and Canterbury to the port of Dover, has been in constant use for nearly two thousand years, and thousands upon thousands of pilgrims travelled this way to bow their knee at St Thomas' shrine. This is the route of kings and princes, the route which Chaucer's pilgrims took, the route that carried soldiers, merchants and statesmen on their way to the continent and saw their return, broken or triumphant. At Canterbury, they might stop to ask a blessing at the shrine or come, like Henry V on his return from Agincourt, to give thanks for a victory. This was the route that travellers from the north of England would take, and many from all parts of the land would make their way through London, both so that they might see the capital and because there was greater safety on the well used roads. Perhaps some pilgrims from East Anglia would take a ferry across from where Tilbury was to grow to Gravesend on the southern shore of the Thames, and from London there were boats to both Gravesend and Dartford where travellers could join the route. There were complaints against the watermen at the Assize Court of Canterbury in 1293 that they were over-charging— asking for one penny fare to Gravesend when it was claimed that the proper toll was only a halfpenny. The same charge was brought again in 1313. (Would that today's Price Commission had to concern itself with such stability over twenty years!) These Thames watermen used to salute a statue of St Thomas on Lambeth palace by raising their caps whenever they passed.

Despite the building of a modern motorway which takes to the high downs and by-passes the towns, Watling Street is still one of England's busiest roads and anyone attempting to follow in the pilgrims' steps will have to have a very vivid imagination to recreate the atmosphere of the Middle Ages, as well as lungs and ears immune to the fumes of the internal combustion engine and the din of traffic.

London was not only a great city with sights to attract the tourist pilgrim, it was a logical starting point for a journey to St Thomas' shrine, for it was

The thirteenth-century common seal of the City of London shows St Thomas seated, wearing the pallium and with his cross, in the act of giving benediction. Below is a view of the city with St Paul's in the centre surrounded by the spires of the other city churches and the square keep of the Tower of London on the right. (*Museum of London.*)

closely linked with Thomas and there were many reminders of him to attract the pilgrim's devotion. Thomas was a Londoner—he liked to be known as Thomas of London and London was proud to claim him as a citizen. The seals of the Mayor and Corporation of the City bore his effigy, and on their accession new Lord Mayors went in procession to the church of St Thomas of Acon (Acre), built upon his birthplace, and then to St Paul's where a solemn *de profundis* was sung by his parents' tombs.

This church, and the hospital of which it formed part, was founded by Thomas' sister Agnes and her husband Thomas fitzTheobald on the site of Gilbert Becket's house in Cheapside, was served by a master and brethren and was endowed with all 'the lands and appurtenances that sometime were Gilbert Becket's', as the Elizabethan antiquarian John Stowe records. A grammar school was opened there in the reign of Henry VI, and at the Reformation the hospital was bought by the Mercers' Company and the church reopened as the Company Chapel in 1541. Rebuilt after the Great

Fire of 1666, and again in 1884, it was once more destroyed in the 1940 blitz. A new hall and chapel now mark where Thomas was born. There was a stained-glass window in the original chapel, showing Henry II being scourged by the monks of Canterbury, which Thomas Cromwell's investigator pointed out in his report at the Dissolution.

When Chancellor, Thomas had had charge of the Tower of London and there Henry III built an oratory dedicated to him, while in the great stone bridge built across the Thames six years after Thomas' death there was another chapel dedicated in his honour. Until that time there had been only wooden bridges to cross the river at London, but in about 1176 Peter of Colechurch, the priest who had been responsible for the repair and construction of the last wooden bridge in 1163, began a stone bridge a little to the west of it. According to Stowe the river was diverted by a trench cut for the purpose running from 'east about Radriffe, and ending in the west about Patricksey, now termed Batersey'.[1] It was thirty-three years before the bridge was finished, and Peter Colechurch, who died four years before his work was completed, was buried in the chapel in 1205. The new bridge had nineteen arches, with the chapel about the centre. On either side houses and shops were built, their rents helping to pay for its upkeep, while King John gave land to provide an income towards building and upkeep, various taxes were assigned to its support and tolls were levied on merchandise passing both over and under its arches. The revenues were assigned to those made responsible for its care—at one time the convent of St Catherine's near the Tower, at another Henry III's queen—but they did not always use the money for its proper purposes and the bridge sometimes fell into such disrepair as to become dangerous. Until the middle of the eighteenth century this remained the only bridge across the Thames at London and the furthest place downstream at which the river could be crossed.

The houses on the bridge were several stories high, with cellars in the thickness of the piers, and the arches were narrow so that there were frequent accidents when boats were dashed against the bridge. Sometimes the inhabitants fell into the river when their homes were in bad repair. (In 1481 a whole block of houses fell into the river.) It was a crowded community: by the middle of the fourteenth century 138 tenants were paying rent to the bridgemaster.[2] The thirteenth arch from the city side was formed as a drawbridge to enable boats with tall masts to pass, and by it was a tower over the roadway on which, from the end of the thirteenth century, the heads of criminals were placed, impaled upon pikes. Timber islands called 'starlings' were built around each pier to reduce the damage to the main structure from water and ice, further narrowing the navigable space. The chapel of St Thomas was the first building on the bridge to be completed. Built on the middle pier, downstream, it was apsidal in form with high windows and decorated pinnacles. The main chapel was on the level of the street with a crypt underneath, built into the bridge itself, which could be entered from above or from a landing place with stairs at water level. After the Dissolution it was converted into a grocer's shop and also used as a paper warehouse.

In 1212 there was a fire in Southwark and many people had taken to the bridge either to escape, or to view the conflagration, when the wind carried some burning material to the north end of the bridge and set it alight. The people on the bridge could not leave it that way and before they could escape the other way the south too was alight. 'Then came to aid them,' records Stowe, 'many ships and vessels, into which the multitude so unadvisedly rushed, that the ships being drowned they all perished. It was said, that through the fire and shipwreck there were destroyed about three thousand persons, whose bodies were found in part, or half burnt, besides those that were wholly burnt to ashes and could not be found.'

St Thomas did not save those souls—and surely, anyway, Stowe must have been wildly exaggerating for this would have been a prodigious tragedy in a city with a population of not much more than 30,000. Either his protection or the more airy aspect of the houses on the bridge do seem to have made it a healthy place: during the Black Death in 1349, when half the country's population died, and the great Plague of 1665, which carried off forty per cent of London's population, only two deaths are recorded of people living on the bridge.

At the beginning of the reign of Edward I so little attention had been given to bridge repairs (the income going into the pocket of the previous queen) that the bridge was becoming ruinous. A severe winter with frosts eating into the heart of the structure caused five arches to collapse. Other bridges in the country suffered too, including the one at Rochester on the Canterbury route. Four London guilds were founded to look after and repair the bridge and, in addition to these and the usual tradesmen's guilds, there was another whose purpose was to aid its members in going off on pilgrimage to distant shrines.

London Bridge continued to play an important part in the history of the capital, but we must return to our pilgrimage and set off across the Thames, for there are many memories of the pilgrims and of St Thomas in Southwark on the other bank.

It was here that 'mad Matilda' warned the archbishop to 'fear the knife'. The church of St Mary Overie still stands on the right, although the priory has long gone and the church, now a cathedral, is today known as St Saviour's; while beyond the cathedral, among the warehouses that still line the river, is a wall with a great rose window, all that survives of the palace of the bishops of Winchester, where Thomas stayed on that attempted last visit to the capital. Here, in Elizabethan times, were the stews of London and the beargardens and theatres at which the plays of Shakespeare and his contemporaries were performed. To the left of the bridge was the Hospital of St Thomas—founded, some claim, by the saint, and certainly named in his honour. At the Dissolution the church was bought by the citizens of London and the hospital repaired for the care of the poor and sick, Edward VI adding to its endowment. Nothing survives of the original building.[3]

There was a busy high street leading down from the bridge and it was lined by numerous inns. John Stowe, writing in the sixteenth century, looks back to Chaucer's time when he describes the

> many fair inns, for the receipt of travellers, by these signs, the Spurre, Christopher, Bull, Queene's Head, Tabarde, George, Hart, Kinge's Head, etc. Amongst the which, the most ancient is the Tabard, so called of the sign, which, as we now term it, is of a jacket or sleeveless coat, whole before, open on both sides, with a square collar, winged at the shoulders; a stately garment of the old time, commonly worn of noblemen and others, both at home and abroad in the wars, but then (to wit in the wars) their arms embroidered, or otherwise depict upon them, that every man by his coat of arms might be known from others: but now these tabards are only worn by the heralds, and be called their coats of arms in service; for the inn of the tabard, Geoffrey Chaucer, esquire, the most famous poet of England, in commendation thereof, writeth thus:

> > '*Bifil that in that seson, on a day,*
> > *In Southwerk at the Tabard, as I lay,*
> > *Redy to wenden on my pilgrymage*
> > *To Caunterbury with ful devout corage,*
> > *At nyght was come into that hostelrye*
> > *Wel nyne and twenty in a compaignye,*
> > *Of sondry folk, by aventure yfalle*
> > *In felaweshipe, and pilgrimes were they alle,*
> > *That toward Caunterbury wolden ryde.*
> > *The chambres and the stables weren wyde,*
> > *And wel we weren esed atte beste.*'[4]

Within this inn was also the lodging of the abbot of Hide (by the city of Winchester), a fair house for him and his train, when he came to that city to parliament.

The famous Tabard survived Stowe's day but was almost certainly destroyed in the fire which swept Southwark in 1676, although perhaps rebuilt after the old plan. In its later guise it was known as the Talbot—a dalmatian dog—but even that phoenix does not survive today, for it was demolished, with some regret, in 1875. It is easy to find where it stood provided you remember its change of name, for the courts to the left of the street are all named after the inns that stood around them: King's Head, White Hart, George Inn, Talbot, Queen's Head and Spur Inn Yards. Cross Newcomen

Street and there follows Mermaid Court—that other famous inn where Shakespeare, Ben Jonson and their cronies are known to have supped. Of all the inns only a small part of the old George remains—post 1676, but nevertheless in the style of the inn yards, with balconies around, in which Shakespeare's strolling players used to give performances—and where today plays may still be seen during Southwark's summer festival. Perhaps some of these features would have been much the same two centuries earlier.

Apart from the George Inn there is little to suggest the pilgrim times in Southwark, but the Borough High Street does still retain a number of older houses, and the shape and feel of an old high street which reminds one at least of Dickens' or even Dr Johnson's London and gives a sense of continuity although the heavy traffic thwarts attempts to conjure any real atmosphere of the past. In the Middle Ages, and even up to Shakespeare's time, there were many fine houses of prelates and nobles in the neighbourhood, and these houses would have been circled about by gardens and orchards, far different from the present scene.

The way to Canterbury lies along the Old Kent Road, which may be reached by the conveniently named Tabard Street. At the junction of the two roads once stood a cross pointing the way to Bermondsey Abbey, which stood a little downstream of Southwark and may have attracted the attentions of many pilgrims before they set off on the main part of their journey. Here was the 'Rood of Barmsey', a wonder-working crucifix—though not so marvellous as the one at Boxley.

The Old Kent Road is long and more famous from the Victorian music-hall song of a cockney coster that Albert Chevalier made popular[5] than for any particular sights. There are numerous public houses which recall by their

The Tabard Inn, an engraving from John Urry's 1722 edition of Chaucer which may have been drawn from the memory of those who knew the hostelry before the fire of 1676. (*British Library*.)

names that this was the road along which cattle would have been driven in from the lush pastures of Kent: The Dun Cow, The Kentish Drovers, and so on. Perhaps some of them long since were ancient alestakes. At number 320, at the corner of Albany Road, where the two-mile stone from London once stood, is a tavern called the Thomas A' Becket, which marks Chaucer's pilgrims' first stopping place, St Thomas Waterings. There was a pool or stream here, now disappeared or channelled underground, where horses could be watered, and no doubt an alestake for human refreshment, while a more sinister sight might be the corpse of some criminal dangling from a gibbet, for this was a famous execution place for the county of Surrey.

The road now breaks its straight advance to negotiate New Cross and reach the bridge across the river Ravensbourne at Deptford, in the Middle Ages a village well into the countryside. Straight on up the hill, taking what are now called Blackheath and Shooters Hills, the pilgrims came to Blackheath itself where, a few years before Chaucer wrote his *Tales*, the peasants, raised in rebellion by Wat Tyler and John Ball, gathered before their march on London.

Tyler's rebels had come from Canterbury. The Kentish rebels gathered first at Maidstone, where they were joined by bands from other parts of the country, attacked the archbishop's palace and freed John Ball, the revolutionary priest whose simple, communistic version of Christianity was as unacceptable to the rulers of his time as it would be to most people of power today:

> *When Adam delved and Eve span*
> *Who was then the gentleman*

he preached. The peasants made it clear that their enemies were the nobles and the landowning classes, and in particular those powerful barons who formed the boy-king Richard II's council; they proclaimed their loyalty to the king. In June 1381 they marched to Canterbury and were enthusiastically welcomed by the people. They ransacked the palace of Archbishop Sudbury, who was also Chancellor (unlike Thomas he saw no problem in holding both offices—and he did not think much of Thomas either). This was not an undisciplined mob, as the nobility liked to think. On their march to London they met the queen, travelling the opposite way, to Canterbury; their quarrel was not with her and they stood back to give her way—although she, in panic, turned back and fled to London. The citizens of London welcomed the rebels as warmly as had those of Canterbury. They stormed the Tower and dragged out Archbishop Sudbury to strike off his head on Tower Hill. But their idealism lead nowhere. Their vague idea of a Great Society crumbled when, at a meeting between king and rebels at Smithfield, outside the gates of London, one of the nobles rode up and killed Wat Tyler. The boy king, by a stroke of instinctive diplomacy, called out that he was their leader and that they should follow him. The rebels quietly dispersed and then, leaderless and dispirited, were ruthlessly put down and all the concessions which the king had been forced to make were withdrawn. England's first real attempt at a popular revolution had failed.

What did the pilgrims of Chaucer's time think as they crossed the heath? Did the poor dream of rising again and creating an egalitarian society? Did the rich, professing a devout Christianity as they travelled to St Thomas' shrine, question the world they lived in? Perhaps some even thought of Sudbury as a kind of martyr—but he would not have approved of their pilgrimage. Meeting a party on their way to Canterbury he once suggested that they would be better to stay at home and work. He was hated by the common people, not because he was a churchman—there were many other poor priests who joined John Ball and the rebels—but because as Chancellor he helped to levy heavy taxes (which in those days penalised the poor while the rich would often pay out very little), and his Christianity was clearly not that of the ordinary people whose beliefs echoed the principles of the very earliest pilgrims. Perhaps, if the nobles had not been so thorough in their suppression, Wat Tyler might have become a saint.

It is too easy to think of the age of pilgrimage as a time of peaceful devotion. It was a time of violent social change, of civil and national wars as families and factions struggled for power. It was an age of violence and squalor as well as priestly prayers. The corpses hanging from the gibbet at St Thomas Waterings, or any number of others along the road, had probably been condemned for some petty crime that was the only way in which they could fill an empty belly while the nobility, literally, got away with wholesale murder.

From the heights of Blackheath the travellers would look down on the great curve of the river Thames at the shipping sailing to and from the merchants' wharves of London. Below, down by the river, beside the marshes was the village of Greenwich, where Chaucer says the women were shrews. On the heights, where the Royal observatory, Flamsteed House, now stands, Duke Humphrey built a fortified tower when he enclosed the park of Greenwich in 1433. (The royal palace where Elizabeth I was born came later.) It was at Greenwich that St Alphage, Archbishop of Canterbury at the time of Cnut, had been martyred by the Danes. Looking back, the pilgrims would have seen London and the spire of St Paul's rising above the bulk of the Tower of London, but ahead there was still a climb up the rest of Shooters Hill before the descent towards Welling.

The modern traveller is still surrounded by the buildings of the metropolis and will be travelling through the fringes of London for many miles to come —administrative London now reaches out to include the Borough of Bexley —but the medieval traveller had left London behind and entered the county of Kent even before he crossed the wooden bridge over the Ravensbourne. In some respects the Kent countryside must have been like that of today—

apples and cherries were abundant but the hop fields and oast houses which, until the last decade, were such a feature of the scene were not yet known. Hops did not come to England until 1524: before that beer was made from cereals. William Lambarde, although writing thirty years after the end of the pilgrimage, gave a picture of an abundantly fertile land. Although in his time many of the enclosed park lands were being disforested, 'wood occupieth the greatest proportion even til this day'. Great stretches of the Forest of Blean remained near Canterbury and the countryside past Shooter's Hill, near Gad's Hill and beyond Chatham were still heavily wooded. There were no 'great walks of waste ground', but, apart from common land, where the trees ended cultivation was intense. Horses, cattle and sheep were 'the largest of stature in each kind' and the fruit 'the most delicious and exquisite kinds that can be'.[6] Lambarde was a Kentish man and prejudiced, but there is no reason not to believe him. He describes the industries as husbandry, seafaring, working in stone, iron and fuel wood (charcoal) and, most importantly, the making of coloured woollen cloth, for which there was a considerable export trade. Canterbury had its dyers' quarter and alongside the river the famous 'weaver's houses' may still be seen.

The old open fields with strips assigned to different peasants began to disappear early in Kent and, well before the end of the Middle Ages, the land was being divided up into square plots, separated by hedges, which were more convenient for grazing cattle. Sometimes these small, hedge fields were made directly from the original woodland which was being cleared for agricultural use right through the Middle Ages. This was easier in Kent, where the ready availability of pasture made less necessary the availability of open fields for stubble grazing. Nevertheless, it was a wilder landscape than today's, with much smaller settlements and long unpeopled stretches between them.

From Welling there is a gradual climb to Bexley Heath and an undulating route to Dartford and the crossing of the Darent. The name suggests a ford, but there was a regular ferry from the time of Edward II, and in the reign of Henry IV a bridge was built. Here, perhaps, sixteen miles from London, many pilgrims would make their first halt for the night, for it seems there were numerous inns. The north chancel of the parish church was dedicated to St Thomas, and there was once an important chantry here of St Edmund which attracted pilgrims of its own. (St Edmund was an East Anglian king who was captured by the Danes: they tied him to a tree and, St Sebastian-like, shot arrows at him until he died.) From 1349 there was also a wealthy priory associated with the shrine which may have offered hospitality. By the bridge, in 1452, Trinity Hospital was built out over the river (a practice we shall find again in Canterbury), and there was also a house of the Knights Templar, although it may have been only for the use of their own Order.

From Dartford there was a choice of route. The original Roman Watling Street pushed straight ahead to Strood with, in the middle, a slight detour to take in the village of Betsham, a half mile north of Southfleet, but another route from Dartford veered away to the north to skirt Gravesend. Today the main route follows Watling Street, but in the seventeenth century, according to contemporary maps, the northern branch was the major route. Pilgrims may have travelled either way. Certainly some travellers came to Gravesend by river, and it is reported that there were some buildings known as St Thomas' houses which were traditionally a stopping-place for pilgrims,[7] but a great fire swept the town in 1727 destroying most of it, and no evidence seems to survive.

William Shakespeare also gives us evidence that pilgrims used this route for, although he wrote Henry IV Part 1 sixty years after the pilgrimage had ended, memories last longer and, in Act I Scene 2, he has Prince Hal, Falstaff and Poins plotting an escapade at Gad's Hill where 'there are pilgrims going to Canterbury with rich offerings, and traders riding to London with fat purses'. And Falstaff robs a party of travellers, to be himself in turn set upon by Prince Hal and Poins. This is not only evidence that pilgrims used this route but a reminder that here was a place where brigandage was rife and, like Shooters Hill, a favourite spot for highwaymen in later centuries as well. On the other route it is probable that there was a regular halt at Singlewell— the old spelling was Shinglewell, the well with a tiled cover—and a mile further on there is a well near Chalk known as St Thomas' Well. Between the two roads, and accessible from each, is Swanscombe, where there was a shrine of St Hilderforth, who apparently offered particular ease to those suffering from madness or melancholia.

At Strood the two routes join and, as has been suggested, it is possible that some pilgrims travelling up the Old Road came up the west bank of the Medway and joined the London route here. At Strood, as well as the Templar's Manor which has already been described, there was a lazar hospital (the tower of its chapel of St Nicholas survives) on the main London road and a hospital for pilgrims and other travellers founded by Bishop Gilbert de Glanville in about 1190, which was usually known as the Newark or New Work and of which some fragments survived into this century. According to Polydore Vergil, a papal representative sent to England to collect Peter's Pence, once, when Thomas rode through the little town, the people of Strood docked the tail of the archbishop's own horse. This sounds like a corruption of the docking by the nephew of Robert de Broc and, since it was not published until 1546, there was plenty of time for distortion to have occurred. However, the writer says, in consequence the archbishop indignantly cursed those responsible for the outrage and decreed that henceforth their children should be born with tails. Another version of the story places the outrage against St Augustine, and the only sure thing is that it found a place in local folklore.

Rochester, which lies on the opposite bank of the Medway from Strood, was the Roman town of Durobrivae, and some of its ancient walls and ramparts still remain, but before that it was a centre of Belgic civilisation. Rochester was an important stopping place for travellers from the earliest times. Its cathedral was founded in 604.

Approaching from the west, from the hilltops even before they reached Strood, medieval pilgrims saw the same landmarks on the other bank as the traveller does today: the solid mass of the keep of the Norman castle and the squatter tower of the cathedral nesting at its side.

The crossing was probably originally a ford, although the river would not be fordable today; then, at least a century before the Norman conquest, came a wooden bridge which survived, although often in a dangerous condition, until 1387, before being replaced by a fine new bridge of stone which rivalled that of London. On the quayside opposite the site of the original bridge, and to the right of the modern one, stands the Bridge Chapel, founded by the men who paid for the bridge: Sir Robert Knolles and Sir John de Cobham. Here three masses were said each day, 'that travellers might have an opportunity of being present at these offices'.[8] The chapel was restored in 1937 and is now the Board Room of the Bridge Wardens, officers of the trust founded in 1391 to maintain the bridge, to help which Archbishop Morton in 1489 granted an indulgence 'remitting from purgatory all manner of Sins for forty days to all persons contributing towards the repair of the Bridge'.

There are reports of accidents from the old bridge when it fell into disrepair—especially after the bad winter of 1282—and in 1300 Edward I had to make reparation to the owner of a horse that he had requisitioned which was blown right off the bridge into the river and drowned. There is a legend of a minstrel or harper who entertained the pilgrims passing through Rochester; he also was blown off the bridge but was saved by calling on the Virgin and harping a hymn in her honour, even as he was carried by the current of the

Today, as in the Middle Ages, the Norman keep of Rochester castle and the squatter tower of the cathedral dominate the view from the opposite side of the River Medway. The medieval bridge had its foot facing the chapel to the far left of the picture.

tide. Another near drowning is recorded in the miracle books of Christ Church and illustrated in the stained glass of Canterbury. A young lad of Rochester, called Robert, fell into the Medway one afternoon at about three o'clock and was not dragged out until after the bell had rung for vespers. He was senseless and blue in the face and, although he was hung up by his feet, not a drop of water came out of him. He was rolled in a tub to make him vomit, without effect, and many said he was dead. His mother, who as soon as she heard what had happened began to call upon St Thomas, now invoked him again and began measuring the body with a thread, promising a silver thread of the same length if the martyr would save her son's life. Water immediately gushed out of little Robert's mouth and he sat up restored to life.[9]

The bridge foot leads immediately into the High Street, where there is much of historical interest to see, though nothing of the Middle Ages, although there are thirteenth-century vaults beneath the George Inn on the left. It is easier to capture the atmosphere of coaching days and Dickens in this narrow thoroughfare than that of pilgrim times. The castle is, however, a magnificent relic of earlier centuries, and much of the cathedral is surviving Norman work.

About 1080 Bishop Gundulph, who built Rochester castle (although not the surviving keep, which was raised more than half a century later) and the White Tower in London, built a new cathedral, to replace the ruinous Saxon one, and founded a Benedictine monastery. Gundulph's Tower, on the north at the angle of the transept and the aisle, although reduced in height in 1779 by about a third, may have had a defensive purpose. Parts of the crypt also survive from his building, but most that remains is hidden by later work. The west front and nave date almost entirely from the twelfth century, although the west towers were by 1892 so decayed that they were rebuilt, reproducing the arrangement shown in old prints, and the great west window is an insertion of the fifteenth century in perpendicular style. The eastern end of the cathedral was largely rebuilt in the thirteenth century, while the central tower and the west end of the nave were replaced early in the fourteenth, when money seems to have run out leaving six bays of the Norman nave untouched.

Rochester's third bishop, Paulinus, who came to the see in 644, was canonized in 1087, and Bishop Gundulph solemnly translated his relics from the Saxon cathedral to the new Norman one, and placed them in a silver shrine where they attracted pilgrims of their own. The rise of the cult of St Thomas lessened the appeal of St Paulinus' shrine and, before the end of the eleventh century, the church was running so short of funds that the monks melted down the silver of the shrine. One of St Thomas' own pilgrims was to restore their fortunes. This was a baker called William, from Perth, Scotland, a devout man whom it was said gave every tenth loaf that he baked as alms for the poor. He was making his way to Canterbury, and perhaps *en route* for the Holy Land itself, when he came to Rochester and sought shelter at the monastery for the night of May 20th, 1201. In the morning he departed, not, it seems, by Watling Street but southward, towards the Pilgrims' Way. He got no further than Delce Lane, for there his body was found. There was no sign of the valuables which he had carried, or of the servant who accompanied him, who, it was therefore presumed, was the murderer. The body was borne back to the cathedral at Rochester and interred there with great honour. By the tomb miracles began to happen and, at length, in 1256, Bishop Laurence went to Rome and obtained the official canonization of the popular saint. The offerings at his shrine restored the monastery's fortunes and paid for the rebuilding of the cathedral until presumably another cult replaced in fashion that of St William and the rebuilding was brought to a halt. All that remains of the shrine of William of Perth is a simple marble slab in the north-east transept.

To help recapture the image of the medieval church it is worth seeking out the effigy of Bishop John de Sheppey, found embedded in a wall in 1925, and now to be seen in the presbytery. Its immurement preserved its original colours and showed how medieval statues, and indeed many churches' walls, were colourfully painted, not the cool stone we see today. There are the remains of some fine paintings on the walls of Rochester's crypt, and on the northeast pier of the choir is an intriguing painting of a Wheel of Fortune, with dame Fortune at the hub, a king about to topple from position at the top of the arc and figures clambering through the spokes between. Another picture, rather faded now, which greeted travellers as they came through the west door into the south aisle shows St Christopher, protector of travellers until the Vatican recently pronounced him purely legendary, with the infant Christ upon his shoulders. There are paintings elsewhere too, and visitors should not miss the splendid carving of the arch around the door which led from the southeast transept to the chapter house.

In 1137 and 1179 the cathedral was ravaged by fire—although since the nave and west front are of mid-century date the damage cannot have been so serious as records suggest. Perhaps it was this fire, although the record books at Canterbury give it a date of 1177, which was the occasion of another miracle of St Thomas. A pilgrim, lodging in Rochester on his return from Canterbury, could find no berth except in the hut of a baker by the name of Gilbert. The hut caught fire, and the pilgrim saved it by leaping on to the roof with a phial of St Thomas' Water. Fixing it upon the end of a pole, like a spear's point, he used it to drive back the flames while the rest of the city was consumed. It is perhaps noteworthy that for once neither the name nor origin of the pilgrim are mentioned, or any other substantiation of the story given.[10]

From Rochester the pilgrims carried on along the Roman road, through Chatham, where there was a leper hospital just past the Rochester city wall, and over the open land of Rainham Down to Newington, a famous stage in the pilgrimage where they would have surely rested at the cross set up in the midst of the town. This marked the place where, on his final return to Canterbury, Archbishop Thomas had descended from his horse and confirmed a large number of the local children. The Canterbury miracle books record no less than fourteen miracles happening here. Six are cases of sight being restored to the blind, one is a girl half-paralyzed and dumb following a curse who was restored to health, while others are cures of lameness and deformity. Brother Benedict refers to many other cures at Newington of which 'the truth has not been perfectly sifted by us' and refrains from listing them, but he does include the strange way in which candles miraculously lit themselves, and a case where seven candles bought at the tomb became eight when Newington was reached.[11]

It became the custom among many pilgrims to present at the shrine a candle of the same height as themselves: being 'measured for a candle'.

Before Thomas' archiepiscopate there had been a nunnery at Newington which had been given the manor of Newington for its support, but there had been such conflict between the abbess and her sisters that they had strangled her in her bed and tipped her body into a pit, thereafter pointed out as the Nun Pit. The king reclaimed the manor and sent the sisters to the Isle of Sheppey. Later Henry II installed seven priests in their place—but one of them was murdered and four of his brethren were implicated in the death.

Only three miles past Newington is Sittingbourne, a town which probably owed its growth to the pilgrimage, and some of its taverns were established in pilgrim times: the Lion gave hospitality to Henry V on his return from Agincourt. West of the town, just off Water Lane Head, was Schamel Hermitage, with a chapel dedicated to St Thomas, and to the east there was a leper hospital at Swanstree.

The road now traverses a number of hills, rising to the height of Beacon Hill, one of many places equipped with signal beacons along the route, and then drops down to Ospringe where it is still possible to visit the Maison Dieu. In fact very little survives of the hospital, founded by Hubert de Burgh and re-endowed by Henry III in 1234. St Mary of Ospringe originally consisted of accommodation for pilgrims and other travellers, homes for pensioners, a chapel and quarters for its priests. The king added a chamber (*Camera Regis*) where he and his suite could lodge when travelling the Dover Road. The strain put upon the finances of the establishment by royal visits, and the practice of installing royal pensioners at the hospital (not as ordinary inmates of course) made the situation worse—and the foundation does not seem to have been a very stable one. Several times feudal dues were waived because 'its goods barely suffice for the maintenance of the Master and brethren and of the weak and infirm persons there'.[12]

In the 1470s all the brethren died, and they were not replaced. The secular priests also left and the Master too, leaving the house deserted by 1483 so that the buildings reverted to the crown, while the Master, held responsible for all St Mary's debts, was declared an outlaw. Eventually, in 1516, the hospital was dissolved and its income given to St John's College, Cambridge, who continued to maintain the chapel and the chaplain's house but let out the rest.

The main part of the hospital was on the left of the road from London, with the present buildings opposite. The chapel and infirmary have not survived and what is left may be part of the brethren's buildings or the Camera Regis. The house now shown to the public on the right of Water Lane and that on the other side of the lane form what is left. Both are built on undercrofts and only the stone part of the buildings is original, the upper portions being constructed after the pilgrim period.

Pilgrims would certainly have found hospitality in Faversham, either in the numerous inns or at the abbey, which was a prosperous foundation. It was established by King Stephen, who was buried there, as also were his queen and his son Eustace. Excavation has shown that the church was grandiose in scale. Among its relics was a portion of the true cross, presented by Godfrey de Bouillon. Part of the abbey gatehouse survives in number 80 Abbey Street, and the low stone building leaning against it was once the gatehouse chapel. This house has another claim to fame, for it was here in 1550 that Thomas Arden, a former mayor of Faversham, was murdered by his wife, her lover and his henchmen. The case became so famous that Holinshed included it in his history and it is the subject of *Arden of Faversham*, a play published in 1592 and once attributed to Shakespeare.

On the creek not far from the abbey are medieval warehouses, and Abbey Street, which runs down to the market place, is lined with sixteenth- and seventeenth-century buildings, some of which date from pilgrim times. The house of the abbey bailiff became a tavern—the Globe, now a private home known as Globe House—and there are excellent examples of Tudor and later domestic architecture. Just off Abbey Street is the parish church of St Mary of Charity, whose pierced-obelisk steeple atop its eighteenth-century tower belies the much older church beneath. Chancel and transepts were rebuilt in the fourteenth century after the townsfolk had attacked the church in 1301 and, although Victorian restoration has disfigured some features, there are intriguing misericords for those who care to seek them out and some fine wall paintings, including nativity scenes with the magi and the shepherds, and a crucifixion.

The church was in the patronage of St Augustine's at Canterbury, but their jealousy of Christ Church did not prevent the north aisle of the church being dedicated to St Thomas, and at one time having a wall painting of his martyrdom. There was also an altar, to Saints Crispin and Crispianus, who, according to tradition, were shoemakers who fled from Roman persecution and settled in Faversham at the end of the third century—they are less known for their own lives today than because, as Shakespeare ensured that no one

The house where Arden of Faversham was murdered in 1550 had only recently been adapted from the entrance gate of the great abbey founded by King Stephen. The flint wall to the rear was part of the gatehouse chapel.

would forget, it was on their feast day that the battle of Agincourt was fought.

Faversham would probably be the last overnight stop for pilgrims on their way to Canterbury, if they did not press on to their destination, for it is only ten miles from the cathedral city. The way now lies up Boughton Hill and through Boughton Street into the Forest of Blean, the reputed haunt of footpads, smugglers and highwaymen. The thick trees no doubt gave protection to the outlaws of the Middle Ages too, for it is for this stretch, so near to their goal, that the Canon's Yeoman hurried to catch up Chaucer's pilgrims to travel with them into Canterbury.

The modern traveller emerges from the wood before he reaches Upper Harbledown, and in the distance may sight the roofs and towers of Canterbury; but the pilgrim traveller would still have been hemmed in by trees until he dropped down into the valley and the clearing made by the hospital at the village of Harbledown, where he might find himself mingling with travellers who had come to Canterbury along the Old Road from the west.

11 The Golden Angel

Woot ye nat where ther stant a litel toun
Which that ycleped is Bobbe-up-and-doun,
Under the Blee, in Canterbury Weye?

THE LITTLE VILLAGE of Harbledown, close by the Blean Forest, is where Chaucer sets the telling of the Maunciple's delightful moral tale of the crow who told the truth to his own ill. It is the last place that he mentions on the road to Canterbury, and his pilgrims are nearly at their destination.

From Upper Harbledown the road drops down and then steeply up again—bob-up-and-down is an apt nickname—and on the right, just above the road, is the ancient church of St Nicholas. It was here, in 1174, that Henry II, having ridden hard from Southampton, dismounted from his horse to begin his penance. Did Chaucer's pilgrims break their journey here? The poem records no devotional stops at any point along the way but perhaps, like Henry, they went into the church to pray. It belongs to an ancient hospital to whose inhabitants Henry gave an income of twenty marks a year. The hospital was founded in 1084 by Archbishop Lanfranc for the relief of lepers, and the nave of the church of St Nicholas dates from his time, although the north wall was pierced for the addition of the north aisle a hundred years later and the south aisle was added in the fourteenth century. Lanfranc provided for sixty inmates, half men, half women and 'skilful, patient and kindly . . . watchers' to care for them. This must then have been on the edge of the forest, for a charter of Henry I calls it 'the Hospital of the Wood of Blean' and gives the inmates permission to clear ten perches of thicket all around. Thomas permitted them a one-horse cart to collect timber each day' and Henry II's grant is to the 'leprous of Herbaldown', so we may imagine that by his time the hillside had been cleared and was flourishing pasture.

Gradually the scourge of leprosy disappeared from England and the inmates became the generally sick and aged. At the end of the thirteenth century they were given uniforms: a hooded tunic for the brethren and for the sisters dark russet cloaks with white veils and black over-veils, and in winter hoods of black wool. Their living quarters were several times rebuilt and today are a row of almshouses built in 1840.

The Hospital is reached today up steep steps on the right, about halfway up the hill, which lead to a timbered gatehouse. The road is a steep and deep-cut hollow way, a little wider today perhaps than when Erasmus passed this way returning from Canterbury. He came with Dean Colet, but describes the visit in a dialogue discussing pilgrimage between 'Ogygyus' and another. Ogygyus (Erasmus himself) described what happened:

Not far from Canterbury we came into a great hollow and straightway, morover bowing so down, with hills of either side, that a man cannot escape, nor it cannot be avoided, but he must needs ride that way. Upon the left hand of the way, there is an almshouse for old people, from them runneth one out, as soon as they hear a horseman coming, he casteth holy water upon him, and anon he offereth him the overleather of a shoe bound about with an iron hoop, wherein is a glass like a precious stone, they that kiss it give a piece of money.

Gratian [his companion, Colet] rode upon my left hand near the alms-house, he cast holy water upon him. He took it in worth not so. When the shoe was proferred him, he asked what he meant by it, saith he, it is St Thomas shoe. Thereat he fumed and was very angry, and turned toward me: what (saith he) meane these beasts, that would have us kiss the shoes of every good man? Why do they not likewise give us to kiss the spittle, and other filth and dirt of the body? I was sorry for the old man, and gave him a piece of money to comfort him withall. [1]

None of the brethren waylay you in the road today, although the 'glass like a precious stone' can perhaps still be seen in a large oval crystal set into a bowl which is known as 'Becket's shoebuckle'. It is on display in the hospital's hall, together with other treasures, but to see them and to visit the church you must ask for the sub-prior at number six.

The Norman flint-built church now has a fourteenth-century roof with tiebeams and kingposts, and until 1815 there was a thirteenth-century screen right down the centre of the nave to separate the brethren from the sisters of the hospital. There are still axe-carved thirteenth-century benches and stalls to be seen and some fine fourteenth-century glass with pretty borders of Canterbury Bells and fleurs de lys. This glass was in private ownership in Canterbury during the last century but was found to fit the stone tracery of the windows exactly, purchased for a pound, and restored to its original home. There are also fourteenth-century wall paintings of the Annunciation on the splays of the east window. The east end of the south aisle was formerly a chapel dedicated to St Thomas.

The floor of the church has a pronounced slope, probably to make it easier to wash after the lepers had attended service, but it is a feature that occurs in other churches built to hold large numbers of pilgrims: it has been suggested that dirt they brought in from the highway made frequent cleaning necessary. [2]

The Black Prince's Well at Harbledown, reputed to have healing waters, especially useful for eye conditions.

Behind the almshouses and lower down the hillside is a spring, once reputed to have healing properties. Tradition claims that the Black Prince drank from it in 1357 and that, as he lay dying, asked for some of this healing water to be brought. It is now known as the Black Prince's Well, and a simple stone arch with a keystone bearing the Prince of Wales' feathers stands over it. The carving is probably not ancient for it does not appear on a woodcut of the well made in 1845.[3]

As medieval travellers on the London Road came over the hill from Harbledown to descend what is now Mill Lane they would have seen glittering in the distance before them the sight they had been waiting for: the gilded figure of the Archangel Michael shining above the solid bulk of the Norman cathedral. This famous golden angel surmounted the pyramidal roof of the sturdy central tower of the old cathedral, announcing the glory of God to all corners of the world.

We do not see that golden figure today when, a little further down the hill, where the road joins the A2, we see the cathedral rising in the distance across a great expanse of tarmac and through a tangle of traffic signs, lamp standards and articulated lorries. The splendid perpendicular architecture that still manages to dominate this ugly highway (given the grand title of Rheims Way!) was not built until two centuries after Thomas death. The earlier pilgrims would have seen the solid west front of Lanfranc's cathedral with its tiered central tower, much lower than the later one, and with similar but slimmer towers on either side of the facade. In a pictorial plan drawn to show the 'new waterworks' (see page 37) these towers too seem to have their own golden cherubs—or are they rather podgy weathercocks? Gervase describes them as 'gilded pinnacles'. In the further distance, beyond the cathedral's towers and the encircling walls of Canterbury the pilgrims would also see the even taller church of the Abbey of St Augustine.

St Augustine's now is little more than a few ruins and an outline on the grass, and the dominant feature of the scene is the great central tower of the cathedral, Bell Harry Tower, built about 1500. The west front and southwest tower date from the early fifteenth century and the northeast tower replaced Lanfranc's original only in 1832 to give today's almost too perfect symmetry.

It is easy to imagine the devout, their spirits lightened by prayer in the chapel of St Thomas at Harbledown, their bodies refreshed by a draught from the healing well, coming over this last hill and seeing the roofs of Canterbury before them and the noble fabric of Thomas' own church, falling upon their knees as they looked down at their journey's end as other pilgrims did when they saw the city of Jerusalem. I doubt if you would feel that urge as you come upon the scene today. But the pilgrims did not follow the route that the lorries take—that is an 'improvement' of very recent years and not the ancient Watling Street, nor the Old Road of prehistoric times.

A turning to the left, called London Road, suggests another, if not the original, route and leads down to the church of St Dunstan where Henry II put on his penitential shift. A coursed flint wall is probably the only surviving part of the Norman church but, despite Victorian restoration, there are still attractive features in decorated and perpendicular style. It was to this church that Margaret Roper, daughter of Sir Thomas More, brought her father's severed head when it was taken down from London Bridge. It is buried now in the Roper vault beneath the church.

Turning sharply right into St Dunstan's Street, the traveller looks straight down to the West Gate of the city. This is the only gate remaining of the seven which pierced the medieval walls of Canterbury. Long stretches of the walls remain, built of flint in the fourteenth and fifteenth centuries. At the southwest corner of the city is the keep of the Norman castle, built with bands of Caen stone between the flint, probably in the early part of the twelfth century. In 1817 the upper courses of its walls were demolished, but it was probably never as high as the one at Rochester. Also within the city walls is the Dane John (probably from *donjon*, the medieval French word for a great square tower like that of the castle, and misused in English in the word dungeon). It was probably a motte, an earth mound which would have been fortified with a wooden palisade and keep. It is uncertain whether it is Norman or was built much earlier, for Canterbury has been fortified since Roman times. The Dane John's present form dates only from 1790 when it was reshaped as part of the gardens in which it stands.

The approach to the West Gate is lined with attractive seventeenth- and eighteenth-century houses and inns, some of them perhaps older, which served those travellers arriving at the city after curfew. On the left a gateway-arch of moulded brick is all that stands of the Roper's family home.

At the foot of St Dunstan's Street flows a branch of the river Stour, clear in its shallow bed with the green weed streaming in the current. In the Middle Ages it was crossed by a drawbridge let down from the gate, which could also be closed by a massive portcullis, the grooves for which can still be seen. The present West Gate, two massive round towers with a narrow arch between them, was built by Archbishop Sudbury in 1375–81. There are machicolations above the central arch, a jutting terrace with holes in its floor through which debris and missiles could be poured down upon attackers. The predecessor of this gate had a chapel over it dedicated to the Holy Cross and when it was replaced a new church was built just to the south. During the Middle Ages this church had a fraternity of Corpus Christi which presented a miracle play.

The city accounts carried a number of entries of payments in connection with a play about St Thomas performed upon St Thomas' Eve. There was a pageant cart, drawn through the principal streets of the city by ten horses, which was set up with a representation of the altar in the transept of the cathedral and presented a very realistic version of the martyrdom. The four knights appeared and struck down the martyr, his blood flowed and an angel turned and waved its wings, welcoming him to heaven. In the years

West Gate, Canterbury, a fine example of city fortification.

1503 and 1504 there are payments for wood, nails, tallow and other materials
and for labour for building the cart, a penny for beer to refresh the craftsmen,
material to make St Thomas' costume, for washing his vestments, for forging
armour for the knights, for painting heads for the angel and for St Thomas,
for candles, paint, the hire of a sword and for garaging the cart in a barn.
One penny is also recorded as payment for the operator who crouched inside
the altar to make the blood flow and the angel spin after the saint had died.
Other charges for replacements and expenses appear in 1513 and 1514 and
again in 1521 and 1522, so the play was almost certainly an annual occurrence.
It was banned after the destruction of the shrine, but revived during the reign
of Mary Tudor.

Ahead through the West Gate lies St Peter's Street, now, as in the Middle
Ages, the main street of the city. It is an attractive medley of brick and half-
timbering from all periods, the double overhanging stories of the sixteenth
century mixing with modern shopfronts, churches and public buildings.
Some areas of Canterbury were flattened by the bombs of World War Two,
but most of its streets still follow the medieval pattern and but little of
historical value was destroyed. In one sense there was a gain, for the destruction of medieval Canterbury made possible the excavation of the layers
beneath, and much more was learned about the Roman town of Durovernum

over which it had been built. A mosaic pavement of a Roman house of the second-third century can still be seen below ground level to the east of Butchery Lane. Some of the inelegant modern buildings which have arisen are not so welcome, although the restriction of certain areas to pedestrians does compensate a little for the acres of ugly car park that the traffic planners find desirable.

In the sixth century Canterbury was the capital of Ethelbert, King of Kent and later ruler of southern England. This Ethelbert married Bertha, the Christian daughter of a Merovingian king, and she worshipped in the church of St Martin which survived from Roman times and was presumably restored and reconsecretated for her devotions. It was also enlarged and partially rebuilt in the seventh century. It was to Ethelbert's and Bertha's court that St Augustine came to convert those Saxons, or Angels as he called them, whom he thought so like angels when he saw them offered in the slave market of Rome. St Martin's became his headquarters but, according to Bede's history, when he succeeded in converting the king he was given another surviving Roman church, long converted to pagan use, which became the first cathedral, dedicated to the Holy Saviour—or Christ Church as it is usually called in English. The missionary archbishop also founded an abbey, dedicated to St Peter and St Paul, where he himself was buried and which is now known as St Augustine's. Here too were laid to rest the Saxon kings and other saintly archbishops: St Laurence, St Mellitus, St Justus, St Honorius, St Deusdedit, St Theodore, St Berhtwald, St Tatwin, St Adrian (all Augustine's successors as archbishops) and relics of St Mildred all lay in the abbey, close by the shrine of Augustine himself and the Saxon kings from Ethelbert on. The abbey claimed the burial of all Canterbury's archbishops and was long in rivalry with Christ Church to whom it eventually had to concede this right.

At Christ Church there were the remains of later archbishop-saints and other relics—by the time of Theobald's archiepiscopate they included St Audoen, St Wilfrid, St Odo, St Dunstan, St Elfheah, the heads of St Swithin and St Fursey and relics of St Blaise. So many holy cadavers brought many pilgrims to Christ Church and to St Augustine's long before Thomas' martyrdom, and provision was made for their accommodation at both establishments. At St Augustine's a guest hall stood a little to the south of Fyndon's Gate, and at Christ Church there were both the Cellarer's Hall and the North Hall for visitors. These opened onto the west side of the Green Court, the secular part of the priory, just inside its main entrance gate (today there is another gate to go through first) and which kept the guests away from the monk's quarters. Both halls are marked on the 'waterworks' plan, being labelled Domus Hospitum and Aula Nova, and the fine Norman entrance stair to the latter still survives.

When the cult of St Thomas brought many more pilgrims to the city further provisions had to be made. Over the years the accommodation in the priory was expanded. The New Lodgings, thirty metres in length and ten wide, were built where the Deanery now stands on the east side of Green Court, and on the south Prior Chillenden built some better chambers to accommodate rather higher-class visitors. To the east, beyond the cathedral, is 'Meister Omers', another of Chillenden's more comfortable additions, built into the perimeter wall of the monastic precinct. It is used today as a boarding house of the King's School, and after Victorian 'restoration' it is difficult to believe that this flint-walled building with its 1860 windows is really a genuine survival from 1400. It has been suggested that Chillenden's Chambers were not built to accommodate an excess of pilgrims but in the hope that better accommodation might attract more of them, for by 1400 numbers were considerably less than in the heyday of the pilgrimage.

At the opposite end of the scale a few poor pilgrims might find accommodation at St Thomas' Hospital, or the Eastbridge Hospital as it is also known, which was built across the Stour on the west of the main street, where St Peter's Street changes its name to become the High Street. Traditionally this hospital was founded by St Thomas; although that is generally thought unlikely, its first known master, Ralph, is believed to have been one of Thomas' nephews. There is a document extant which names an Edward fitzObold of St Peter's Street as the builder of the hospital, and it is most probably that he was the founder too. It could not have been very well endowed, for in 1203 Archbishop Hubert Walter gave the hospital the tithes of certain mills 'being moved thereto by the poverty and necessitous condition

The original Norman stair which led up to Christ Church Priory's 'new' guest hall

of the Hospital'.[4] At the beginning of the fourteenth century they received a royal licence to beg in the streets to raise money but this led to imposters asking for alms, and in 1312 the Sheriff and Bailiff of Canterbury were instructed to arrest anyone who fraudulently passed themselves off as agents of the Master or Brethren. St Thomas' has a chapel, a hall (presumably used as a refectory) and undercrofts to each, the rear of which formed the dormitory.

The rules of the foundation obliged them to 'receive wayfaring and hurt men' who might stay one night only, or more if they were too sick to depart, and there were beds for eight men and four women. They were allowed twenty loads of wood each year and fourpence a day for each person was allotted to provide their needs and sixpence a week for beer. Other costs included twenty shillings a year for a poor woman (who was to be over forty years) to wait upon them, and £10.6s.8d for a chantry priest to serve the chapel. The sums reflect that spiritual guidance was considered much more important than physical care: such hospitals did not set out to cure the sick—they cared for the soul rather than the body, strengthening it as the body decayed and preparing it for the life to come.

Part of the hospital's income came from land in the Forest of Blean, for which the rent was paid in kind: 'cocks and hens, a hundred and nineteen, and a third part of a hen, and a half a hen', an awkward computation that must have been easier to collect when it was eventually compounded for cash at the rate of 2½d for a cock and 3d for a hen.

Since the Reformation the hospital has passed through many vicissitudes: supressed during the reign of Edward VI it passed into the hands of the king and was used for the wounded garrison from Calais in the following reign. Refounded by Archbishop Parker, it was again disestablished and sold, and for a time the chapel was used as a school, but under Archbishop Whitgift it recovered its estates and was given new statutes. Today it still provides for ten brothers and sisters living in and an equal number living out. The inmates now have rooms in later buildings beyond the original hospital and visitors may see the old accommodation.

The street frontage dates mainly from the second half of the fourteenth century. Through the low doorway, made lower because the modern street level is above that of medieval times, there is a small vaulted hall with a tiny chapel to the left. On the floor above is the chapel proper, and behind, at right-angles, is the late twelfth-century room originally used as the main hall and refectory of the hospital. It is an elegant room, divided by an arcade of three arches and the traces of original oil paintings, parts of which have been carefully restored. There is an attractive figure of Christ in glory set within a mandorla, with the symbols of the Evangelists set around the almond shape in semicircles against its sides in a way characteristic of English work at the time, and echoed today in Graham Sutherland's tapestry in Coventry Cathedral. Only the eagle of St John is now clearly visible; the others have almost gone, as has a mural showing the martyrdom of St Thomas.

Directly beneath the refectory, a few steps down from the street level, is the undercroft which was the pilgrims' dormitory. There are supporting pillars down the length of the room and, to the right, partitions from pillar to wall separate each bay into a separate sleeping cubicle. The dormitory would accommodate eight men. Perhaps the women slept elsewhere, or perhaps there was originally some less permanent division as well. There is a small area in one corner up some steps which looks out over the Stour and which was probably a washing area. Only to the rear is one aware that the hospital is actually built out over the river.

There were other hospital foundations in Canterbury: one for Poor Priests is a little distance along Stour Street behind St Thomas', and clergy might have found a welcome there, although it was mainly a house for sick and aging priests. Part of the building was once the house of Adam of Charing, who was responsible for turning back Thomas' boat when he was trying to flee England, but the hospital was rebuilt in stone in 1373. The foundation was certainly before 1224, for a party of Franciscans, the first in Canterbury, stayed there on their arrival. They were later established at the Greyfriars, built across the river a little closer to the High Street. Parts of their surviving building are Saxon, but most of the friary buildings and their church have now disappeared, leaving only a small gabled building standing on two pairs of stone arches across the river. It is not clear what this surviving building was used for; John Newman[5] suggests that it may have been the warden's lodging, since there is a fireplace in the upper storey, while Laurance Goulder[6] proposes that the large room upstairs was a dormitory. He points out that a loose board in one of the lower rooms can be raised and that a similar device probably made it possible for the friars to catch fish from the river beneath, and perhaps to draw up water for their ablutions.

There were other hospitals where a bed might also have been found. That of St John in Northgate is the earliest almshouse in Canterbury, founded in 1084 by Archbishop Lanfranc—who had the chapel here divided as at Harbledown to separate men from women. It is still in use, although only the south nave of the chapel survives in the modern buildings, and the walls of the old hall now encircle part of the garden. In Castle Street was Maynards' Hospital, but the present building on the corner of Hospital Lane was not erected until 1708. Other monastic houses which might give a pilgrim shelter included the Austin Friars, which stood where the 'bus station does today; the Friars of Penance (known in England as the Friars of the Sack from the fabric of their habit), which was north of St Peter's Street; and until the fourteenth century a Convent of St Sepulchre (although so poor that it could have offered little to female travellers who knocked upon its gate). Blackfriars, built across the northern reaches of the Stour, was probably most able to offer accommodation. Given land beside the river by Henry III in 1237, the friars built a church and monastic buildings on both sides of the river, and an old print shows them linked by a parapetless bridge. What survive are the refectory on the east bank and what is thought to have been the guest hall on the opposite bank. Both date from the thirteenth century but the frater has been added to in the middle of the eighteenth century, when it became a Methodist meeting house, and is partly used today as a Christian Science reading room. The pulpit, from which a brother would have read the Latin scriptures and other sacred books at mealtimes, makes a strange spiritual companion to Mary Baker Eddy's texts. The guest hall now largely consists of comparatively modern work, although features of walls and windows from the fourteenth century still survive.

For those who preferred the freedom of an inn to the hospitality of the church there were many hostelries within the walls as well as those outside the West Gate. Most famous was one known as the Chequers of the Hope at the corner of Mercery Lane. The name may have derived from the squared cloth used to help in counting money (from which the word exchequer comes) placed over a barrel (hoop), or the chequer part may have been a gaming board—chess was then thought of rather as a game of poker might be today, and would be played in taverns.

It is here that Chaucer's pilgrims lodge in the continuation of the *Canterbury Tales* known as the *Tale of Beryn*:

> *They toke hir In, & loggit hem at mydmorowe, I trowe,*
> *Atte 'Checker of the hope,' that many a man doith knowe.*

The famous inn was largely destroyed by fire in 1865, but stone arcading survives on the ground floor and old pictures are another guide to its original appearance.

The author of the *Tale of Beryn* describes a garden at the rear: while the rest of the party go out to amuse themselves and see the town the Wife of Bath and the Prioress, too tired for sightseeing, take a short stroll there 'to see the herbis growe' which were so useful for 'sew and surgery' (cooking and medicines). The inn had a dormitory of one hundred beds and old descriptions suggest a building rather like an Elizabethan coaching inn but whether it was like that in the Middle Ages we cannot be certain.

In 1796 William Gostling wrote:

Great part of this lane seems formerly to have been for large inns. One part of the Chequer . . . takes up almost half the west of it, and another part, with its gates, reaches some way down High St, but perhaps not so far as it once did, a new house having been built there, and great alterations have been made almost everywhere. The corner shop indeed shows, by arches each way, in what manner the ground floor was built, and some others were joining to them within the memory of man, but now the whole being converted into tenements and shops, many of the windows sashed, and the well-timbered upper stories cased with roughcast: the extent of the old house cannot be guessed at but by its roof. Going thro the gate of it, we find on our left a staircase leading up to a gallery, which probably went round the whole court, when larger than it is now. Another also appears to have been above it, but it is now become part of several houses which wanted the room these galleries took up.[7]

Mercery Lane, with the Chequer of the Hope on the left and Christ Church Gate and the west towers of the cathedral beyond.

The Chequers, and the shops which have succeeded it, are actually built on land owned by Christ Church, and the building was originally put up as a pilgrim hostel by the priory. Prior Chillenden rebuilt the houses of Mercery Lane about 1400, and if one looks beyond the present divisions of the buildings, the modern shop fronts and the Georgian accretions, it is possible to recognize the massive timber framing and overhanging upper stories of the late Middle Ages in many of the streets outside the great gate to the cathedral precincts. Lenley's furniture shop in the Butter Market, the nearby Burgate Restaurant, the Cathedral Gate Hotel, the building on the corner of St Margaret Street facing Mercery Lane, and Boots on the opposite side of the lane from the Chequers, can all be identified as following the long dormitory plan of the pilgrim hostels,[8] and some of them still serve the same purpose, although the long dormitories have given way to a maze of smaller rooms and the accommodation provided is more luxurious than five centuries ago.

A view from a hotel room across to the flood-lit towers of the cathedral in the evening quiet, or down into the Butter Market at breakfast time, gives the visitor a feeling of old-world peace very different from the hustle and bustle of the shoppers, office workers and milling tourists of daytime Canterbury. But it is a sentimental error to think that tranquility was a quality of the past. The Middle Ages had no noisy lorries or loud car radios, but the over-merry crowd falling rowdily out of the inn at closing time and shattering the quiet of the Butter Market and the jostling crowds hurrying about their business are probably much like their medieval ancestors and closer to the lively scene of Canterbury at the height of the pilgrimage. Today there are not so very many hotels and lodging houses in Canterbury and no place at all in monasteries or charitable hostels. Those long dormitories lined with mattresses may have housed more medieval travellers than there are modern tourists sleeping in the city—yet in jubilee years this was nowhere near enough, and many must have been put up by the townsfolk in their homes. In 1420 the bailiffs and the citizens made all the arrangements for bed and board of the hordes of visitors, and in 1520 a post was set up in the main street to display the provisions made with 'letters expressing the ordering of vitell and lodging for pylgrymes'.

The Priory's revenue from offerings rose from an average of £426 a year at the beginning of the thirteenth century to £1,142 in the year of the Translation, but by 1535 was as low as £36. (By then pilgrimage in general was in decline, yet at the Norfolk shrine of Our Lady of Walsingham receipts in that same year were £260.) This suggests a tremendous falling off in numbers, particularly when allowance is made for the devaluation of money (although the great debasement did not happen until the next decade), but pilgrims were by then largely from the poorer classes, and individual offerings were small. Although the popularity of Canterbury against other shrines was low there were still sufficient pilgrims for them to be responsible for much of the trade of the city.

After the supression of the monasteries the many hosteliers and alehouse-keepers were hard put to make a living. John Hales, an officer of the Exchequer reporting to Thomas Cromwell, pointed out the hardship which the loss of pilgrims brought. 'Please,' he wrote, 'allow the city of Canterbury to have a mill, of late belonging to St Austin's [Augustine's] Abbey. A great part of their yearly charges used to be paid by victuallers and innholders, who made their gain out of the pilgrims which heretofroe came to the said city, but do not now continue. It is like that they will not be able to pay their yearly charge without this grant.'[9]

To judge by the medley of languages and accents to be heard in the streets of Canterbury today the modern pilgrim again represents a considerable contribution not only to Canterbury's income but to Britain's. Their offerings and response to the Cathedral Chapter's appeals are helping to preserve the fabric of Christ Church, much of which, including the gorgeous thirteenth-century coloured windows, is sadly in need of repair and protection from the ravages of time and the pollution of contemporary life.

There is much to see in this historic city as well as the splendours of Christ Church itself, but how many of today's visitors realise that, although Thomas' great shrine is no longer in the cathedral, there are still in Canterbury what are claimed to be genuine relics of the saint, for visiting which the Roman Catholic church will still give the penitent faithful an indulgence.

The Roman Catholic church of St Thomas is in the heart of the city on historic Burgate Street. Built in 1876, it escaped the bombs which destroyed the buildings opposite, but it has little architectural interest. Displayed above the altar of a chapel in the south aisle are two reliquaries. One contains a piece of bone about two and a half inches long, and probably a finger, the other has a small piece of a vestment worn by St Thomas and another small piece of bone. The finger bone came from a collection of relics in St Nicholas' Abbey at Tournai, and the other relics were authenticated by a bishop of Gubbio, in Italy, in 1794 and verificated by Cardinal Wiseman and Cardinal Bourne. Except on special Catholic festivals you will not find queues of pilgrims waiting to kneel before them. Most of today's pilgrims are looking for a longer history and a finer architecture than this church has to offer—mere relics are not enough. The crowds are drawn by the glories of Christ Church itself and the aura that still surrounds the empty space where Thomas, chancellor, archbishop and saint, once lay within his shrine.

12 Corona Sancti Thomae

The knyght and al the feleshipp, and no thing for to ly,
When they wer all I-loggit, as skill wold, and reson,
Everich after his degre, to Chirch then was seson
To pas and to wend, to make hir offringis,
Righte as hir devocioune was, of sylvir broch and ryngis.

THUS THE ANONYMOUS AUTHOR of the *Tale of Beryn* brings Chaucer's pilgrims to their journey's end, for the pilgrimage is not a journey for its own sake: its culmination is the church and shrine of Thomas. And it is a culmination that loses none of its effect by the anticipation which has been building on the way, as Erasmus of Rotterdam makes clear in his somewhat satirical description based upon his visit with Dean Colet:

> The church which is dedicate to St Thomas doth stretch up upon height so gorgeously that it will move pilgrims to devotion after off, and also with his brightness and shining he doth light his neighbours, and the old place which was wonted to be most holy, now in respect of it, is but a dark hole and a little cottage. There be a couple of great high towers, which do seem to salute strangers, afar off, and they do fill all the country about, both far and near, with the sound of great bells.[1]

The cathedral church still makes its impact upon the senses, particularly if the bells are pealing from the Bell Harry Tower. Approached along narrow Mercery Lane and the Butter Market, Christ Church gate and the cathedral towers block the view. This entrance to the cathedral precinct, as distinct from the monastery, was built in 1517, at the end of Goldston II's priorship, to replace an older gate dating from the reign of Henry III, while in Norman times the precinct wall was closer to the cathedral and there was a gate a little to the east.

Beyond the arch the green lawns of the precincts give space to view the grand exterior, with its ancient Norman arcadings and the stone traceries, soaring battlements and pinnacles of later centuries stretching away towards the east and reaching into the sky. The usual entrance is by the sturdy south porch, beneath the southwest tower. The figures that fill the niches are nineteenth-century ones but above the arch is a worn panel which survives from the Middle Ages. It shows the altar of the Sword's Point which stood in the transept where Thomas died. The shattered sword of Richard le Breton lies in front of it. According to Erasmus the now blank panel next to it once showed three of the murderer knights.

Inside the nave the great length of the cathedral is not at first apparent, partly because of the prodigious height of the nave itself and partly because the view east is screened, first by the pierced strainer spanning the crossing arch, put there to help the piers support the weight of the tower above, and then by the pulpitum screen at the top of its flight of steps. The nave is more recent than the eastern parts of the cathedral, being erected by Prior Chillenden between 1378 and 1410. In the Middle Ages the nave was not planned to accommodate large congregations, but to give space for chantry chapels and for burials. Parts of it would have been screened off: the space beneath the north-west tower for use as the archbishop's consistory court, the eastern end of the north aisle as a Lady Chapel. There was an altar on the low platform at the east end of the nave, where the modern nave altar stands, but behind it was a stone screen with doors on either side to give access to the transepts, which are also work of Chillenden's period. There was an upper chapel of St Blaise in the northwest transept, built over the altar of St Benedict, which was demolished after the martyrdom, but otherwise this transept was left untouched for several decades after the rest of the church had been rebuilt, presumably because of the sanctity attached to it. When the perpendicular work was set over the Norman in 1468 the floor level was maintained, making necessary the rather complicated stairways that are seen today. In Thomas' time the steps up to the choir and down to the crypt were similar in arrangement to those on the other side of the crossing.

From the top of the steps beneath the crossing the westward view of the nave is dominated by the magnificent perpendicular window, much of which is filled with ancient glass, though not all in its original position. The great window in the martyrdom shows Edward IV and his family and was given by him after he had visited the cathedral.

The choir is cut off from the nave by the stone pulpitum, the screen which separated the monastic part of the church from the public part. The iron gate in the small central arch permits a view to the sanctuary and, beyond, to the site of the shrine. Usually pilgrims would be directed along the aisle of the choir to avoid disturbing the monks, but when the choir was not in use, they would have been permitted to pass this way. A monk stationed here (his seat is still at the south side of the platform) watched over their behaviour. As they passed he may have sprinkled them with holy water from a stoup beneath the archway. The marks made by the chain on which the sprinkling stick was hung are visible on the north side of the arch.

In the years before the Translation in 1220 pilgrims had three stations of

The nave of Canterbury Cathedral, looking west. (*British Tourist Authority.*)

pilgrimage to visit in the cathedral. First they would go to the martyrdom; some perhaps would be taken there directly from the hospitum, along the covered pentise way, through the cloister and in through the very door by which Thomas had made his last living journey. After the altar of the Broken Sword they would go to the high altar, the place where Thomas' bier had lain, and then they would descend to the crypt to visit the tomb.

We know what this looked like from the pictures in the miracle windows at the east end of the cathedral. It was a rectangular sarcophagus with oval holes in the sides through which the coffin could be seen and touched. It stood at the east end of the crypt, behind where the chapel of Our Lady of the Undercroft is today and between the first two pillars where the new crypt opens out from the old.

After the Translation, there were five stations for the pilgrim for he would still visit the martyrdom, the altar and the site of the original tomb (where a piece of Thomas' skull, mounted in gold, was offered to the devout to kiss), and then there would be the altar of the corona, that portion that was sheared from Thomas' head, which was kept at the extreme east of the cathedral, and the magnificent shrine itself.

Today they are all gone. Devout King Henry VIII, Defender of the Faith and benefactor of the Church, changed his mind about St Thomas when his break with Rome and the Reformation of the English Church brought a new attitude to saints and shrines and images. During his stand against the Church of Rome there were many who reminded Tudor Henry of the similarity of his position with that of his Angevin predecessor, and reminded him of Henry II's fate. Thomas had dared to oppose the king—worse, he won! It was a precedent not to be tolerated. Henry VIII had already been excommunicated in 1535: doctrinally he was a devout Catholic but, since he had made himself head of the Church and did not recognize the Pope, the excommunication did not concern him. But he had to show that those who oppose the king do not win, nor sit in heaven among the saints. Thomas was to be demoted. In 1538 Henry issued a proclamation[2] which declared:

As much as it appereth now clerely, that Thomas Becket, sometyme Archbyshop of Canturburie, stubburnely to withstand the holsome lawes establyshed agaynst the enormities of the clergie, by the kynges highnes mooste noble progenitour, kynge HENRY the second, for the common welthe, reste, and tranquillitie of this realme, of his frowarde mynde fledde the realme into Fraunce, and to the bishop of Rome, mayntenour of those enormities, to procure the abrogation of the sayd lawes, whereby arose moch trouble in this said realme, And that his dethe, whiche they untrely called martyrdome, happened upon a reskewe by him made, and that as it is written, he gave opprobrious wordes to the gentyllmen, which then counsayled hym to leave his stubbernesse, and to avoyde the commocion of the people, rysen up for that rescue. And he nat onely callyd the one of them bawde, but also toke Tracy by the bosome, and violently shoke and plucked hym in suche manor, that he had almoste overthrowen hym to the pavement of the churche, So that upon this fray one of their company perceivynge the same, strake hym, and so in the thronge Becket was slayne, And further that his Canonization was made onely by the bysshop of Rome, bycause he had ben a champion to maynteyne his usurped auctoritie, and a bearer of the inquitie of the clergie, for these and for other great & urgent causes, longe to recyte, the kynges maiestie, by the advyse of his counsayle, hath thought expedyent, to declare to his lovynge subiectes, that notwithstandynge the sayde canonization, there appereth nothynge in his lyfe and exteriour conversation, whereby he shuld be callyd a sainct, but rather estemed to have ben a rebell and traytour to hi prynce: Therfore his grace strayghtly chargeth and commandeth, that from henceforth the sayde Thomas Becket shall not be estemed, named, reputed, nor called a sayncte, but bysshop Becket, and that his ymages and pictures, through the hole realme, shall be putte downe, and avoyded out of all churches, chapelles, and other places, and that from hence forthe, the dayes used to be festivall in his name, shall not be observed, nor the service, office, antiphones, collettes, and prayers in his name redde, but rased and put out of all the bokes . . .'[2]

By the time that this was issued the shrine had already been dismantled and its riches carried away.

A papal bull of Pope Paul III repeats the excommunication of Henry and contains the story—not confirmed elsewhere—that Henry had the long-dead Thomas called for trial and condemned when he failed to return to earth to face the charge (shades of Northampton once again). It was even rumoured that Thomas' body had been arraigned before the Star Chamber as a traitor. There was a precedent. In 896 Pope Stephen VII had had his predecessor exhumed and charged with unlawfully usurping the papal throne. The corpse was dressed in full pontificals, seated on a throne in St Peter's, tried, found guilty and stripped of his dignities. After the three fingers with which he had given the papal blessing had been hacked off the months-old corpse was cast into the Tiber.

It does not seem likely that anything like this happened to Thomas' body: such stories were probably Catholic counterpropaganda, but we do not know for sure what did happen to Thomas' remains. Stowe, writing half a century later, says that they were burned. There was great excitement when in 1888 a stone coffin was discovered under the paving of the crypt and thought to contain the bones of St Thomas—but they were not. Unless new evidence emerges we shall never know what happened to Canterbury's greatest relic.

Since we cannot visit the shrine and stations of the pilgrimage we must rely on the reports of those who saw them to begin to appreciate what the culmination of a pilgrimage was like. We can join with two different kinds of pilgrims: the company that we have already got to know in the *Canterbury Tales*, and Erasmus and Dean Colet under the guise of Ogygyus and his friend Gratian.

We join the fourteenth-century pilgrims of the *Tale of Beryn* at the church door where:

> . . . *the knyght, of gentilnes, that knewe right wele the guyse,*
> *Put forth the Prelatis, the Person, and his fere.*
> *A monk, that toke the spryngill with a manly chere*
> *And did as the maner is moillid al hir patis,*
> *Everich aftir othir, righte as they wer of states.*

While the knight goes forward to the shrine the Pardoner and the Miller
stare at the stained glass trying to work out the stories that it shows until the
host of the Tabard urges them:

> . . . '*let stond they wyndow glasid!*
> *Goith up, and doith your offerynge! yee semeth half amasid!*
> *Sith yee be in company of honest men and good,*
> *Worchith somwhat aftir, and let the kynde of brode*
> *Pas for a tyme! I hold it for the best;*
> *For who doith after company, may lyve the bet in rest.'*
>   *Then passid they forth boystly, goglyng with hir hedis,*
> *Knelid a down to-fore the shryne, and hertlich hir hedis*
> *They preyd to seynt Thomas, in such wise as the couth;*
> *And sith, the holy relikis, each man with his mowith*
> *Kissid, as a goodly monke the names told and taught.*
> *And sith to othir placis of holynes they raughte,*
> *And were in hir devocioun tyl service wer al doon;*
> *And sith they drowgh to dynerward, as it drew to noon.*

Goggle-headed at the splendours of the church, and weak sinners though they
be, they nevertheless tell their beads and pray as well as they know and
devoutly kiss the relics.

A century and a half later our pair of sophisticated intellectuals are somewhat cooler in their reactions. Erasmus's Ogygyus is first impressed by the
'great wideness of the place' and then by the closeness with which the monks
guard the eastern part of the church. They visit the transept of the martyrdom
where 'in the altar is the point of the sword that stirred about the brains of
this blessed martyr . . . the holy rust of this grat I devourly kissed for love of
the blessed martyr.'

Inventories survive of the equipment of this chapel in 1500 and 1503. There
was an image of St Thomas placed in a niche or under a canopy above the
altar with three tapers kept burning before it, and on the altar gold rings set
with sapphires which had belonged to St Thomas and St Andrew which had
'great and wonderful virtue for relieving the eyes of sick persons'. The point
of le Breton's sword, with its special set of coverings (removed when it was
displayed), was placed on or over the altar probably together with the pom-
mel of the hilt, which was also listed. Under a 'great beryl' or crystal were
placed other relics. In addition to those of St Thomas this altar also displayed

relics of Saints Stephen, Laurence, Maria Jacobe, Salome, Marcello Papa, Sebastian and Anastasii.

After the transept of the martydom Ogygyus

> went under the crowdes [underground; that is, into the crypt] which is not
> without his chaplains, and there we saw the brain pan of that holy martyr
> which was thrust quite through, all the other was covered with silver, the
> overpart of the brain pan was bare to be kissed, and therewithall is set
> forth a certain leaden table having graved in him a title of saint Thomas of
> Acrese [Acre]. There hang also the shirt of hair, and his girdle with his
> hairen breeches wherewith that noble champion chastened his body, they
> be horrible to look upon, and greatly reprove our delicate gorgeousness.

Our pilgrims then came up into the choir, upon the north side of which they found a great collection of relics being shown: skulls, jaws, teeth, hands, fingers, whole arms. When Ogygyus 'had worshipped them all, we kissed them, that I thought we should never have made an end, but that my pilgrimage fellow which was an unmete companion for such a business, prayed they make an end of setting forth their relics'.

Gratian, Ogygyus' companion, was now offered an arm with red flesh still left upon it, which 'he abhorred to kiss', and the priest at last put the relics away. Then they looked at the display upon the altar: riches in respect of which 'a man would account both Midas and Cresus beggars'. Ogygyus admits that he was then overcome with a desire to have such relics at home, but quickly repented and decided to ask St Thomas' forgiveness before he left the church.

Next they were taken to the vestry where they were shown vestments of velvet and of cloth of gold, St Thomas' pastoral staff, a robe of silk and 'a napkin full of sweet blood, wherewith the saint Thomas wiped his nose and his face, these things as monuments of ancient soberness we kissed gladly'. Ogygyus then explains that not everyone sees these treasures but that he was closely acquainted with Archbishop Warham, who had written them a letter of introduction. Clearly they were being given the full VIP tour.

Next they climbed the steps behind the high altar 'as it were into another new church, there they showed us in a chapel the face of the blessed man overgilded and with many precious stones goodly garnished'.

The prior now came out to greet them; he showed them the great shrine and had the cover raised for them. Ogygyus explains the he did not actually see the saint's bones for

> that is not convenient, nor we could not come to it, except we set up
> ladders, but a shrine of wood covered a shrine of gold, when that is
> drawn up with cords, then appeareth treasure and riches inestimable . . .
> The vilest part and worst was gold, all things did shine, flourish, and as it

The stairs trodden by generations of pilgrims on their way to St Thomas' shrine. (*British Tourist Authority*.)

were with lightning appeared with precious stones and those many and of great multitude: some were greater even than a goose egg. Divers of the monks strode thereabout with great reverence, the cover taken away, all we kneeled down and worshipped. The prior with a white rod showed us every stone, adding thereto the French name, the value, and the author of the gift, for the chief stones were sent thither by great princes.

Other reports confirm the magnificence of the shrine. A Venetian traveller at the end of the Middle Ages described the tomb as beyond belief:

Notwithstanding its great size it is covered with plates of pure gold; yet the gold is scarcely seen from the various precious stones with which it is studded, as sapphires, balasses, diamonds, rubies, and emeralds; and wherever the eye turns something more beautiful than the rest is observed. Nor, in addition to these natural beauties, is the skill of art wanting, for in the midst of the gold are the most beautiful sculptured gems, both small and large, as well as such as are in relief, as agates, onyxes, cornelians and cameos, and some cameos are of such a size that I am afraid to name it; but everything is far surpassed by a ruby, not larger than a thumbnail, which is set to the right of the altar. The church is somewhat dark, and particularly in the spot where the shrine is placed; and when we went to see it, the sun was near setting and the weather cloudy; nevertheless I saw that ruby as if I had it in my hand. [3]

'That ruby' was the famous Regale of France, presented by Louis VII. Louis was three times married (one of his wives being Eleanor of Aquitaine) but had only one son. When he was getting old he wanted to have the fourteen-year-old Prince Philip crowned, but the boy disappeared while out boar-hunting and Louis was distraught. Then Louis had a vision of St Thomas, whose protector he had been in life, and was promised the safety of his son if he would make a pilgrimage to Canterbury. Philip was found by a charcoal burner and brought safely back to court, but the king's advisers were against him going to England for he was sick and Henry II was hostile to him. However, Thomas appeared again and threatened disaster if he did not keep his vow. Louis left France with a brilliant retinue, and Henry II went to meet him at Dover and escorted him to Canterbury, where Louis stayed to pray for a full two days. He made an offering at the shrine of a gold cup and this fine jewel, and gave the monks 100 casks of wine a year from his cellars at Poissy-sur-Seine.

The Icelandic *Thomas Saga Erkibyskups* recounts the giving of the Regale more colourfully, although it erroneousy makes the donor Louis' son. [3] It tells how Philip, being ill with leprosy, was told by his mother to vow to give the jewel to St Thomas—who had once desired it of his father. No sooner had he made the vow than 'the leprosy fell clean away from him into the bed-clothes, and so utterly, that he stood up in that same twinkle of an eye, thoroughly healed and with his skin so clean, and his breast so whole, as if he had never ailed ought in his lifetime'. [4] But, like his father, Philip was loth to part with the gem. He made the pilgrimage to Canterbury but there conferred with the archbishop, who agreed to ransom the stone for a sum twice what had been paid for it when it had been bought from the Emperor Charles. Philip went to the altar and speaking as though to St Thomas, told him:

'Blessed be thou, worthy lord Archbishop Thomas, for all thy mercy in the restoration of my health, which through thy merits thou didst bestow upon me. I have now ransomed to myself this carbuncle by a twofold price, the very one which erst I vowed that thou shouldst be the owner of, and now I pray thee that thou bless the stone, for the honour and spiritual healing of myself and my successors.'

Having spoken thus he lifteth up his hand with the ring on it in such a manner that the back of the hand turned towards the shrine, and therewithal having made the oval of the carbuncle to touch the shrine in the middle as he turned to his following, making ready to array himself for his departure. But being about to fit the gauntlet to his hand, lo, the lustre is gone, for, indeed, the gold setting was empty. Turning then towards the altar he perceiveth forthwith, that the very carbuncle discovered where it was gone, whereof the king deemeth needful to go once more to the altar and to behold how these things had come to pass . . . the carbuncle was so masterly set in the centre of the front face of the shrine, as if the master wright had set it there himself in the beginning. Philip said, 'If you prefer jewel to wealth I shall nevertheless not take back what I have given to the church, be it all thine together.'

After the wonders of the shrine Ogygyus and Gratian were taken down into the crypt again, to the chapel of Our Lady of the Undercroft, the beautiful perpendicular chantry built in the latter part of the fourteenth century. At first it was dark but when candles were brought they 'saw a sight passing the riches of any king'. This secret treasure, well guarded behind 'iron grats', was shown only to special visitors. There was yet more to see, for next they were taken up to the vestry and there a great coffer covered in black leather was opened up and everyone knelt down to worship around it. Inside were

certain torn rags of linen cloth, many having yet remaining in them the token of the filth of the holy man's nose. With these (as they say) saint Thomas did wipe away the sweat of his face or his neck, the filth of his nose, or other like filthiness with which man's body doth abound. Then my companion Gratian, yet once again, got him but small favour. Unto him, an Englishman of similar acquaintance and beside that, a man of no small authority, the prior gave genteely one of the linen rags, thinking to have given a gift very acceptable and pleasant, But Gratian therewith little pleased and content, not without an evident sign of displeasure, took one of these between his fingers, and disdainingly laid it down again, made a mock and a mow at it after the manner of puppets, for this was his manner, if anything liked him not, that he thought worthy to be despised. Whereat I was both ashamed and wonderously afraid. Not withstanding the prior, as he is a man not at all dull witted, did dissemble the matter, and after he had caused us drink a cup of wine genteely he let us depart.

Perhaps most visitors today would have a somewhat similar reaction to Dean Colet's if offered such relics as dirty handkerchiefs to kiss, and such devotions have no place in the ritual of the Anglican communion of which Canterbury is now the mother church. Nevertheless, the thousands who now

The chapel of St Thomas. The verger is standing on the site of the shrine, marked by the ending of the decorative tiles and the broken line of the paving. The tomb is that of the Black Prince, son of Edward III. Above it hang his funeral achievements: helm, gauntlets and surcoat. These are modern facsimiles, for the originals have been carefully restored and are exhibited elsewhere in the cathedral. (*British Tourist Authority.*)

walk through the church each day and stand in the martyrdom transept listening to an earphone commentary on the events of 800 years ago are there precisely because it was upon that spot that Thomas, Archbishop of Canterbury was killed. Reverently they will walk up the steps that pilgrims over centuries have worn into deep hollows, and stand trying to imagine what the great shrine was like as they gaze at the empty space where it once stood.

The shrine was broken up four hundred years ago, filling two great chests with gold and precious stones, each of which needed six or seven strong men to carry it out of the church, and it took 26 carts to bear away the treasure. Except for the regale, which Henry VIII had set into a ring, we do not know what became of it—and even the regale seems now to have disappeared (although it is known that Mary Tudor still had it and, Catholic queen though she was, did not give it back to Canterbury).

Although the shrine has gone, its position is clearly defined by the broken pattern of the pavement and the ending of the decoration in marble tesserae and stone tiles with incised patterns filled with coloured mastic. The complex geometrical design marks the western side of the shrine where an altar would have stood against it. It is bordered to north and south by roundels which show the signs of the zodiac, the months, and virtues overcoming vices. Along the sides of the empty area, a rut worn into the stones shows where generations of pilgrims' toes have rubbed as they knelt on the step around the shrine.

In the glowing windows of the chapel can be seen a picture of the shrine. It is in the fifth window from the left (north) at the very top, and shows Thomas appearing to a sleeping monk. Less clear representations appear in other panels. It did not necessarily look exactly like this picture—medieval artists were allowed a lot of licence—and in trying to imagine its appearance the surviving shrine of St Edward the Confessor in Westminster Abbey is a useful guide. This was built about fifty years after that of Thomas, in the time of Henry III. It was to an earlier shrine that Thomas and Henry II translated King Edward's body in 1163. The marble tomb of Archbishop Walter, who died in 1205, although far less sumptuous than the shrine would be, is also a helpful guide to style. The Westminster shrine shows the stone supporting structure and, in addition to the descriptions already quoted, John Stowe tells in his *Annals* that the shrine 'was builded about a man's height, all of stone, then upward of timber plain, within which was a chest of iron, conteining the bones of Thomas Becket . . . the timberworke . . . on the outside, was covered with plates of gold damasked with gold wier, which ground of golde was againe covered with jewels of gold . . .' All the upper part was kept hidden beneath a wooden cover when not being shown, and to guard the treasure of the shrine there was a watching chamber high above in St Anselm's tower at the east end of the south choir aisle—and one source, how reliable it is difficult to judge, even claims that a band of ferocious dogs was kept near at hand to help the watcher.[5]

Where the altar of the Corona once stood the Chair of St Augustine is now placed. This is not the original chair, which may have been destroyed in the fire of 1174, but probably dates from the time of the Translation. It has an elegance matched with a solid certainty that recalls the way in which Christ spoke of his Church being founded upon a rock. The words referred to St Peter, but to Christians in the Middle Ages they might equally have meant St Thomas.

The windows of the Corona (or Trinity Chapel as it is more correctly called) and those which flanked St Thomas' shrine contain some fine ancient glass—and a little inferior nineteenth-century work. The glass at which the Miller and the Pardoner goggled is still one of the glories of Canterbury.

When Dr John Layton came to destroy the shrine on Henry VIII's orders he failed to destroy the windows around the chapel of St Thomas, which portray the miracles which Thomas performed and even show the saint himself. The window that upset Thomas Cromwell's man at the chapel in Cheapside was destroyed but, in Oxford, the east window of St Lucy's chapel in Christ Church Cathedral shows St Thomas being struck down; the local officials removed only the saint's head, leaving the rest of the window intact. Elsewhere in Oxford, a window in Duke Humphrey's library at the Bodleian, which shows the flagellation of Henry II, was left untouched, and up and down the country many depictions of St Thomas' life and martyrdom were overlooked. Nevertheless, it is surprising that these windows recording Thomas' sanctity were allowed to remain.

Some of the stories which these Canterbury miracle windows tell have already been recounted, but before leaving the cathedral take another look at them. Today we remember Thomas as a martyr and as a political figure, but to the people of the Middle Ages it was his miracle-working that made him such an important saint: without his reputation for miracles he would scarcely have attained such major rank.

Stephen of Hoyland is in the upper part of the third window with William Patrick lower down; Henry of Fordwich is to the bottom of window four, while higher up is Thomas appearing in Louis VII's dream. In window six three pictures tell the story of little Robert, who fell into the Medway, and at the top of window ten four panels show the story of John from Roxburgh. Some big groups among the lower panels, which are most easily seen, devote sequences to a single story. Here are three of them:

The lower six panels of the fifth window recount the story of Eilward of Westoning who, attempting to obtain restitution from a debtor, was wrongly accused by that man of theft and hung around the neck with things he was supposed to have stolen. Blinded and castrated in punishment, having been judged by ordeal by water, he made his way to Canterbury led by his little daughter. At Bedford one of his empty eye sockets began to itch and he removed the dressing covering it and found that he could distinguish light and dark. A new eye was growing, and at length all his mutilations were restored.[6]

To emphasise the truth of this strange healing, monk Benedict adds a lengthy comment of authentication, emphasising that Eilward had been mutilated by his enemies who would not have spared him, so that there could be no doubt that he had indeed been lacking both eyes and testicles.

The lower eight panels of window six tell the story of the family of Sir Jordan fitzEisulf. His son, stricken dead with plague, was after two days brought back to life with St Thomas' water brought by pilgrims who were given hospitality, and a pilgrimage of thanks was vowed within a certain time. But the vow was not kept, and Thomas sent a blind leper with warnings of disaster if they did not hasten to his tomb. Another son now died, but at last the pilgrimage was made; the last stained glass scene shows Sir Jordan pouring offerings of gold and silver coin on to the tomb.[7]

In window eleven the lower eight panels all tell the story of William of Gloucester, a workman of Thomas' old rival Roger Pont l'Evêque, who was buried by a fall of earth. First he called upon Christ and upon the Virgin, then Thomas' name came into his mind and he called for the martyr's aid. A woman had a vision that William was still alive beneath the earth and, when she sent her son to the place (Benedict says it was the town crier), and he put his ear to the ground, groans were heard and William was soon dug out. On his release he made his way to Canterbury to make thank-offering at the shrine.[8]

When the pilgrims had marvelled at all these wonders and made their way out of the cathedral, were their feelings very different from those of sightseers

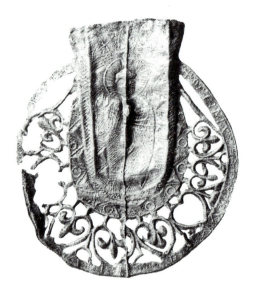

An ampulla of lead, made to contain the Water of St Thomas and as a pilgrim badge. (*Museum of London.*)

today? The modern visitor may explore the cloisters and other remains of the monastic house, but he will find no monks to portion out a few drops of St Thomas' Water for him, and not all pilgrims of the Middle Ages would be given a measure of the miracle-working fluid. But all would go out into the town to buy their pilgrim tokens, like the pilgrims of the *Tale of Beryn*, who

> ... *as manere and custom is, signes there they boughte,—*
> *For men of contre shuld know whom they had soughte.—*

There was a variety of types to chose from, to be pinned upon the tunic or sewn upon the hat; figures of St Thomas on horseback giving a blessing, heads of the martyr, Canterbury bells and little ampulla to hold the wonder water, or at least to remind people of it—some of them inscribed with the legend *Optimus egrorum medicus fit Thoma bonorum* (Thomas is the best physician for good people that are sick).

No badges of St Thomas are sold today; instead a replica of an eighth-century cross, which may be worn as a brooch or pendant, is offered. But one hopes that the modern tourist is more honest than the anonymous poet makes the Miller and the Pardoner, for while the other pilgrims chose their signs and

> *Ech man set his sylvir in such thing as they likid:*
> *And in the meen while, the Miller had I-pikid*
> *His bosom ful of signys of Cantirbury brochis;*
> *Huch the Pardoner, and he, pryvely in hir pouchis*
> *They put hem aftirward, that noon of hem it wist,*
> *Save the Sompnour seid somwhat, and seyd to hem 'list!*
> *Halff part!' quod he, pryvely rownyng on hir ere ...*
> *... They set hir signes uppon hir hedis, and som oppon hir cappe,*
> *And sith to the dynerward, they gan for to stappe ...*

And so, their vows completed and indulgence won, the pilgrims could begin their journey home, a journey perhaps as fraught with dangers and with pleasures as their journey to Canterbury.

EPILOGUE

Today the Cathedral Church of Christ sells no indulgences, only post-cards, guidebooks and souvenirs. It welcomes offerings, but preferably in cash or by covenant, and calls upon the services of professional fund-raisers to launch its appeals for sorely needed funds to keep the fabric of the church repaired and the choirboys trained.[1]

A panel from one of the miracle windows of Canterbury Cathedral. At the top St Thomas, seemingly issuing from his shrine, appears to a monk. On the left, Roger of Valognes (near Cherbourg) has his foot bathed at the shrine; right, an unidentified woman makes an offering at the tomb; bottom, Godwin of Boxgrove gives away his clothes as a thanks-offering for the cure of his leprosy. (From *The Ancient Glass of Canterbury Cathedral* by Bernard Rackham.)

There is no shrine of St Thomas to visit, only an empty space, but the visitors which throng to see its remaining glories come each year not in their thousands but in their millions. Canterbury is still the Mother Church of England, and, through the English Church, of Anglicans and Episcopalians all over the world. If the coachloads of tourists who walk beneath the great gate and into the soaring nave each day are more like the lively band who travelled with Chaucer than the solitary palmers, they perhaps emerge with as great a sense of wonder. For Christians the work of the Church goes on, vital in our materialistic world; for others the high, cool vaults, the glorious glass and the echoes of history still provide a place for reflections and refreshment of the spirit. The clicking of cameras and the explanations of the guides fade into the background as the spirit of centuries drifts over them. At evening, when the visitors are few, it is easy to imagine the crash of sword on stone in the dark shadows.

Thomas is not forgotten. Whatever happened to his bones, today his face and name are out there in every other shop in Canterbury.

Bibliography

Edwin A. Abbot, *St Thomas of Canterbury, His Death and Miracles*, Adam & Charles Black, London, 1898

George Burton Adams, *Constitutional History of England*, Jonathan Cape, London, 1935

Anon., *Charing Church and Parish*, undated

Anon., *The Tale of Beryn* (ed. F. J. Furnivall & W. G. Stone), Trubner, London, 1887

Anon., *The Friars, Aylesford*, undated

Geoffrey Baskerville, *English Monks and the Supression of the Monasteries*, Jonathan Cape, London, 1965

Hilaire Belloc, *The Old Road*, Constable, London, 1910

Morris Bishop, *The Horizon Book of the Middle Ages*, American Heritage, New York, 1968

Julia Cartwright, *The Pilgrims' Way*, John Murray, London, 1911

Geoffrey Chaucer, *The Canterbury Tales* (ed. A. C. Cawley), Dent, London, 1958

Rotha Clay, *The Medieval Hospitals of England*, Methuen, London, 1909

William Cobbett, *Rural Rides*, Dent, London, 1948

C. G. Crump, *The Pilgrim's Way*, in *History* XXI, 81

David C. Douglas and George W. Greenaway (eds.) *English Historical Documents*, Vol. II (1042–1189), Eyre and Spottiswoode, London, 1953

Alfred Duggan, *Thomas Becket of Canterbury*, Faber & Faber, London, 1967

Desiderius Erasmus, *The Pylgremage of Pure Devotyon* (anon. trs.), London, 1540

Raymonde Foreville, *Le Jubilée de Saint Thomas Becket*, S.E.V.P.E.N., Paris, 1958

Garnier de Pont Sainte-Maxime, *La Vie de Saint Thomas Becket* (ed. Emmanuel Warbury), Librairie Ancien Honore Champion, Paris, 1936; and *Vie de St Thomas le Martyr de Cantobrie* (trs. J. Shirley), Phillimore, Canterbury, 1975

Gentleman's Magazine, 1722

Gervase, *Chronicle* (Rolls Series), 1879

J. Allen Giles, *The Life and Letters of Thomas à Becket*, London, 1846

Robert Hall Goodsall, *The Ancient Road to Canterbury*, privately printed, 1959

William Gostling, *A Walk in and about the City of Canterbury*, Simons and Kirkey, Canterbury, 1796

Laurence Goulder, *Canterbury*, Guild of Our Lady of Ransom, London, 1962

George W. Greenaway, *The Life and Death of Thomas Becket*, Folio Society, London, 1961

Donald J. Hall, *English Medieval Pilgrimage*, Routledge, London, 1966

Edward Hasted, *The History of the Ancient and Metropolitan City of Canterbury*, Canterbury, 1799; and *The History and Topographical Survey of the County of Kent*, Canterbury, 1797

Sidney Heath, *Pilgrim Life in the Middle Ages*, T. Fisher Unwin, London, 1911

William Hutton, *St Thomas of Canterbury*, Nutt, London, 1899; and *Thomas Becket*, Cambridge University Press, 1926

Sean Jennet, *The Pilgrims' Way*, Cassell, London 1971

J. J. Jusserand, *English Wayfaring Life in the Middle Ages*, T. Fisher Unwin, London, 1920

David Knowles, *Thomas Becket*, Adam & Charles Black, London, 1970

William Lambarde, *A Perambulation of Kent* (written 1570), Baldwin, Craddock and Joy, London, 1826

William Langland, *Piers Plowman* (ed. W. W. Skeat), Oxford, 1924

J. Wickham Legge and W. H. St John Hope (eds.), *Inventories of Christ Church Canterbury*, Constable, London, 1902

Sheila Lewenhak, *The Merchant Adventurers*, Jackdaw Publications, London, 1967

Howard Loxton, *The Murder of Thomas Becket*, Jackdaw Publications, London, 1971

Eirikr Magnusson (ed.) *Thomas Saga Erikbyskups*, The Chronicles and Memorials of Great Britain and Ireland during the Middle Ages (Rolls Series), London, 1875–83.

W. J. Millor and H. E. Butler, *Letters of John Salisbury*, Nelson, London, 1955

R. J. Mitchell & M. D. R. Leys, *A History of London Life*, Longmans, London, 1958

Ian Nairn and Nikolaus Pevsner, *Surrey*, Penguin, Harmondsworth, 1969

John Newman, *North East and East Kent*, Penguin, Harmondsworth 1969; and *West Kent and the Weald*, Penguin, Harmondsworth, 1969

Nikolaus Pevsner and David Lloyd, *Hampshire*, Penguin, Harmondsworth, 1973

Colin Platt, *The English Medieval Town*, Secker & Warburg, London, 1976

A. F. Pollard, *Henry VIII*, Jonathan Cape, London, 1970

S. E. Rigold, *Maison Dieu, Ospringe*, H.M.S.O., London, 1958; and *Temple Manor*, H.M.S.O., London, 1962

J. C. Robertson (ed.), *Materials for the History of Thomas Becket Archbishop of Canterbury* (Rolls Series), London, 1875–83

John Stowe, *The Annales of England*, London, 1592; and *A Survay of London*, London, 1603 (Dent, London / Dutton, New York, 1965)

William Somner, *The Antiquities of Canterbury*, London, 1703

Jonathan Sumption, *Pilgrimage*, Faber & Faber, London, 1975

Francis Underhill, *The Story of Rochester Cathedral*, British Pub. Co., Gloucester, 1969

William Urry, *Canterbury Under the Angevin Kings*, Athlone Press, London, 1967

H. Snowden-Ward, *The Canterbury Pilgrimages*, Adam & Charles Black, London, 1904

Francis Watt, *Canterbury Pilgrims and their Ways*, Methuen, London, 1917

William Wey, *Informacion for Pylgrymes*, London, 1498

William Woods, *England in the Age of Chaucer*, Book Club Associates, London, 1976

Hugh Ross Williamson, *The Arrow and the Sword*, Faber & Faber, London, 1947

Richard Winston, *Thomas Becket*, Constable, London, 1967

Christopher John Wright, *A Guide to the Pilgrims' Way and North Downs Way*, Constable, 1977

Jacobus de Voraigne, *Life of St Thomas* (from the Golden Legend), London, 1510?

Isolated references to State Papers and other general documentary sources have not been included within this bibliography.

Notes and Sources

Introduction
1   *Materials for the History of Thomas Becket* II, 15

Chapter One: The young lawyer

1   *Materials* III, 15
2   *Materials* II, 302–3 (see also IV, 7)
3   *Materials* IV, 6
4   Several sources place his earliest education at Merton Priory. I follow Alfred Duggan's suggestion that it is more likely that he went to a city grammar school first instead of after Merton (see A. Duggan, *Thomas Becket*, 221).
5   *Materials* II, 361. Other sources say that Thomas worked for a sheriff, it is reasonable to assume that they were one and the same.
6   Morris Bishop, *The Horizon Book of the Middle Ages*, 96
7   *Materials* III, 15

Chapter Two: The seal and the sword

1   Matilda had married the Count of Anjou.
2   Walter Map, *De Nugis Curialium* (Of Courtiers' Trifles), printed in *Anecdota Oxeniensis* Vol XIV (1914), 237–42
3   *Materials* III, 24–5
4   *Materials* IV, 255
5   *Materials* III, 29–31
6   *Materials* III, 34
7   *Materials* III, 34–5
8   *Materials* III, 35
9   *Letters of John of Salisbury* (ed. W. J. Millor and H. E. Butler). The quotations are from letters numbered 121 and 120 in this collection. See also 129, a letter from Archbishop Theobald to Thomas himself, 128, and pp xxxvii–viii.
10 *Materials* III, 181
11 *Materials* IV, 17–8

Chapter Three: The mitre and the ring

1   Garnier, lines 486–90. *Saga* I, 82 makes Winchester's words seem a little more confident and gives Thomas's reply 'God's hidden will and yours seem to be alike in this. I give my assent, although in great fear.'
2   *Saga* I, 106
3   Garnier, lines 541–5
4   *Materials* III, 99–100
5   *Materials* III, 38ff and 192ff
6   'Water in which straw had been boiled' is the way William fitzStephen describes it, but he probably misunderstood the dried herb used.

7 Garnier, lines 741–50. 'God's eyes!' was Henry's favourite oath.
8 *Materials* III, 45–6
9 Some authorities place this letter a month later.
10 *Materials* V, 48–9
11 *Materials* IV, 202
12 *Materials* IV, 202–3
13 *Materials* III, 270
14 *Materials* IV, 204 '*salvo ordino nostro*', III, 273–4 '*salvo ordino suo*'
15 *Materiais* IV, 27
16 *Materials* IV, 32
17 *Materials* V, 88–9
18 *Saga* I, 180
19 John the Marshal had taken the oath on a service book, not the Bible, and therefore might be suspected of trying to leave himself technically free to commit perjury. *Materials* III, 51
20 *Materials* II, 326–7
21 *Materials* II, 332–3

Chapter Four: The obstinate exile

1 *Materials* IV, 57
2 *Materials* II, 332–3
3 *Materials* III, 332,
4 Garnier, lines 2216–20
5 *Materials* II, 290–1
6 Alfred Duggan, *Thomas Becket*, 150
7 *Materials* V, 178–9
8 Giles I, 327–30
9 Giles I, 330–1
10 Thomas also suspended Bishop Jocelyn of Salisbury for appointing John dean at the king's request, despite the taking of the oath.
11 *Materials* III, 423
12 *Materials* III, 425
13 Giles II, 160–1
14 Bishop Gilbert actually set out to appeal to the pope who, taking pity on the ageing prelate, who took several months to reach even Milan, authorised others to absolve him, provided that he swore to follow the pope's instructions over the dispute.
15 *Materials* VII, 147–9. These decrees were probably never fully implemented. See Knowles, *Thomas Becket*, 124–5 note.
16 *Materials* III, 466
17 *Materials* VII, 334
18 Giles II, 284–5
19 This practice of passing the Kiss of Peace fell into disuse except among canons and deacons when they are gathered for High Mass in a cathedral, but a freer form has recently been revived in many churches as a symbol of union among the laity.
20 *Materials* III, 470. *Matthew* Chap IV, verse 9
21 *Materials* III, 116
22 Giles II, 295
23 *Materials* III, 119

Chapter Five: Dark December

1 Not, as the King James's Authorised Version has it 'Peace and goodwill towards men' (*Luke* Chap II, verse 14) which is a mistranslation.
2 Gervase, *Chronicle* (translation published in *The Gentleman's Magazine*, 1722).

3 *Materials* III, 128
4 There are several versions of this phrase which has echoed down the centuries. Henry spoke in French, the biographers wrote in Latin, we know it translated into English. William fitzStephen describes only a meaningful look.
5 The writers describing the scene of the murder are identified in the text. The main narrative is from Edward Grim, who stood by Thomas and had his arm slashed.

Chapter Six: The hooly blisful martir

1 *Materials* III, 518–9
2 *Materials* II, 27
3 *Materials* III, 147–8. It is not clear whether this took place during the night or in the preparation of the body for burial next day. Not all accounts refer to the vermin and indeed the soldiers ransacking the palace discovered two further sets of clean hair-cloth garments which suggests that there is some contradiction here.
4 *Materials* III, 522. Again a deliberate parallel is drawn by Herbert of Bosham with Christ's passion.
5 *Materials* II, 290
6 *Materials* III, 150
7 *Materials* III, 150
8 *Materials* II, 162ff (Benedict III, 64)
9 *Materials* I, 213 (William II, 52) and II, 245 (Benedict IV, 74)
10 *Materials* I, 251 (William II, 91)
11 *Materials* II, 128 (Benedict II, 18)
12 Caesarius of Heisterbach, *Dialogus miraculorum*, ed. J. Strange, Cologne, 1851 Vol II, 127–8
13 *Materials* II, 967 (Benedict II, 51)
14 *Materials* I, 282–3 (William III, 24)
15 *Saga*, 176
16 Gervase *Chronicle* I, 248–9
17 Hugh Ross Williamson, *The Arrow and the Sword*
18 Margaret Murray, *The God of the Witches*
19 Sean Jennet, *The Pilgrim's Way*, 49
20 *English Historical Documents*, Vol II, 375
21 David Knowles, *Thomas Becket*, 154
22 Gervase I, 3–29
23 *Materials* II, 44 (Benedict I, 13)
24 *Materials* II, 66 (Benedict II, 13)
25 *Materials* II, 46 (Benedict I, 14)
26 *Materials* I, 296ff (William III, 41); II, 266 (Benedict VI, 3)
27 *Materials* I, 276–7 (William III, 18)
28 *Materials* I, 539–40 (William VI, 161)
29 *Materials* II, 153ff (Benedict III, 51)
30 *Materials* I, 539 (William VI, 158)
31 *Materials* II, 67 (Benedict II, 16)
32 *Materials* I, 528–9 (William VI, 147)
33 Gervase I, 3–29
34 *Letterbooks of the Monastery of Christ Church Canterbury* III, 26–8
35 *Calendar of Venetian State Papers relating to English Affairs* (RS) I, 42
36 *Calendar of Entries in the Papal Registers relating to Great Britain and Ireland* (RS) XI, 685
37 Jonathan Sumption, *Pilgrimage*, 293
38 *Letterbooks of Christ Church* III, 340, 344–5; Raymonde Foreville, *Le Jubilée de St Thomas Becket*, 191
39 A. F. Pollard, *Henry VIII*, 84

Chapter Seven: To be a pilgrim

1 *In Gloria Martyrum*, quoted Sumption, 24
2 *Indulgentiarum Doctrina*, 1967
3 Guibert of Nogent, *Gesta Dei per Francos*
4 *Letters and papers illustrative of the reigns of Richard III and Henry VII*, ed. J. Gairdner (RS) II, 97–8
5 Sumption, *Pilgrimage*, 107–8
6 12 Richard II Cap 7
7 When that April with his showers sweet
The drought of March hath pierced to the root
And bathed every vein in such liquor (sap)
By virtue of which it flowers . . .
8 *Materials* I, 290 (William III, 33)
9 Sidney Heath, *Pilgrim Life in the Middle Ages*, 36
10 Quoted Sumption, *Pilgrimage*, 124–5
11 Statute of Winchester
12 The examination of Master William Thorpe in *Fifteenth Century Verse and Prose* (ed. A. W. Pollard) 97ff
13 J. J. Jusserand, *English Wayfaring Life in the Middle Ages*, 89
14 William Dugdale, quoting a charter of Henry VI's reign
15 Heath, *Pilgrim Life*, 204
16 Rotha M. Clay, *Medieval Hospitals of England*
17 Rolls of Parliament III, 26 (AD 1377)
18 Quoted in Jusserand, *English Wayfaring Life*, 132–3
19 Statute 23 Edward III Ch 6 and 27 Edward III St 1 Ch 3
20 Parson's Tale, lines 1102–3
21 *Piers Plowman*, Book V, lines 344–50
22 *Materials* II, 105 (Benedict II, 60)

Chapter Eight: The Pilgrims' Way I

1 C. G. Crump, History XXI, 81: 'In the fourteenth century they went from Winchester to Alresford not by the lanes up the Itchen valley among the Worthys, but by the straight road over the downs, and so by Alton and Farnham to Guildford. From Guildford they went up to London by Ripley and Kingston, as men go today; and from London they went, like Chaucer's pilgrims, to Canterbury. And that road is marked on the fourteenth century map in the Bodleian Library, of which Richard Gough published a facsimile in the first volume of his *British Topography* in 1780.'
2 Hilaire Belloc, *The Old Road*
3 Christopher John Wright, *A Guide to the Pilgrims' Way and North Downs Way*
4 William Thorn Warren, *Guide to Winchester*, 1950, 52

Chapter Nine: The Pilgrims' Way II

1 Heath, *Pilgrim Life*, 174
2 William Lambard, *A Perambulation of Kent*, London, 657–8
3 Jennet suggests that there must be an ancient causeway running beneath the modern surface.
4 John Newman, *North East and East Kent* (The Buildings of England)
5 Anonymous guide *Charing Church and Parish* (I particularly like Mr Dios— Mr God—burning down the church!)
6 Julia Cartwright, *The Pilgrims' Way*, 179

Chapter Ten: The London road

1 John Stowe, *A Survay of London*, 23
2 R. J. Mitchell and M. D. R. Leys, *A History of London Life*, 157
3 A new hospital chapel, built in 1702, now serves as the chapter house of Southwark Cathedral and an old operating theatre discovered in a sealed up part in recent years is now open to the public. When London Bridge railway station was built on the site of the hospital it was transferred to new premises on the bank of the Thames opposite the Houses of Parliament which have themselves recently been extensively rebuilt.
4 Stowe, 367–8; Chaucer's spelling has been replaced instead of that of Stowe.
5 'Wot cher!' all the neighbours cried,
'Who'er yer going ter meet Bill?
Have yer bought the street, Bill?'
Laugh! I thought I should 'ave died,
Knocked 'em in the Old Kent Road!
6 Lambarde, *Perambulation of Kent*, 205–7
7 Francis Watt, *Canterbury Pilgrims*, 99
8 Heath, *Pilgrim Life*, 250
9 *Materials* II, 226 (Benedict IV, 62)
10 Materials II, 186–7 (Benedict IV, 6)
11 Materials I, 310 (William III, 57 and 58)
12 S. E. Rigold, *Maison Dieu Ospringe*, 6

Chapter Eleven: The golden angel

1 Desiderius Erasmus, *Peregrinatio religionis ergo*, the translation is from the first printed English edition *A dialogue of two persons, devysyd and set forthe in the latine tonge by the noble and famous clerke Desiderius Erasmus intituled The Pylgremage of Pure Devotyon*, published c 1540. Since the extracts are of some length the spelling has been modernised to help the reader.
2 Heath, *Pilgrim Life*, 212
3 If walkers coming from the Pilgrims' Way turn up the path on the right before reaching the main road they will pass the well on their way to the hospital.
4 Clay, *Medieval Hospitals*
5 Newman, *North East and East Kent*, 229
6 Laurance Goulder, *Canterbury*, 112
7 William Gostling, *A Walk in and about the City of Canterbury*, 56
8 I am indebted to Miss Ann Oakley, the Cathedral Archivist, for this information.
9 *Calendar of Letters and Papers of Henry VIII*, XIII(2) 1142 dated 20th Dec 1538

Chapter Twelve: Corona Sancti Thomae

1 Erasmus, *Peregrinatio religionis ergo*
2 Proclamation issued at Westminster 16 November, Henry VIII, 30 printed by Thomas Berthelet the king's printer.
3 Loxton, *Murder of Thomas Becket*, V
4 *Saga* II, 217
5 Watt, *Canterbury Pilgrims*, 42
6 *Materials* II, 173–82 (Benedict III, 2); I, 155–8 (William II, 3)
7 *Materials* I, 160 (William II, 5); II, 229–34 (Benedict IV, 64)
8 *Materials* I, 253–6 (William III, 1); II 261–3 (Benedict VI, 1)

Epilogue

1   Contributions to the Canterbury Cathedral Appeal should be sent to The Chapter Office, 8, The Precincts, Canterbury, or in the US to The American Committee to Save Canterbury Cathedral, Suite 7210, 350, Fifth Avenue, New York, NY1000.

Acknowledgements

MANY PEOPLE have helped with this book in many ways. My debt to the scholarship and superior Latin and Norman–French of many previous writers on the subjects involved is amply evidenced by the bibliography but I should particularly like to thank Dr William Urry, who, despite his own long-promised book on Thomas and his pilgrims, guided me from his deep knowledge when I first wrote about Becket, Miss Ann Oakley, his successor as Cathedral and City Archivist at Canterbury, Mr Charles Long, Sub-Prior at Harbledown, and all those unknown people who told me of local traditions in my travels along the pilgrim routes. The staff of the British Library, the London Library, Camden Libraries and Canterbury City Library have all given invaluable help. The translation of Edward Grim's text in Chapter Five is reproduced from *English Historical Documents* by courtesy of the publishers, Messrs Eyre and Spottiswoode, and illustrations (which are individually credited) are reproduced by courtesy of The British Library, the Trustees of the Bodleian Library, the Museum of London, the British Tourist Authority, the French Government Tourist Office and the Mansell Collection, while Jonathan Cape Ltd kindly allowed me to borrow negatives originally made for my 'Jackdaw' on the murder. The photograph of one of the miracle windows at Canterbury is reproduced from *The Ancient Glass of Canterbury Cathedral* (Lund Humphries) by courtesy of the Friends of Canterbury Cathedral. I must also thank Hilary Evans for preparing prints from my own negatives, Lawrence Easden for help with the map of pilgrim routes and many other things, and my editor, Paul Barnett, without whose encouragement and enthusiasm this book could never have been written.

INDEX

Page numbers in italic type indicate illustrations. Sub-headings for persons are in chronological not alphabetical order.